# ADAPT AS AN ARCHITECT

A Mid-Career Companion

RIBA Publishing

Randy Deutsch

© Randy Deutsch 2021

Published by RIBA Publishing, 66 Portland Place, London, W1B 1AD

ISBN 978 1 85946 951 4

The right of Randy Deutsch to be identified as the Author of this Work has been asserted in accordance with the Copyright, Designs and Patents Act 1988 sections 77 and 78.

All rights reserved. No part of this publication may be reproduced, stored in a retrieval system, or transmitted, in any form or by any means, electronic, mechanical, photocopying, recording or otherwise, without prior permission of the copyright owner.

British Library Cataloguing-in-Publication Data
A catalogue record for this book is available from the British Library.

Commissioning Editor: Elizabeth Webster
Assistant Editor: Clare Holloway
Production: Sarah-Louise Deazley
Designed and typeset by The First 47
Cover illustration by Bruce Bondy
Printed and bound by Pureprint Group

While every effort has been made to check the accuracy and quality of the information given in this publication, neither the Author nor the Publisher accept any responsibility for the subsequent use of this information, for any errors or omissions that it may contain, or for any misunderstandings arising from it.

www.ribapublishing.com

## Contents

| | |
|---|---|
| IV | Acknowledgements |
| VI | Preface: You must change your life |
| 1 | Introduction: Twenty years of experience versus one year of experience twenty times |
| 10 | Prologue: Adapt |
| | |
| 26 | **Part I** |
| 27 | Chapter 1: Relate |
| 45 | Chapter 2: Remain |
| 63 | Chapter 3: Rebound |
| 79 | Chapter 4: Flourish |
| 97 | Chapter 5: Shift |
| | |
| 116 | **Part II** |
| 117 | Chapter 6: Pivot |
| 134 | Chapter 7: Reinvent |
| 150 | Chapter 8: Rewire |
| 170 | Chapter 9: Reinforce |
| 188 | Chapter 10: Reintegrate |
| | |
| 203 | Epilogue: Thrive |
| 214 | Appendix: Reboot |
| 217 | Notes |
| 218 | Index |
| 220 | Image Credits |

## Acknowledgements

Thank you to RIBA Publishing Director Helen Castle, senior commissioning editor at RIBA Publishing Elizabeth Webster, production and design assistant Sarah-Louise Deazley and copyeditor Liz Jones, and graphic designer and typesetter Alex Synge, all of whom helped turn this idea into a book. Thank you to the many selfless and esteemed contributors who shared their insights during a most inconvenient peak-pandemic time: Alexandra Pollock, Alison Brooks, Alistair Kell, Allister Lewis, Andrew Pryke, Andy Watts, Angela Mazzi, Angela E Watson, Aurélie de Boissieu, Chithra Marsh, Danei Cesario, David Swain, Diane Reicher Jacobs, Don Semple, Nicole Semple, Donna Sink, Duane Carter, Elliot Glassman, Emily Grandstaff-Rice, Evan Troxel, Evelyn Lee, Henry David Louth, Joe Cliggott, John Edwards, John Gresko, Justin Martinkovic, Lora Teagarden, Mary Shaffer, Matt Dumich, Meghana Joshi, Michael Riley, Oscia Wilson, Philip Twiss, Randy Guillot, Rob Rothblatt, Sara Beardsley, Sarah Harrison, Su Stringfellow, Susan Morgan, Stephen Drew, Ted Hyman, Tom Lee, Thomas Mozina, Trina Sandschafer, Virginia E Marquardt, Zoe Hooton; representing the following companies: FXCollaborative, Alison Brooks Architects, Ayre Chamberlain Gaunt, BAM Design, Grimshaw, GBBN, Shepley Bulfinch, Buttress Architects, Skidmore, Owings & Merrill (SOM), Studio Gang, Holly Street Studio Architects, Krueck + Sexton Architects, Kuklinski + Rappe Architects, Rowland Design, Ayers Saint Gross, WSP Built Ecology, Arrowstreet, HMC Architects, Slack Technologies, Zaha Hadid Architects, HDR Architecture, Laing O'Rourke, Taylor Design Architects, Martinkovic Milford Architects, RATIO, Mead & Hunt, SmithGroup, Little Diversified Architectural Consulting, BDP (Building Design Partnership), Google, Gensler, Red Leaf Architects, Adrian Smith + Gordon Gill Architecture, Harrison Stringfellow Architects, Macdonald & Company, ZGF Architects, Perkins&Will, Kahler Slater, HMC Architects, HPA Chartered Architects. Due to word count restrictions only a fraction of their insightful responses made the final cut. There is enough lived wisdom, oral history and sound advice on the proverbial cutting room floor to fill an enticing second volume (hint to my editor, if you are reading this). Once again, I am indebted to illustrator Bruce Bondy of Bondy Studio for his dedication to excellence, carrying the torch for hand drawing and for his always compelling drawings. And to Sharon, Simeon and Michol for standing by me as I continue on my career path less travelled.

## Dedication

Even more than architects who leave the profession each year are those who remain never to reach their full potential; who subsist instead of persist; who may have found their niche but one that no longer resembles the path they pursued. This book is for them.

# Preface: You must change your life

Fig 0.1: Architects may not be the most adaptable animal. Camels – illustrated throughout this book – are perfectly adapted to their natural environments. But humans are the most adaptable species

**The best way out is always through.**
**– Robert Frost**

At mid-career, you are either on a career path or you are not.

Joining the executive level is not the goal of every architect, especially for the emerging and rising cohort of professionals, including the majority who work in firms too small to have such things.

Which is a good thing, as aspiring to firm leadership is no longer the only option, and leadership can occur at any rung of the company ladder.

Some are not sure how they arrived on the path they are on, while others may want to explore how to get off their current path to try another within their organisation or field without making any unnecessary or catastrophic career mis-steps.

Some, through no fault of their own – especially with the current pandemic and economic recession, may have been forced off their path for unforeseen reasons, and are wondering which way to turn or what their next steps ought to be to ensure this doesn't happen again.

You've come to realise that *how you arrived at where you are won't help you with where you want to go* (running counter to a sentiment that, until now, has helped employees climb within their organisation).

**Preface: You must change your life**

You may be asking yourself: How do I persevere as a practitioner while remaining rejuvenated, relevant and resilient – without losing sight of how to leverage and capitalise on my existing knowledge and skills?

Many architects – even as soon as five years into their post-college careers – say that they no longer use *anything* they learned in school. So how can rising design professionals make the most of what they've acquired along the way – their experience and expertise, but also their relationships and network – to help their careers remain effective, fulfilling and long?

We seek to be mentored by those who have persevered and who thrive in their careers. By those who know which of the four qualities for a fulfilling career in architecture – perseverance, resilience, brilliance and prescience – are really required. We would all like to become resilient throughout our career, and learn how to do so without becoming hardened, reticent or withdrawn. And to be able to anticipate what is on the horizon so we can be prepared.

Along with the first book in this series, *Think Like An Architect,* this book, *Adapt As An Architect: A Career Companion* aims to support, nurture and promote the growth of architects in the developing stages of their careers.

This – my sixth book – is my most personal. I share stories, triumphs, reinventions and massive failures alongside those of others, all with the intention of helping you on your own path.

The book's premise is simple: how to make the most of your career prospects without having to leave the profession or industry. Architecture as a career certainly doesn't make staying easy, especially for those who find themselves nearing mid-career, or in the thick of it.

You don't need a book in order to leave architecture and go and work for a startup – you only need apply – whereas remaining an architect in architecture, on the other hand, requires a community.

This book aims to introduce you to one.

## What triggered my interest in helping mid-career architects stay in architecture?

I came to write this book as a result of four recent experiences.

In spring 2019 I once again led my university architecture programme's Chicago Studio, where my graduate architecture students and I visited 32 firms. During walk-throughs of these offices I hung back and wondered *where are all the older architects?* Everyone seemed so young – especially considering so many older architects who were set to retire in 2008–10 had supposedly remained due to depletion of their retirement savings during the 2008 Great Recession. *Where were they?*

It is true we didn't walk through sole-proprietor offices – most of those we visited were small, medium-sized and large firms in a single US city, Chicago. Had mid-career architects left to open their own offices? It turns out, *yes,* as 80% of architecture firms in the UK and US have fewer than ten people. The 32 firms were an admittedly small sample, but in 2019 I also visited and spoke in firms throughout the US and in the UK and what I saw supports what I witnessed elsewhere.

The second thing that led to me to write this book is an apparent lack of mentoring at mid-career. I say apparent, as there is scant research to support this, and not all those who you'll meet in this book agree on this point. However, most have experienced a decline in mentoring at mid-career, and this book seeks to understand this phenomenon and, as much as a book can, fill this gap.

Third, in 2010 I celebrated 25 years in the profession without a redundancy – and what happened next, let's just say for now, made me an authority on career reinvention.

Finally, from 2017–19 while travelling around the world speaking about my research (published in my third book *Convergence* and, more recently, *Superusers*), everywhere I went someone inevitably came up to the dais after my keynote, handed me their business card and asked if they could buy me a cup of coffee. Well into their careers – even if they were *asking for a friend* – they wanted to know some version of: Is there still a place for them in the profession? Should they keep at it or look for work elsewhere? And, inevitably, should they learn Revit, or coding?

They were mid-career architects looking for something – yes, the 4Cs: coffee, conversation, camraderie and companionship, but also direction and hope. I empathise, for I had found myself in similar straits several times throughout my career. An architect reaching out for support needs courage; at mid-career you are given little direction.

Through my work as an architect, professor, book author and public speaker I have benefitted from meeting and engaging with active, vibrant, brilliant, nurturing souls – fellow architects all. I reached out to 50 of them in the midst of the COVID-19 pandemic to share their thoughts with me, and now – along with my own advice and findings – with you.

The chapters that follow are loosely modelled on the conversations you might have over coffee at your regular haunt with 50 of your favourite mentors. Here I've collected the wisdom of many from firms of all sizes, a variety of roles and geographic locations to help you get back in the game; to persevere; to leverage what you already do; to reach the next level; to segue into something else so you become the architect you always imagined you would be, only with children and a mortgage and all the better for it. Admittedly a coffee doesn't last long enough to touch on and reinforce everything it is important to do to ensure that your career stays on track.

So, consider this book a series of coffees (or dare I say it, teas).

I wrote both this book and *Think Like An Architect* during the global pandemic of 2020, against a backdrop of economic recession and uprisings against racial justice. Unlike *Think* – which is backed by research found in nearly 400 articles and books – I made this a much more social book for you and me by inviting architects from around the globe (all appropriately socially distanced) to share their insights into what it takes for an architect at mid-career to persevere and thrive.

Think of them for the duration as your mentors. As with any mentor, you don't have to agree with and use everything they say. Apply what works for you now, and return to the book later for insights and suggestions for how to proceed in a way that is less fraught and more joyful, fulfilling and rewarding.

## Some answers to your questions

The book is in two parts. Part I focuses on Relevance – doing what you are doing today, only better and smarter. Part II is about Reinvention – doing something different, but not so different that you have to leave the field to do it.

I anticipated the questions you are, if not asking, thinking concerning this career phase – whether you're just starting out in the field and curious what lies ahead, or in the throes of mid-career. I posed tough questions to the architect mentors, existential questions, challenging questions – questions that made them think at a time that was not particularly conducive to thinking; questions forged by experience, representing a great deal of thought and research.

Central questions of the book include: How do we become relevant, and once we have proven our value and relevance, how do we remain so? Why do some mid-career professionals flourish, while others struggle or become obsolete? How can we be more like those who carry on and thrive? What can we do now to assure our career longevity and survival? What advice would you have for a mid-career architect who would like to stay in the profession but is finding it increasingly difficult to do so? What advice would you give to a mid-career architect who sees no clear path to leadership within their current organisation? Have you experienced mid-career reinvention/self-disruption/self-transformation in your role, and how has it worked out for you? Do you miss your former role? What impact, if any, do mid-career pressures have on how you experience work as an architect? What can firms and professional organisations do to help female architects stay? Is work-life balance achievable and desirable? Have you visualised outcomes for where you are today, or would you describe your career as a happy accident … and does it matter? What role does career planning play versus serendipity?

Throughout the book I share hard-earned career tips and advice that have worked for me and others. The responses to these questions aren't scientific and this is not a sociological academic study, but as with the best of things crowdsourced, they're convincing, insightful and to my estimation, accurate. And for these reasons, they'll be helpful to you as you grow in your career.

The book assumes you are an architect, have studied architecture or want to be an architect. This book also has some baked-in assumptions based on my biases. I believe architects are reflective and cultivate self-knowledge; that they are self-motivated – driven – and self-directed; that they continually question; that they are sceptical (in *Think Like An Architect* I refer to architects as *amiable sceptics*); and that they are optimistic – they have to believe what they design will get built, and when it does that it will have a positive impact on others. There are a staggering number of qualified architects who just leave the profession, but this book assumes you want to stay, or are trying to stay, or want to be convinced to stay. This book is here to help.

## Why now?

As a mid-career architect you have lived and worked through a period that included the dot-com boom and bust, 9/11, the 2008 Great Recession, understaffed firms that struggled to survive, the bull-market run that followed, and now the pandemic which has brought that run to an end and some firms to their knees. 'Nuff said.

## Why architects?

In most fields, professionals need to adapt. We *all* need to adapt due to the pandemic and the resulting economic recession. So, in what way – if at all – are architects different from, say, orthodontists? Why not *Adapt As A Dentist?*

The fact that every project has a different site means that architects must be comfortable with ambiguity. They work with a constantly changing array of technologies. Their work is impacted by political, economic, regulatory and social change and uncertainty. Architects design environments that adapt to people's needs, and are adept at adapting history to modern needs, and old ideas into new designs. And because I am an architect, I believe in the value of the architect, in how the architect thinks, and want to see architects persevere and thrive well into the future.

Architects adapt words to drawings and drawings to 3D models which they adapt to new buildings and existing buildings to new uses. Take the illustration on the book cover. The Elbphilharmonie Hamburg by Herzog & de Meuron is an adaptive reuse project – one of the largest and most recognised in recent years. Notice how the waterway splits into two paths at the building? This book is all about career paths splitting in two (or more) throughout one's career, and pivoting or deciding which to take when it's still your decision – and what it means when it's not. The illustration is a metaphor for adaptation, and architects' 'fork in the road' career decisions.

Fig 0.2: The Elbphilharmonie Hamburg by Herzog & de Meuron is an adaptive reuse project. In a way, our careers need to be adaptive reuse projects

## Why mid-career?

Coming out of the 2008 recession, the Emerging Professional's Companion (EPC) was a free resource offered by the National Council of Architectural Registration Boards (NCARB) in the US to assist interns (now architectural interns or emerging professionals) to earn IDP (now AXP) training towards licensure. But where was a similar resource for mid-career architects, many of whom lost their jobs or had to reinvent themselves following the last recession, as many will need to do so again coming out of the current one?

There is a lot of material, information, mentoring and support for emerging professionals. As the average age of both RIBA and AIA members is 55, younger members need enticing to join what is perceived as an older-person's organisation at a time of declining civic engagement. There is also attention lavished on those at the top nearing the end of their careers, especially on the occasion of their becoming Fellows of their respective professional organisation. But nary any attention on the mid-career architect who, in many cases, is left to sink or swim.

Mid-career architects represent the heartwood, the sweet spot, of the firm and profession – not too junior, nor inexperienced; not too senior, nor out of touch or expensive. They *make* the firms they belong to. They may not always be getting their hands dirty – though often they are – but instead they make things happen, which is every bit as important, ensuring that there is work for others to do for months to come. There is little career information or guidance available for the majority in the central 10–25 years in the field, and that is why they are hungry for insight, wisdom and shared experience.

## Why *adapt*?

The word *adapt* could be seen by some as too reactive for a book which seeks to empower an individual. Is it?

Why not *change* or *develop* or *grow* as an architect? Why is adapting so important? In other words, ought architects be driven from within and – damn the torpedoes – venture forth full steam ahead irrespective of the environment they find themselves in?

We all – some sooner, some later – come to find that career growth *requires* adaptation. 'Because that's just the way I am' said no one with career longevity. But most of all, architects need to adapt due to constant change.

## Why me?

As a university professor and until recently an administrator, I care about future architects in the university, seeing them continue on and grow in their careers. I have dedicated my career to teaching, engaging and nurturing the next generation of architects – helping them adapt to constant change – and want to see them flourish not only on entering the field but throughout their careers. But I also care about the mid-career architect and what they may feel is lacking: a voice, direction, opportunity, hope. In fact, in 2010 I delivered one of my first conference talks, at KA Connect, entitled *The Reemerging Mid-Career Professional's Companion,* addressing what I saw as a gap in our profession.

People want to have something rewarding and satisfying to do – they want purpose and meaning in their lives: a good job can satisfy those needs. They also want to be paid a decent wage so they can secure the material things that any life requires, and they want time so they can enjoy life beyond the office. I get that – and designed my career to see if it was possible to have all this and more by treating my career in architecture as a series of experiments. In this book I'll share with you some of what I learned.

## Why companion?

A book not only informs but can emote and empathise: this is one of those books. I've aimed to write a book that *gets* you and the circumstance you find yourself in – a book you can turn to again and again as challenges and opportunities arise – supporting and providing guidance for mid-career architects at a developing stage in their careers.

So, pull up a chair or 50, pour a cup and relax. What follows are the post-keynote conversations I wished I'd had the opportunity to have, with other architects present to listen in and add their hard-won wisdom.

# Introduction: Twenty years of experience versus one year of experience twenty times

Fig 0.3: Just as animals adapt to the conditions of their environments, so do architects

Skidmore, Owings & Merrill Project Manager, AIA New York State Board Representative and founder of WALLEN + daub, Danei Cesario AIA, RIBA, NOMA has never valued her intuition more than right now. That expands across the gamut of her life, personally and professionally. On 3 March 2020 she turned to her husband and said, 'This coronavirus is about to rock our world in an unprecedented way.' He laughed at her ominous comment and told her to relax. 'A week later,' says Cesario, 'companies started enforcing work-from-home directives. By that point, I was already working remotely from my fully stocked home and reassuring my teams, because I responded to my intuition with preparation. Now, nearly three months on [at the time of writing], many furloughs and paused projects later, we understand our business models and our teams better. The pandemic has pushed us to challenge the way we work and interact, and what we focus on. The pandemic has concretised the way that I have approached my life and career. It has been an unhappy global occurrence; my hope is that we can garner some good from this unique shared experience.'

This book, and my previous, *Think Like An Architect,* were both written during the worldwide COVID-19 pandemic, subsequent worldwide recession and uprisings against racial injustice. Just as my first four books on design technology relied on practice-based research and on interviews with industry stalwarts, this book represents a return to form as it contains a variety of voices of women and men in the industry like Danei Cesario, from a variety of firm sizes and roles.

Part of that is by design – the voices in this book aside, research from books and articles will only go so far to provide readers with an understanding of how to advance in their careers. Part is by circumstance – reaching out to individuals at a time of social distancing and social isolation, when most are working or in my case teaching from home, provided an opportunity for social engagement from however far afield.

Because they were largely working from home, one could argue that the pandemic provided some of the design professionals who lend their voices, experiences, perspectives and insights to this book, if not with that most hard-to-come-by resource – time – then a chance to consider their own careers with some distance and objectivity. A pandemic has a way of putting things that matter into perspective, while sidelining the trivial. As Samuel Johnson retorted, 'when a man knows he is to be hanged in a fortnight, it concentrates his mind wonderfully'.[1] One other outcome is that the pandemic forced everyone to adapt. What better example of adaptation than during a pandemic: restaurants, architects, students, professors, literally everyone has had to adapt in these challenging times.

## Global crises

The COVID-19 pandemic has allowed us to see how we live and practise through a new lens. In many ways, it gave us perspective to become comfortable with our individual identities rather than [this being] gleaned from where, how and who we worked for. It was a great equaliser and illuminated the disparities among socioeconomic strata.
**– Emily Grandstaff-Rice**

It is requiring us to look at how we work, the efficiencies of work, how we communicate with our teams, leadership and clients. And seeing how we need to adjust the types of services we provide our clients to remain relevant.
**– Virginia E Marquardt**

The pandemic will undoubtedly change the way the role of the architect exists as a business, but it's far too early to see how this will impact on individual careers or decisions.
**– Alistair Kell**

Many of the decisions Shepley Bulfinch principal Angela Watson FAIA has made are resonating in today's changed world. Has the pandemic made her reconsider some of the decisions she made, careerwise? 'I've always tried to embrace new tools to find better ways to communicate,' says Watson. 'In fact, that has been one of my big endeavours over the last few years. Communication is the key for people be able to collaborate with each other, and collaboration is at the heart of what we do as architects. Being really good at it is key, but it's not so simple. This is especially true when people are in different locations. To get better at it and make better connections across the firm, we have composed teams across offices. While not always easy, this gave everyone an opportunity to practise communicating remotely. When our whole firm started working from home in mid-March of 2020, that practice paid off. People were able to work together to invent new meeting protocols, inside and outside of teams.'

While the situation helped her firm to adapt, there were other unforeseen advances that took place. When Watson's firm grew to include multiple offices and she moved to one of the smaller ones, she experienced first-hand that communicating in an equitable way was harder. 'When we were distributed in various conference rooms in different cities, group dynamics had an impact on effective communication, separating us into groups as opposed to connecting us as one firm,' says Watson. 'We were working on making that better, and one of our challenges was to change behaviour that was rooted in many years of meeting in person only. By working remotely, everybody had to communicate virtually from their individual workspace. This dramatically changed meeting dynamics. Assuming adequate bandwidth, everybody was on an equal footing, regardless of which city they were in or if they were an outspoken person or not. Our tools that we're using to communicate with each other now allow some of those differences to be equalised.'

Fig 0.4: Design session at Angela Watson's firm, Shepley Bulfinch

As the pandemic is ongoing, impacts at the time of writing – on roles, people, firms, industry and society – remain to be seen. 'This pandemic has had to make us more resilient, smarter and efficient in order to survive it,' says architect and director of HPA Chartered Architects Zoe Hooton. 'For my career, it has made me step up as a leader.'

During the pandemic, most have learned to use their digital tools in more nuanced ways: survival mode versus enhanced mode for heightened engagement. 'Technology is awesome – but only when it is tailored so that it is in the background and supports you – not the other way around,' says founding principal of Holly Street Studio, Diane Reicher Jacobs AIA. 'I have fallen in love with my iPad Pro during the quarantine; I now know the million things this baby can do.' Moving forward, she will be more measured and focused in directing the work of her firm. 'There are many things the pandemic exposed in terms of crumbling infrastructure, housing inequity and basic human needs for public space,' Jacobs adds. 'I am going to be even more proactive in pursuing work of higher value. I will be a bit more outspoken, toward arrogance. I will make rest more of a priority.'

## Great recessions

As today's mid-career architects either graduated during or managed to maintain their jobs during (or despite) the 2008 recession and the 2020 recession, these cannot be ignored. The architecture profession lost a substantial number of future architects over this long period, with only the best and brightest (and luckiest) graduates finding jobs. Many architects in this cohort left the profession to find more secure careers.

The experience of successfully navigating their careers during the 2008 recession is unique to this group, though circumstances will likely be similar for those who make it through the ongoing pandemic and its associated recession. Additionally, because as many as 30% of architects left the profession after the 2008 recession, there is a 'hole' in the number of mid-career architects, increasing their value in the current marketplace.

What strategies were successful for this group in surviving the first recession?[2] Do these strategies apply in the 2020 recession, and potentially hereafter? Do the architects in this group hold an 'unfair advantage' because of their relative scarcity? If so, how is this advantage being exploited for career advancement? Can and should mid-career architects prepare for future shocks, including future Great Recessions? Is managing uncertainty a key skillset needed to survive these recurring life events? How should one deal with redundancy – as that can happen to anyone, regardless of preparedness? What are the lessons that we can take from this group's experience, and how might they apply today as we weather another economic downturn?

As an entire book could be devoted to these questions – and in a way, this one is – we'll focus here on this last question as it applies to mid-career architects, and on some of the others elsewhere in the book, for beside the impact of the 2008 recession this group has also experienced a revolution in design technologies.

What strategies can mid-career architects attempt to remain relevant in a rapidly changing digital world? What value does experience bring to the architectural process today? How can that value be quantified? How can the mid-career architect best communicate this experience to younger, more tech-savvy architects? These questions will be addressed in a later chapter.

In a sentence, to successfully navigate an economic downturn, Great or otherwise, it would be wise to be proactive, to emphasise relationships – to reach out to others before you need them so they will be there when you do – and to segue into a new market before you need it, so when the shoe drops, you're prepared.

Survival is largely about communicating what value you deliver, and it's about agility – recognising where the needs are *now,* and reframing what you do in terms of the work that needs to be done. In the 2008 recession, focused almost exclusively on housing projects, my firm had to shift from designing market-rate and affordable housing to deals that were then attractive to banks – looking at where loans would be made. You could argue that this was always the case – it can be a subtle shift – but nonetheless reframing the emphasis from designing buildings to appealing to loan officers was significant for our survival.

Fig 0.5: Team meeting at Alistair Kell's firm, BDP

Value to a business, based on the economic circumstances, and a degree of luck are needed to navigate any downturn, advises BDP principal Alistair Kell. 'The skill and project experience, education or healthcare buildings by example, may be valued when there are project opportunities, but as workload softens work-winning is key. Those capable at delivering projects may be seen as less vital than work-winners, and by mid-career your position and skills within a business tend to be assumed.'

Diane Reicher Jacobs's firm weathered the 2008 recession by doing on-call work with various municipalities. 'We knew that the work would not be glamorous, but set our sights on a different measure of success – building relationships and fixing problems. Turns out two of our most decorated, award-winning designs came out of this period,' she says, adding, 'just when we weren't focused on that sort of thing.'

Weathering an economic downturn is more about mindset and personal fortitude than career position, believes architect and principal of Martinkovic Milford Architects Justin Martinkovic. 'The real question is "how do architects position themselves to be more resilient and less affected by market forces outside of our control?" The framework of the owner–architect construct may not be the way to do it.'

## Mid-career defined

Architectural careers evolve slowly. Nearly every building is unique, a prototype, so there's a continuous learning curve. Technologies and regulations can change over the lifespan of one project. It can take ten years in a practice before an architect sees a project through from beginning to end. You need patience and stamina. Most good architects are seeking that moment where they can stand beside a building and say, 'I did that, I made that happen.'
– **Alison Brooks**

I'm 63 years old and I still feel like I am mid-career; this is such an exciting profession, the clients and projects are so amazing, I am not at all tired or bored. When the process of exploration stops, that is when it will be time to stop and go learn to play golf …That hasn't happened yet, when it does, I think I will know it.
– **Ted Hyman**

If you consider that architects on average qualify around the age of 28–30 and will practise for 30–40 years, 10–25 is probably about right [for mid-career] but a very broad range! That said, it does take time to develop a career within a company. However, ten years is too late to be thinking long term about a career, and it is important to have aspirations and goals [from the outset] even if they change.
– **Philip Twiss**

When exactly mid-career begins is up for debate. This book defines mid-career as 10–25 years into one's career. In the UK, once you have passed your Part 3 examination you are a qualified architect. Head of architecture and design at Macdonald & Company Stephen Drew RIBA Associate would argue that after three years as an architect you are mid-career. 'It takes seven years to get to become qualified,' explains Drew. 'So, ten years total. It is at this point that the person's career either goes up a gear or stagnates.'

Architect and principal-in-charge at HMC Architects Virginia E Marquardt AIA is entering her 21st year in the profession, and says that it feels like she's just starting to hit her stride and mid-career point. 'With our life expectancy being longer than [that of] our parents and grandparents, I'm planning to work another 20–25 years, well into my sixties before I retire,' says Marquardt. 'And retirement may be consulting half the year, while travelling and relaxing the other half.'

Fig 0.6: HMC principal-in-charge Virginia E Marquardt leading a meeting

Despite exceptions, most of the architects in this book believe the definition of mid-career as 10–25 years is appropriate. '[From] 0–10 years you are learning on a steep curve,' says Martinkovic. 'At ten years you should have the landscape of our profession surveyed, and you should know where your interests lie and where strengths and weakness measure up against the broader industry. Excepting, perhaps, the first one or two years of orienting to the industry, we should be thinking about our career trajectory throughout our career. We should challenge our assumptions constantly. We should push our own growth and learning. We should consider alternative paths, even if only as a thought exercise.'

That said, most believe that architects ought to consider their career path well before arriving at mid-career. 'It is way too late to start planning your career ten years in,' says senior associate at Arrowstreet Emily Grandstaff-Rice FAIA.

Architect at Rowland Design Donna Sink is representative too, in that she agrees that after ten years one is mid-career, but also that an architect can remain mid-career for as long as they want. 'The truth is: there is no choice about being resilient in one's career; we all have to be, no matter what point in our career we are at,' says Sink. 'The first 10–15 years can be a time to try different things: working in a corporate or boutique firm; specialisation in something like curtain walls or healthcare; residential design versus commercial, marketing, historic restoration. But even after two decades doing one or another type of work, an architect can take the skills they have and pivot to a different area within architecture or even to a different field altogether. The "young architect" awards in our field typically use age 40 as a cut-off; at age 50 one is really hitting one's stride as an architect, and many architects use retirement as an opportunity to shift into a slightly different field, like consulting.'

Fig 0.7: Adrian Smith + Gordon Gill Architecture director Sara Beardsley (far left) leads the Yongsan team meeting

'The amount of planning needed is a constant process, but the intensity of it at different periods can depend on the career,' says director at Adrian Smith + Gordon Gill Architecture Sara Beardsley AIA. 'Some careers have a series of milestones in quick succession early on – becoming licensed, leading a first project, for example – and then the path to the next big step may take quite a bit longer,' says Beardsley. 'Taking this next big step into "middle management" or, at a smaller/mid-sized firm, the role of principal – marks that one may have arrived at "mid-career",' she says. '10–25 years is the right definition. It will vary by person, and by the educational or previous career path the person may have taken before becoming an architect. It also varies by the maturity of the individual and how naturally they fall into leadership roles.'

### ASK THIS

The COVID-19 pandemic has not made Joe Cliggott reconsider career decisions to this point. 'However,' he says, 'it has been a time of reflection, personally and professionally; a time to question worth, value and what is essential to the community. There will be a newfound appreciation for a lot that we've taken for granted, and hopefully a greater attention to communities that have suffered the most.'

### ASK THIS

Concerning career narratives: architects with 10–25 years of experience are interested in building a long-term narrative for their careers. Look back on your career mid-stream, and ask yourself: How does what came before, leading to today, form a thread or career story that I can explain to someone?

## TRY THIS

For those who have been chastened by the pandemic, Sara Beardsley says the following: 'Having experienced the last ten or so years of my mid-career in relatively good economic times, I have found the pandemic to be a humbling experience; it has given me more gratitude for what I do have – and it has reinforced the importance of all of the remote-working and communication technology that I was fortunate to become well versed in during my mid-career. I do not think I would have done anything different, other than perhaps making a point to remember what is important every day over those past ten years. The pandemic will, in some ways, bring the world together in order to face common problems that we are all vulnerable to. It will also help us as architects consider more ways that design can be linked to healthier living and to protecting people from disease.'

## Prologue: Adapt

Fig 0.8: The extent to which architects fit into their working environment is a big part of the adaptability equation

### The only architects that are doomed are the ones that won't adapt.
– Zane Gray

Due to COVID-19, HMC Architects' K-12 practice had to pivot to understand from their school districts how they could best support and service them. Principal in charge at HMC Architects Virginia E Marquardt and her partners reached out to them to discover what is keeping them up at night: learning from parents, teachers and students the pros and cons of distance learning and how they would like to see it improved or tweaked; learning what the CDC, the state education system, and local health departments will be requiring of schools to reopen; and learning what this means for them as an architectural solution and service. 'We are not sure just yet, but we want to help and support our school districts, and we are learning and researching how we can best help and support them,' says Marquardt. 'And as we help and support each district, there will be a different solution for each, because each has its own challenges and needs.'

During this time of increased home working, HMC Architects' LA K-12 studio, which Marquardt leads, provided full-time construction administration services, producing 50% construction documents for a comprehensive high school modernisation/seismic retrofit, and new two-storey classroom building project. 'We have all learned how to work and collaborate virtually with each other from each of our homes,' says Marquardt, 'instead of in the office where we had face-to-face discussions.'

Every morning the project leadership teams meet first to plan the day and work through challenges, then the entire team meets to update each other regarding the previous day's progress: 'Anything we have learned, and what we each plan to accomplish that day, holding each other responsible,' Marquardt says. Then throughout the day, project architects meet with their architecture and engineering team members to work different aspects of the project and coordinate with each.

Fig 0.9: HMC principal-in-charge Virginia E Marquardt working remotely during the pandemic

'I'm amazed at how well my team is working together and ensuring the success of the project,' says Marquardt, who is also working with clients in this manner, holding weekly all-owner/architect meetings to continue to identify and work through open scope and design items. For their projects in construction, the architects are still on site one to three days a week, practising social distancing by holding owner/architect/constructor (OAC) meetings in their own trailers, and then walking the site together (with the proper PPE, 2m apart), to observe and resolve in-field conditions.

The architects were able to accomplish this transition during the pandemic in large part because they planned well in advance. 'We're fortunate that HMC Architects has been thinking about what it looks like and what is needed to support working from anywhere for some time,' says Marquardt, having over the last year rolled out the tools and resources necessary for employees to do this. One example of this is that new employees were provided with laptops or tablets, replacing desktop computers, and the firm moved to a VoIP phone system. They also started utilising software for virtual meetings, chatting and sharing documents, and they moved to cloud work-sharing. 'Not everything was in place when we decided as a firm to work from home a week before the order was given,' Marquardt admits, 'but we were better prepared, and with our IT department and digital practice's support, the move was pretty smooth. Sometimes the mental aspect of being safer at home has been harder to manage.'

Just as architecture firms and teams have had to adapt in these pandemic times, so too have individual architects. As Marquardt has grown and moved into different positions and been promoted, gaining new skills, knowledge and experiences – and importantly, learning to let go – she has had to remain adaptable. 'I'm a person that likes to control my environment and my work,' says Marquardt. 'Now that I'm a principal in charge, I've had to learn to trust my team more than ever and give that control to them. It has not been easy, and every day I learn how to let go even more, to trust more – what that means and looks like – because I have to trust my team to do their job, their role, if I'm going to have their trust and support, and for them to have buy-in and take full responsibility. And I have a different role and responsibilities I must see through, too.'

Being an architect, navigating the obstacles in the course of a career, requires ongoing adaptation, which in turn requires mindfulness and self-awareness on the part of the architect. You can't just adapt once and relax, rest on your laurels, take a victory lap then move on.

Adaptation isn't one and done. It isn't something you do and then are immune from through the vicissitudes of time, chance, circumstance and fortune. You've got to be vigilant and keep at it.

## When to adapt, when to stand firm

My career so far has spanned changes to credential proceedings, an economic recession, furloughs and now a global pandemic. With every external challenge, I have been challenged to become more flexible in the way I operate as an architect and as a person.
**– Danei Cesario**

That level of adaptability and flexibility has allowed me to stay gainfully employed through the peaks and troughs. It has built confidence in my skills to know that I can positively contribute to any environment – whether that environment is an engineering firm, an exhibit space, a university lecture, an expeditor's office, a committee or my team.
**– Danei Cesario**

Adaptability is about continuing to remain curious and using our design thinking skills and knowledge to listen to our clients about their needs and then collaborate with them to develop strategies, processes and design solutions to help meet our needs.
**– Virginia E Marquardt**

Why adapt? What does it mean to adapt as an architect? First, it means to alter or adjust yourself while you are and continue to be an architect. It implies adapting on your terms *and* adapting on others' terms – there needs to be some give and take on the part of the architect. You can have a plan, an idea for what you want to achieve and accomplish in your career, but you must also learn to roll with the changes. Looking in the rearview mirror of recent history, our careers can be seen as a series of adaptations amassed over time, versus having been designed or predestined.

This last criterion implies a level of flexibility and agility, which may be tendentious as architects can be rigid types – a necessary trait for those responsible for the health, welfare and safety of the public. Architects require a certain rigidity beyond which they will not bend.

So, the flexible and adaptable architect is in stark contrast to the stiff and upright, immovable and set-in-their-ways architect. As the rate of change in the world increases, architects must learn to adapt faster.[3] In addition to being able to adapt to novel situations, being resilient and agile, recommended survival skills[4] include the ability to navigate around distractions and impediments, and pivot when the road ahead is fraught. To adapt is the key to survival.[5]

Simply put, be flexible and easy to work with. You decide the things you as an architect can learn to live with, but here is where you need to have a hard stop: gravity, codes, ethics, equity, your health and wellbeing, family. Careers are long, and life is full of surprises, so architects also need to adapt to change.

## Adapting as a coping mechanism

People use adaptive coping mechanisms as survival tactics, but also in order to experience less stress.[6] During the 2020 pandemic, architecture firms adapted by printing eye shields and PPE, proving that both architects and architecture firms can, when required, quickly and deftly adapt to their new reality.

Imagine that while you are working on a high-rise headquarters your client – the CEO – asks you to design her vacation home: a building type and scale your firm has never worked on. Or you're a specialist in healthcare architecture and a pandemic rolls around. You become the go-to person to respond to media questions concerning the need for temporary health facilities, and are asked to lay out an ICU in a pre-existing convention centre. 'Those types of healthcare facilities are not my specialism' would be one possible response – however unhelpful and ungracious, nor strategic. 'Let's see who we could work with on adaptive reuse, and I'll chime in as necessary' would be another – one that requires thinking on your feet, and no small amount of adapting what you do for the demands of the moment.

Perfectionism is another form of rigidity. Architects aren't expected to be perfect – the standard of care that they are expected to achieve is based on what a similar architect in a similar situation might achieve. Adaptability requires a bit of not perfectionism but *imperfectionism:* veering from the rules when required to (who has ever won a design competition without breaking at least one rule?); letting people off the hook when the situation demands; adlibbing and improvising instead of always doing things by the book – in other words, the sort of behaviour that would drive a perfectionist mad. This is not to say that architects shouldn't specialise. Yet, architects who are unable also to generalise can be seen as being brittle or having difficulty adapting when facing new situations. *When all you have is a hammer, everything looks like a nail.*

The ability to adapt of course is not limited to architects. The human body is incredibly adaptive to new environments and situations, and as new problems arise. When organisations model themselves on living organisms, they do so because it enables them to adapt rapidly to changes and restructure themselves quickly.[7] For example, consider what happens in the brain of a blind person proficient at reading Braille. The visual centres in the brains of blind people when learning Braille register what their fingers are 'seeing'. In other words, their fingers register in the part of the brain that would have been responsible for seeing.[8] How long did this change take? Less than a week. An example of neuroplasticity, the visual cortex can adapt and repurpose itself.

*That's* adapting.

When painter Chuck Close was paralysed from the neck down, or when glass sculptor Dale Chihuly flew through a windshield in a head-on car accident then later dislocated his right shoulder in a bodysurfing accident, or when architect Chris Downey lost his vision mid-career due to a brain tumour and now designs buildings focused on acoustics and accessibility – they thereafter had to modify how they worked.

*That's* adapting.

Your architectural education and training can of course be adapted to other uses, meaning architects can be adapted for other uses, too. This is the beauty of transferable skills. Just as their buildings are formed through adaptive reuse, so too architects adapt to different environments and external situations: new jobs, careers, titles, roles, responsibilities and technologies.

Architects must know how to adapt to constantly changing situations throughout their careers. They learn mid-design that the site is smaller than they were led to believe – or that their client purchased the property next door and wants to expand. Or mid-construction they find there are objects or obstructions below grade that may hamper progress pouring foundations. On fast-track projects with compressed schedules architects adapt to an increase in speed and decrease other aspects accordingly. Cut in budget? Change in material selection or availability? Architects adapt.

Architects need to adapt, change, evolve: to the company's needs, to changing environments, even to the future.[9] There's the continuing need to adapt to always-evolving disruptive technology. In your career, unless it is in its final throes, you will find yourself adapting to parametric tools, computational tools, generative design software, automation, AI and machine learning (aka *adaptive* computation).

The faster the changes, the faster we must adapt and evolve to the changing environment. You might think that with the rise of machines and robots they would have an advantage over people when it comes to adapting to sudden change, but in fact the opposite is true: because machines need to be reprogrammed, humans are more adaptable than machines and can respond more quickly to changes.[10]

Whether architects *should* adapt is another question. Some feel that architects adapting implies they are weak, acquiescing to others' demands rather than directing others on what ought to happen – changing, challenging, fighting, questioning. So, are we not to say *adapt,* as doing so appears to make an architect less likely to fight or improve the situation? How do we know that what we are adapting to is beneficial or good for us? And, how important is adaptability throughout the course of a career?

## From literate, to adaptive, to transformative

For starters, as consultants and service professionals, architects work in a service industry. Adjusting and adapting to others doesn't show weakness: it's expected and it's your job. Adapting throughout your career is important, but it isn't the be all and end all. (That would be self-transformation and reinvention, covered in a later chapter.) This concept comes from EdTech – the idea of moving from literate, to adaptive, to transformative: where if you can operate a device you are considered *literate;* if you can operate an app that helps you read on the device you are considered *adaptive;* and, if the device enables you to do something you couldn't before, you are using the device in a *transformative* way.[11] Sometimes using the device in an adaptive way is what you need, other times you want to aim to use it transformationally.

The fact is, change happens and architects need to adapt – yet we don't always know *what* we are adapting to. So, there is always some risk involved. I wrote this book in part to make adapting less risky and more rewarding for you.

Here's why we need to take on some risks. Being unwilling or unable to adapt throughout your career will ultimately lead to your demise as a design professional. Adapting *as* an architect – while remaining in the role of an architect – is the focus of this book, and in the pages that follow takes on many guises. Some architects adapt by learning to play the game in order to find themselves on the path to the C-suite and firm leadership, some adapt by pivoting to a different role or position, or by reinventing themselves at a career inflection point, to name just three.

Some adapt to midlife pressures – the realities of ageing and ageism; family and work-life balance; successfully navigating an economic downturn – and the various paths to career longevity. Some are able to visualise a successful outcome (and *in*come) for themselves, while others make it up as they go and wouldn't have it any other way. In this book we'll look at all of these, as well as the importance of perseverance, resilience, talent and prescience;

how training and mentoring impact one's ability to adapt and ensure one's continued relevance; the best time to switch firms or take on a parallel role; how to become unstuck; we also address near-constant change in the profession.

The focus is on adapting *as* an architect – for the architect who studies architecture and intends to become an architect, becomes one and *remains* one. How does one do this? There are as many career paths, roadmaps and ways to do this as there are unexpected bumps along the way. Unless you are practising in Australia – which, until recently, hadn't experienced an economic recession in nearly 25 years – regular economic downturns and recessions are predictable, even cyclical. However, the one that cratered the economy in 2008 and again with the pandemic in 2020 were neither. Architects who persevere adapt.

Can you prepare in advance for both the inevitable economic downturns and the unpredictable cataclysms? Yes – by having a plan in place should the unexpected occur.

*That's* adapting.

Just as animals adapt to the conditions of their environments, so do architects. If architects are hired by an employer based 50/50 on their potential and fit, to the extent that the architect fits into their new environment, is a big part of the equation. Architects may not be the most adaptable animal (ants, camels – illustrated throughout this book – and especially alligators are perfectly adapted to their natural environments), but humans are the most adaptable species. People live on every continent except Antarctica, and are adapted to virtually all of our planet's terrains and climates.[12] These are examples of situational adaptability, the kind of challenges we face in our rapidly changing workplaces.

What makes architects especially good at adaptation? Is it the fact that we're visual learners? As architects, we believe we're especially adapted to learning by seeing images. Most of us won't attend a lecture unless there are slides – *You promised there would be slides!* – because humans are gifted at remembering images. *Homo sapiens* is particularly adapted to learning in ways that are vivid, visual and experiential, in what is referred to as 'the picture superiority effect'.[13]

Architects have been concerned with adapting, and addressing adaptability as far back as Vitruvius in the *Ten Books,* where it is declared that 'decorations of the polished surfaces of the walls ought to be treated with due regard to propriety, so as to be adapted to their situations, and not out of keeping with differences in kind'.[14]

## The adaptable architect

And yet there's a reason this book isn't titled *Adapt Like An Architect* (like the first book in this series, *Think Like An Architect*). Not everybody would agree that architects have this whole adaptation thing down, that people ought to emulate the way architects adapt (they shouldn't, at least not yet) – just as others ought to emulate the way architects think (they should). This book is very deliberately entitled *Adapt As An Architect* because it is about how to adapt *while* you are an architect. In a perfect world, no matter what is thrown your way, you adapt. And that means you make the most of things; you make the situation not only copacetic and amicable but, all things considered, optimal.

Buildings for the most part are predictable – they behave in predictable ways. If you can model it, you can simulate it, and are able to more or less predict how buildings will behave. People, on the other hand, aren't. Yes, neuroscience and behavioural economics can predict how people will generally act in a given situation, but no one can predict how everyone will behave – it's more a percentage, it's a range. Architects aren't like product managers churning out widgets. What architects produce must adapt to changes of site and location; different users and their needs, which change due to preferences, the economy and trends.

But what about people – who are more unpredictable? Who may have communication styles different from your own? Who may have different goals and ambitions and priorities? How do architects adapt to them? Because adapt they must if they are to persevere and prosper in their career – indeed, if they are to have a career. When presenting, you adapt by reading the room, gauging everyone's mood, attuning yourself to what is going on in other people's heads, where everyone's knowledge level is – and with this input you decide how to proceed. Taking in data and feedback, you constantly assess and adjust accordingly. That is similar to how architects adapt.

Fig 0.10: The architect should first determine whether theirs is a job, a career or a calling

It is important to state here what adapting is not. Adapting isn't the same as creating a workaround, hack or bespoke solution when facing an unworkable situation. Adapting isn't the same as fudging or rigging the result.

Adaptation is about change – but it is also a response to change. Change of any scale requires our adaptive response. Like everyone, architects have to adapt to new bosses, team members, sometimes even clients. I was once designing a high-rise in a major city, and my boss called me into his office to tell me I no longer had a client. I didn't understand. Apparently, my client had taken his own life the day before. Nothing prepares you for such a situation. In time, when appropriate, you adapt.

To be sure, not all adapting is beneficial. Adapting can take on a negative aspect when we decide, for example, not to fight climate change but instead to adapt to the consequences. 'Climate change deniers might argue that, even if anthropogenic global warming is happening and there will be negative consequences, perhaps it will be cheaper and easier to simply adapt to the changing climate'[15] where it is thought that 'the rich will adapt. The poor will suffer'.[16]

In wanting to improve the world, we are perpetually dissatisfied with the way things are. This perpetual dissatisfaction drives us to adapt. Architects are famously never satisfied – certainly not with the status quo. We're always looking to progress, build on what came before, improve with every opportunity to build, where evolution favours dissatisfaction over contentment. 'Our tendencies toward boredom, negativity bias, rumination, and hedonic adaptation conspire to make sure we're never satisfied for long.'[17]

### Asking the right questions

**Adaptability is key. If you can identify the shifting needs that a project, a practice, a successful career might need, then the next step is to be versatile enough to shift with it. Working in a technology-focused support role, a big component of our work is in identifying and working to the differing needs a team may have. This can be different technologies, different briefs, or just different approaches to the same problem. A key thing that all members of our design technology team learn early on is that you need to be able to see a problem from different viewpoints – the technology specialist, the architect, the client.**
**– Andy Watts**

**I often find myself in situations where I do not have previous experience, not quite sure where to start, but the path to the solution is learning how to ask the right questions.**
**– Emily Grandstaff-Rice**

Before Andrew Yang was a US presidential candidate, he was an entrepreneur working in startups and early growth stage companies as founder or executive. When hiring, one criterion he would use was what he called 'adaptive excellence', looking for people who achieved over time in a combination of academic, athletic, extracurricular, personal and business contexts.[18] He saw these as qualities predicting success in adapting to the challenges frequently seen in startups. While not all of us can rise to this level of achievement – and not all of us need to – the idea of adaptive excellence is one that architects ought to strive for, hire for and create within themselves.

When Emily Grandstaff-Rice was younger, she was fascinated by the painter and sculptor Alberto Giacometti. 'I remember reading a passage from him where he described the artistic process like peeling the layers of an onion – with every reveal you find that there are more below the surface,' says Grandstaff-Rice. She describes her career as a series of moments and experiences – 'never quite a target' – realising that her career path may never have an ultimate destination. Once she arrives at one, 'there is another on the horizon,' she says. 'Adjustments along the way are the key to survival.'

'I thought I would be a firm principal by now,' admits Grandstaff-Rice. 'So many of my friends and peers have achieved that and on my low days, I question why I do not have the same title.' Then she remembers that her path is different: pursuing things at her own pace, having other aspirations besides the title. 'I have experienced disappointments,' she continues. 'I have experienced great success. The key for me is realising that there is growth in both – high highs; low lows. But throughout my career, asking the right questions has guided me to better understand my value as a professional and the impact my work can have in shaping the built environment.'

## Staying curious

Adaptability, or at least the ability to take on new tasks and pressures, is vital. There is no straight-line path between graduate architect and practice principal.
**– Alistair Kell**

Adaptability is important but for it to be strategic, you have to ask questions of yourself and the world. The secret to career longevity is curiosity.
**– Emily Grandstaff-Rice**

As a survival tactic, Red Leaf Architects founding partner Rob Rothblatt has made many subtle adaptations throughout his career that show a willingness to take on tasks others didn't want, or try something new, frequently diving into projects in unusual locations. 'To do Golden 1 Center,' explains Rothblatt, 'I suggested moving to Kansas City for a year, and that worked out well. I had never done a sports project – but I just said "yes", and, using the expertise around, we created the world's first LEED Platinum arena.'

'Is adaptability the secret of longevity?' asks Rothblatt. 'Architects are blessed with nimble minds, curiosity about the world, penetrating perception, and a desire to see through the status quo to a better synthesis. So, they are naturally adaptable. Architects want to do new things, try new things, and most are trained to want to pursue innovation and progressive ideas,' explains Rothblatt. 'That means buildings, ways of designing, or jobs and skills. Young and mid-career architects are pretty savvy at identifying opportunities when they see them. And genuinely don't like being stuck in a rut. Maturing as an architect is a bit like aikido – the martial art where you use the energy and momentum of your opponent in smooth fashion. Career advancement or change often comes from just saying "yes" or asking to try something when one senses an opening.'

## What to keep, what to let go of

Adaptability does give improved resilience. Even if you specialise you do have to be prepared for circumstances to change. Adaptability doesn't necessarily mean making small changes, either – ideally yes, but fail fast and learn from your mistakes. If something isn't working, pause, analyse why it isn't working, and adapt.
– **Philip Twiss**

Most of my successful senior management have two skills. They adapt to change well, and they listen to their clients' requirements. They then take ownership of the change as though it was their idea to start with.
– **Michael Riley**

Diane Reicher Jacobs has a philosophical view on the role of adaptation in one's career, and explains how she adapted to different situations in her career. 'When [the] kids left for college, I put in more time.' 'Though I am not sure if it has been more productive. Otherwise, I have had to adapt my process and toolkit as an architect for each new project and client. [The] trick is to know what to keep so I'm not reinventing the wheel all the time.'

If adaptability is making tiny adjustments until you hit your target, how do you recognise when to make these adjustments? 'If your method of dealing with others, solving a problem, or just getting through your day is causing stress, then it is time for adjustment,' says Jacobs. 'Know where you are needed, and where you must step back. Understand that your employer needs you as much as you need them, and be clear in your offerings, intentions and needs.' She continues, 'Small adjustments come in the form of changing schedules, shifting teams, time away learning something, and a distinct strategy for growth. These focal points should be mutually beneficial to more than one party in order to bring them to fruition.'

That said, Jacobs would not say that she makes adjustments. 'I have a steady spiritual practice that informs this perspective,' she explains. 'I would say that I have remained open-minded and steadily engaged, but also more vocal when things do not feel right. My biggest problem right now is that I am fiercely reluctant to waste time. It is one of our most valuable limited resources, and *so much* of how we operate in our profession wastes time. Even the things that people say are meant to *save* time. This can be clearly seen with technology, collaboration and administration. I am working on how to deal with that, especially in a hyper-collaborative environment. This is one of my unstated goals for my current project. I keep a list of these for personal sanity.'

At the start of your career, you don't always have control over where you work, the people you work with on your team, or who your clients are. By mid-career, your goal may be to have to more and more control over these factors, where you can to a greater extent choose the people and context in which you work. Some architects have described ultimate freedom as being where, if things aren't working out, you can afford to fire a client. For Jacobs, the secret of life is that 'it is a long, linear and singular journey that is constantly informed by who we surround ourselves with and the context that we (most of the time) get to choose. Problems arise if both the people and the context are not of one's choosing. That is stagnation, or worse.'

## Internal versus external forces

Our world is constantly changing, and our profession is constantly changing. As a result, our target is constantly moving as well. That means that I am constantly making tiny adjustments as part of an ongoing learning process. For me the target is to do it better next time.
– Angela Watson

Everything changes all the time. A fixed career is an illusion and a lack of observation of the ever-changing world we are building.
– Aurélie de Boissieu

You must make adjustments and be adaptable, but all will be for naught unless you also have a plan. There is a continuous tension throughout a career between these two polar points: knowing how much to stick with your career path and how much to be flexible in the face of circumstances. It's a variation on the *circumstantial and ideal.* If you stick too closely to your envisioned plan, you could miss out on serendipitous, career-making opportunities that arise along the way. On the other hand, those who are overly flexible may err on the side of over-acquiescence, appearing not to have a backbone. Adaptability is important, but you're at the whim of the wind if you don't also have inner direction.

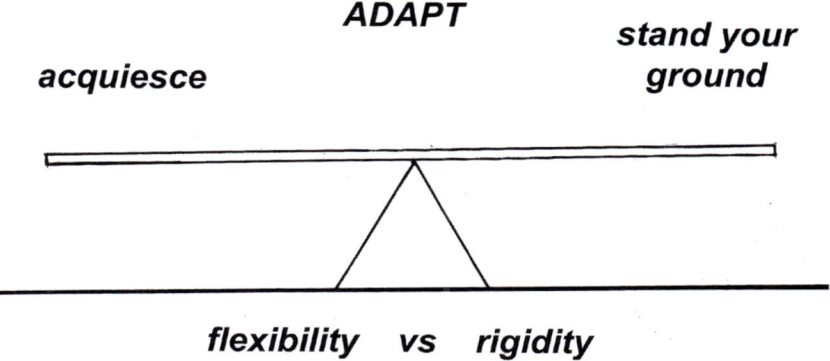

Fig 0.11: Adaptability is all about knowing when to stand firm and when to be flexible

Design principal and vice-president at Kahler Slater Trina Sandschafer sees the importance of adaptability. 'However, you cannot keep adjusting your course without knowing where you are going,' she explains. 'There needs to be both inward reflection about what you are doing well, where you can improve, where you are going – and you counterbalance that with the same questions about your firm and our industry. Knowing where you are going, and where the industry is going, is important. How do you hit the target? Accountability and adaptability.'

Managing principal at HDR Chicago Joe Cliggott believes that the secret to career longevity is the balance between adaptability and perseverance. 'The challenge is to recognise when to change and when to show resolve,' he explains. 'Adaptability in a career goes back to empathy and awareness. If you are aware of your actions and the impact on others, you will start to understand when to adjust.' In Cliggott's own career, the need for adjustments occurred when he was changing firms, and the makeup of the team changed from what he was used to, where a greater diversity of age, experience, gender, race, education background, nationality and work styles meant having to adjust his approaches to communication and management.

Designers deal with ambiguity every day. It has become a truism that designers are comfortable with ambiguity and uncertainty, and that flexibility and adaptation are part of the iterative process of an architect's work. Yet, according to principal and design director at Gensler, Randy Guillot FAIA, 'when faced with similar obstacles in our own careers often that same spirit of iteration is harder to come by'. Guillot further explains that 'adaptability is the willingness to try new things. To try them out, to pivot, take what works and what doesn't work and to use it to move forward. Adaptability may be making tiny adjustments or large ones; the key is to be objective enough to really look at the results and see if what you're doing is getting you closer or farther from what you are trying to achieve.'

So, how do you know when adjustments need to be made? 'Experience, more often than not, is your friend in understanding how to recognise when these adjustments are necessary,' says Guillot. 'That's certainly not to say that architects early in their career aren't able to recognise when to make these adjustments, but their toolbox just is not as full yet in predicting outcomes. The irony is of course that late-career professionals have a harder time making changes traditionally, not recognising their experience is their asset and comfort along the journey.'

### ASK THIS

Imagine a continuum from stagnation (stopping; solid) to adaptation (in the middle) to acquiescing (too malleable; changing face.) Where do you fall along it? Where along the continuum would you like to be more of the time?

## ASK THIS

How do you know if your adapting is working? Ask yourself: Am I moving forward? It isn't always helpful to judge whether something is 'good' or 'bad'. Instead, try *pragmatism* by asking three questions of every piece of career advice you receive: Does it work for me? Is it nurturing? Is it growth promoting? If the answer is yes to all three – go with it.

## ASK THIS

Early in her career, Mary Shaffer kept running into colleagues who already saw their future career paths. Some wanted to start their own firm, some wanted to work in residential design, some wanted to work in healthcare design. 'It felt like they all had a specific goal,' says Shaffer. 'My reactions were immediate. No, I don't want to start my own firm. No, I don't want to be a residential architect.' Shaffer found it easy to decide what she did not want to do, but not what she *wanted* to do. 'The secret to most career success is adaptability and resilience,' says Shaffer. 'Do you bounce back from setbacks? Do you always look for a path forward, or look at things from a different perspective, even with obstacles in your way? Are you always looking to grow?' As for Shaffer, she joined committees in her state AIA chapter, eventually chairing the Architecture in the Schools Committee, where she taught kids of all ages about architecture. 'The connections I made there led to one of my favourite job opportunities, and eventually to a leadership position within our local AIA chapter, which led to another job later in my career.'

## ASK THIS

When things are not going well, it may be time to examine assumptions. Has the situation changed? Is the audience different? Has our goal evolved? **[Angela Watson]**

## ASK THIS

When Angela Watson coaches others, she tends to ask them to think of how their actions might be perceived by others. 'By putting themselves into the other person's shoes they can start to imagine how something might be perceived differently,' explains Watson. 'I sometimes try to help them with examples, mostly of things I have had to adjust. I think examples are a really important mechanism to share how something more theoretical shows up in the real world.'

## ASK THIS

Where are you unmovable/inflexible? Unwilling to move/change/adjust? Why?

## TRY THIS

Find ways to cut to the chase; be comfortable with saying no. This is not just adaptability on an individual level, but collectively. Spend less time in meetings and more time being accountable, so that when the meeting day finally arrives you 'come bearing gifts'. Curtail a bit of teamwork in favour of individual responsibility, minimise the information we feed into technology to create new ideas and create ideas from simple means, using technology as an implementor. Honour our clients' need for complex administrative accountability by setting up systems (with help!) ahead of time. **[Diane Reicher Jacobs]**

## TRY THIS

If you know where you want to head, it's certainly important to make incremental steps forward. Look for opportunities to thrive within your firm or within your professional organisation. I believe it's never too late to try something new; you may discover a new passion. **[Mary Shaffer]**

## TRY THIS

Adaptability is important, and at different scales. It is important to be willing to gradually change and grow, and to be open-minded to new ways of working. I have also found it is important to make big changes when needed, and to re-evaluate where you are personally, if you feel like you are getting stuck or not continuing to grow. These can be signs that you need to make a bigger change. **[Alexandra Pollock]**

## TRY THIS

The secret is adaptability. Every day, there is change in a practice. A lot depends on having the right attitude and personality, as in all professions, but people tend to look at change as good or bad: glass half full or glass half empty. The hardest part for me in architecture is not the practice itself, it is the people management. I have had training in understanding my own personality type and how to best relate to others that are different from me. This allows me to adapt my communications and collaboration with others in a more productive, harmonious way. **[John Gresko]**

# PART I

# 1: Relate

Fig 1.1: Situational adaptability represents the kind of challenges we face in our rapidly changing workplaces

# Attaining relevance is not a one-time thing.

Architects become more relevant by expanding their services beyond traditional practice. To what extent can we expand how we design and deliver design and a variety of different services to our clients, and be OK with the fact that the end result may or may not lead to architecture? By doing so, it will open doors for more opportunities in the future.
– **Evelyn Lee**

As architects, we are equipped to provide design services that influence the ways we experience our cities, homes and workspaces. Our relevance is embedded in that talent, and to remain forward-thinking in an ever-evolving world. Understanding the individualities of the people, cultures and socioeconomic climates we are designing for allows us to create in a meaningful way. Our relevance is borne in the resonance our designs carry.
– **Danei Cesario**

To continually adapt as architects, we need to make small adjustments throughout our careers, especially to the random and unpredictable things life throws at us. This *continual adaptability* gives you an advantage over those who do one thing well and just keep doing it, as in *The Hedgehog and the Fox,* an essay by philosopher Isaiah Berlin based on the Greek poet Archilochus, who wrote: 'the fox knows many things, but the hedgehog knows one big thing'. Hedgehogs tend to do one thing really well and always seem to have a big idea, whereas the more nuanced foxes tend to take different approaches to different problems – so foxes are more adaptable than hedgehogs. If you had to choose, at least for your career, aim to be a fox. Turning to the question of relevance, is the person with the big idea more likely to be relevant, or the person who can adapt to different circumstances?

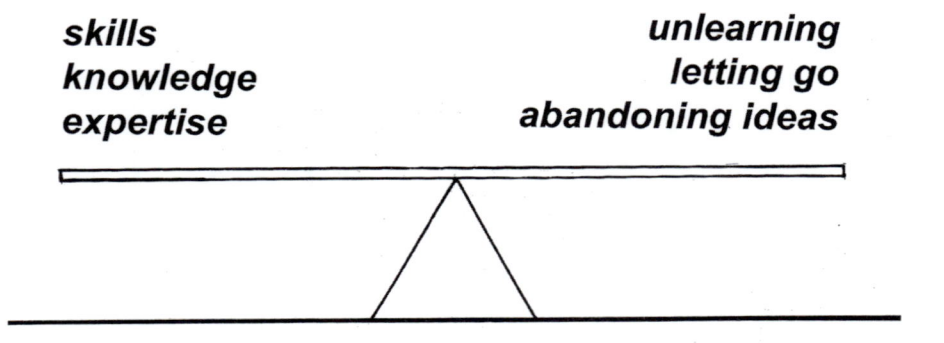

*skills*
*knowledge*
*expertise*

*unlearning*
*letting go*
*abandoning ideas*

Fig 1.2: By mid-career, what we know and learn has to be balanced with what we know and need to unlearn

# 1: Relate

Architects didn't always need to question their importance and role, both with clients and in society. But the current pandemic and events related to social and racial equity have set architects thinking about their relevance. Without the status of being 'essential workers', architects have had to find and create roles in which they can contribute to the wellbeing and welfare of others. So, how do we become relevant – and, once we have proven our value and relevance, how do we remain so? 'The internet quickly transformed the world in less than ten years, supplanting taxi cabs with Uber, travel agents with Expedia,' says managing partner at ZGF Architects Ted Hyman FAIA, 'and architects began to ask themselves "what [do] we need to do to remain relevant?" It is an impossible question to answer without some understanding of what the future will look like. Especially now, with COVID-19 and the context of the total disruption of the world economy because of a small virus, unknown just months earlier, [how can we know] what the world will look like in one year, let alone ten?'

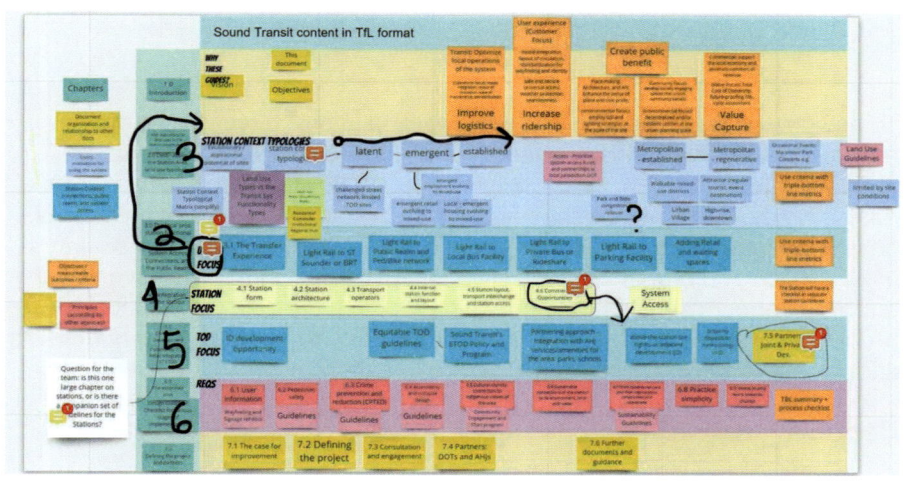

Fig 1.3: While quarantining during the COVID-19 pandemic, ZGF were able to maintain the pace of work and continue their interactive work sessions with clients and consultants using virtual tools like Microsoft Whiteboard

Hyman suggests that architects can remain relevant by addressing the challenges we all face. 'While we ponder what could possibly come next, the answers should be obvious; to remain relevant in the future, climate change and social equity will assuredly remain [the] two biggest challenges to "normal" that we have ever experienced,' continues Hyman. 'Together they have the potential to kill more people and disrupt the world economy well beyond anything we've seen in our lifetimes, including COVID-19. The built environment, the world architects "designed" is the largest contributor to the world's greenhouse gases, and the primary cause of climate change. The cities we have constructed not only contribute carbon but they also contribute to social inequality more than any single factor; well-designed places should be for everyone.'

Fig 1.4: In addition to meetings and work sessions, ZGF team members continued to conduct site walks with contractors and consultants while working remotely during the pandemic. A platform called StructionSite has been invaluable for these virtual site visits

To be sure, architects have been marginalised in part by their own doing – an unwillingness to take on more risk or pass responsibility on to others, and by others who claim to do similar work. 'So how can architects remain relevant? They can take on these issues and others, the ones each of us is passionate about, and with talent and expertise solve some of our society's most challenging problems,' says Hyman. 'Just designing and documenting buildings for our clients is not enough to keep us relevant; we must be problem solvers beyond simply programme, bringing value both to our clients and the larger population.'

## Becoming relevant

I believe an architect's built and unbuilt work is what is judged for its value and relevance, not the author. If as an architect you engage in contemporary culture, in socioeconomic and environmental issues, and you take a critical position that you express through architecture or architectural thinking, you are doing relevant work.
– Alison Brooks

In our profession becoming relevant or being relevant means bringing some unique skill or knowledge to your position that few others have. Maybe it's a strong interest in sustainability, technical knowledge, marketing, management – whatever your interest may be. If you want to be valued, you have to stand out.
– David Swain

There is an order to this: first, we strive to become relevant, then once relevant, we strive to remain so. To begin, how do we know that we are relevant? Or rather, how do we know if our work is vital to others? What evidence is there? By the number of people who follow us on social media, or who retweet, like or comment on our posts? Or that we are given a regular increase in salary by our employer? Does that prove our relevance?

Being relevant isn't a one-time thing, but something you must continually renew. Belonging to a currently unpopular gender (male), race (white), class (upper), age group (middle aged) or demographic (#OKBoomer) can contribute to feeling relevant or irrelevant. To be relevant means to matter more to more people. When what I have to offer has real-life applications, then what I know, teach and share has relevance. To be relevant requires you to be of – or even a little ahead of – your time, living in the moment and up to date, offering insights and knowledge that are applicable and useful to others. To *stay* relevant requires you to shift from where you are today and adapt to where you need to be – the ever-changing world around you. To be relevant means you are in tune with the times; to be irrelevant is to be tone deaf. To stay relevant, you must transform yourself, and keep on top of the latest technology and work processes. Relevance suggests a moving target: you are never relevant forever. Relevant and done is not a thing.

Justin Martinkovic believes that architects are already relevant. 'However, most architects, myself included, sense our relevance has declined, and that our talents and capabilities are not as valued and fully utilised as in the past,' says Martinkovic. 'We view the archetype of the architect as the venerated master builder, yet when we observe our context today, we may feel our profession is marginalised and our work product undervalued. But we, ourselves, hold the key to becoming more relevant.'

'First this means solving the client's problems extraordinarily well, and when possible, creatively adding value along the way,' Martinkovic continues. 'We must communicate well, understand the clients' needs and not put our own interests above those of the client. We must be a true partner to the client, a trusted adviser. To be sure, this relationship works both ways. If a client does not have our best interests at heart the way we have their best interests at heart, we must disengage with that client. Easier said than done, I know, but to work at our best in the owner–architect construct, a constructive working environment is important. We must make buildings and environments for the end users that are always functional and rational, while continuing to find ways to inject our designs with meaning, metaphor and delight. It is in our blood as architects to make our work even more impactful than it was asked to be, but it must always amplify – and must never be at the expense of – the client's goals, the experience of the end user or the greater good. Second, we must realise that we possess a unique talent that fuses art and science, and we utilise a powerful design process through which we perceptively uncover problems and cleverly solve them. We apply these talents and tools to the design of buildings and environments every day, but usually within the confines of the traditional owner–architect construct. If we as architects feel irrelevant, if we feel marginalised or constrained, we should look outside of the owner–architect construct and expand the limits of what it means to be an architect.'

'This is the path of the visionary, the creator, the innovator, the inventor,' continues Martinkovic. 'Rather than outside for meaningful work, we look inside and ask "What is that fire burning inside me? What do I want to contribute to the world? What is my song to sing?" We then find ways to apply our creativity, design thinking, pragmatism and artistry to addressing the challenges that inspire, energise and motivate us. This approach holds the promise to address the problems of today and tomorrow, and to contribute our talents to improving society at large.'

This path is very difficult, admits Martinkovic. 'Outside of the owner–architect construct, who is going to pay us? Does the project require funding? How am I going to enlist help? That is where the entrepreneur mindset can be applied.' Tools such as the ability to think creatively and pragmatically as it pertains to buildings and environments, he adds, 'can be applied to matters of business and organisation. If we as a profession can harness our greatest gifts and talents, if we are daring enough to expand our definition of what it means to be an architect, if we can apply our unique talents to solving significant problems, we can further contribute to the greater good, and relevance will no longer be an issue. In the act of so doing, we may find that fulfilment in our lives is greatly advanced.'

## Increasing your value

We become relevant by learning things other people don't know or developing relationships other people don't have. We stay relevant by becoming historians – collecting a history of steps and reasons and context changes. Knowing the current best practice for how to design an office is an example of becoming relevant. Staying relevant means learning the next version of best practice and the next, as it evolves, and being able to tell the story about why we collectively evolved our best practices.
– Oscia Wilson

We remain relevant by being able to adapt and change. Our relevance as architects is directly related to our understanding of how we bring value with what we do, and how that is recognised by our clients. This should be measured from the viewpoint of our clients instead of our own. As a profession, we often try to convince ourselves of the value we bring by our own measurement. If this is not obvious to our clients and does not align with their needs, then it effectively doesn't exist.
– Angela Watson

Is relevance a choice, or something that is bestowed on you by others? To what extent can you control your relevance? And, what is the relationship between relevance and value? 'Be adaptive, creative and acknowledge the passions that make you unique,' says associate director at Buttress Chithra Marsh RIBA. 'Look at how these can benefit the bigger picture and how you can best contribute.' But how does one stay relevant? 'Be prepared to continue learning,' says Marsh. 'Be connected to the world around you and assess how your skillsets can contribute and benefit wider objectives.

Be prepared to hone your skills and continue learning. Enhancing your professional qualifications with your core ethics and interests will give you a point of difference. This adaptability will be what makes you unique and stand out from the crowd. No two architects are the same.'

Fig 1.5: Associate director at Buttress Chithra Marsh (second from right) participates in a meeting with colleagues

'There is no clear map to success,' adds Marsh. 'It is more of a meander to the finish line, picking up skills and experience along the way. Taking a passive approach and relying purely on the core skills you learn to become a qualified architect are just not enough.'

How is value perceived, and how is it defined by others? 'Architects are commoditised,' explains associate and office leader at Taylor Design John Gresko AIA. 'Our services are widely seen as interchangeable. We are often pitted against similarly qualified firms, and my clients (when setting aside qualifications) tend to take the ones that have lower fees or provide more value for their fee in regard to their cost.'

Consider yourself warned. Gresko offers five hard-to-accept reasons the architecture profession is not as revered in the industry as it was in the past: 'Disgruntled architects have left the profession and joined the client and construction side. I have seen former design-side architects take it out on us from the client and construction side; architects have in the past designed ugly buildings and imposed their will on their clients. We have lost the trust of our clients; Society, in general, doesn't care much for architecture any more – particularly in the US; architecture as a process is not easily understood and we have a hard time describing what we do and our value'; and, lastly, 'We have given up ownership of the building industry and the responsibility to manage costs and scope.'

Beyond what the client asks for, architects need to present the client what they never imagined, delivering what they didn't know they needed. How will our prospects as architects, and thus our value in the eyes of clients and society, increase? 'When we are able to demonstrate a few things,' says

Gresko. 'We take care of our own, and people do not leave the industry and bemoan us from the client and construction side; we design beautiful buildings; we interject ourselves into all facets of society; we find a way to come together as an association of professionals to truly advocate for our value; we have our clients' best interests at heart; and, we are responsible and trustworthy.'

One way for architects to ensure they remain relevant is to have an outward focus. Interjecting themselves into all facets of society is especially important if architects want to remain relevant. There's the reality that, depending on where you grow up, you might be raised and go through school without ever hearing the word *architect* uttered, let alone meet one. Until architects find a way into all facets of society, and into all communities, they will be overlooked.

There's a four-circle Venn diagram I share with my final-semester graduate students, as a segue between their college experience and soon-to-be-entering practice. One circle reads: What does the world need? Another circle: What are others willing to pay for? These are both outward focused. But it's not enough to focus exclusively on the world beyond until you know what it is you can offer. It's important early in your career to identify both interests and strengths, to build confidence, to feel as though you have something of value that others want and are willing to retain. To this end, the third circle reads: What are you passionate about? And the fourth: What are you good at? To become and remain relevant, you need an answer for all four circles. Your sweet spot is where the four circles overlap.

## Relevance through your network

In an image-based culture, it's important not to be distracted by what other architects are doing. Every work is the product of unique circumstances that cannot be replicated; trust your own authorship and subjectivity. If architecture is your vocation, do it on your own terms. Stand by your ideals. The more you practise what you do, and strive for excellence, the more relevant you'll become. Take risks, exert judgement and be tenacious.
– Alison Brooks

Becoming relevant is an organic process of identifying your talents and aligning them with the causes that resonate with you. While validation matters, and it can be inspiring to continue the efforts, contributions to the profession cannot be planned around a value system. You have to continually offer the best you can and hope to benefit others on the way. In order to achieve that, a constant professional evolution is required.
– Meghana Joshi

Another way for architects to ensure their relevance is to turn their attention inward – to what makes them unique. If the industry sees architects as just one option among many to deliver what it is they espouse to deliver, then architects must find ways to differentiate themselves – starting with their expertise. 'One becomes relevant by having expertise: knowledge, interest and enthusiasm in certain areas or specialisms within the profession,' says Sara Beardsley. 'Architecture is very broad and has plenty of related disciplines, including interior design, urban planning, and specialisms such as exterior wall design, building codes and standards, building science. Architects who specialise in a certain typology or scale of building can also build value in their career within that specific area – for example healthcare; residential; public projects; government work; educational work – to name a few. Often an upward career step is made when one has sought-after experience or a specific skill that one firm needs, allowing for a move that is upward into a specific position that is sought after.'

Fig 1.6: One becomes relevant by having expertise – knowledge, interest and enthusiasm in certain areas or specialisms – within the profession

It is often thought that having a singular specialism in architecture will save you from economic recessions and pandemics, but the jury is still out on whether it is better to dedicate yourself to being a generalist or specialist. I side with the generalists, as does Adrian Dobson, practice director at the RIBA, who believes that it is 'in the expansion of skills, and not specialisation, that the work of the architect will survive', and that architects 'are actually better placed than many of our co-professionals to adapt to the requirements of faster, more or less'.[19]

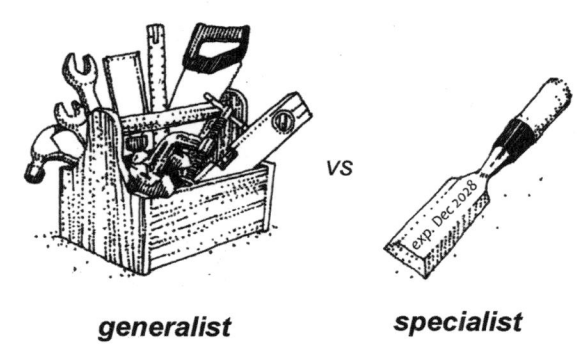

Fig 1.7: Generalists think of their skills as tools in a toolbox, whereas specialists tend to emphasise one tool over another: such an approach can have a use-by date

The problem with using specialisation as a means to differentiate yourself is that specialising has a date stamp. Expertise is important, but with research advancing and the world constantly evolving, your expertise requires upkeep and maintenance to stay ahead of new information. Beardsley addresses this by alluding to your most important source for staying informed: social learning. 'Ways to specialise can also include mastery of certain software or workflows, or having skills in things like contracts or project management, or particularly strong design, or visualisation skills,' says Beardsley. 'Once you have a specific expertise it is important to develop it by networking with others in similar areas of work, sharing knowledge and having a discourse about the best way to design certain types of buildings. Having a great network of consultants and collaborators, and serving on professional committees outside the office, is also helpful in developing and retaining a specific expertise.'

Fig 1.8: Presentation to partners at director Sara Beardsley's firm, Adrian Smith + Gordon Gill

Joe Cliggott concurs on the importance of building and maintaining your contacts. 'First, and foremost, have intellectual curiosity and passion about the work. Second, and [it is] never too early to start, build a professional and personal network. Maintain these two things throughout your career, and value and relevance will follow. You must love the work, and you must have a group of collaborators and patrons to support the creation of the work.' But Cliggott cautions, 'At different times in our careers there are more suitable company structures to support further growth and development. This is a totally personal question; there is not a path that fits all people. While at a simplistic level, all architects and architecture firms are working towards the same goals, the means to get there are extremely different. Firm size, organisation, design authorship, [and] technical and financial management will vary greatly, and the impact is then felt by each team member and how they fit into that process.'

## Continued relevance

*Staying relevant means pushing your work to the absolute limit of excellence, within your client's brief, but also thinking beyond it. In architecture you have to attempt something impossibly great to end up with something that's just really good.*
*– Alison Brooks*

*I taught a design studio for a few years at MIT and found that I learned an incredible amount from working with students, teaching assistants, and the challenge of balancing work at my firm and work for the studio. I learned how to ask questions instead of offering solutions to help students develop their ideas. I believe I've become a much better leader, mentor, designer and colleague as a result.*
*– Angela Watson*

What have you done in your career to remain relevant? Do you feel there is more that you could do – and, if so, what? Have you taken any special courses, received certifications, or explored acquiring additional degrees? As discussed, attaining relevance is not a one-time thing – it has to be renewed continually. 'The notion of relevance is one that I struggle with every day,' says Randy Guillot. 'I believe it is the right struggle to be having every day.' This is not to say Guillot is not good at what he does – he has received awards and accolades, and has been published widely, which he concedes 'is nice and somewhat reaffirming that the path I have been on has been perceived as valuable'.

'But being relevant means charting a course long before the recognition of awards, and fellowships,' admits Guillot. 'It means having a vision of the future for yourself and for the profession. This can absolutely include additional degrees, certifications and courses, but it doesn't have to. The education and career of an architect prepares you to solve problems at different scales and with all different types of people.' Guillot continues, 'The relevance so many of us seek is still grounded in our approach to problem-solving. Much of the world has caught up, embracing design thinking in business and more maker-based educational and professional models, but I believe as architects we have the best of all of these platforms at our disposal.'

So, where should architects direct their attention to ensure their continued relevance? 'I strongly believe that where focus goes, energy flows,' says Guillot. 'My focus has changed and will continue to change over the life of my career, but my energy comes from design. It comes from an unwavering belief that the power of design can create a better world.'

Architects have to consider the impact of emerging technologies and the rise of automation on their continued relevance. 'The magic of the architect is the ability to understand a client, create a personal trust relationship and an emotive design response; the subjective artistry that brings joy to a design, and one that is not simply born of metrics and parametric code,' says senior associate and design director at Gensler Philip Twiss RIBA. 'Although one would have to question whether or not, with the increase in AI, that position will be sacrosanct in the future.' Twiss adds, 'We have to be aware of changing socioeconomic dynamics, seeking out new opportunities, macro trends, and learn to adapt and be flexible. Architects are still relevant but increasingly, as with many industries, many of the processes we undertake can be digitised or codified and can therefore be automated. It is up to us as a profession to keep up with those trends in our sectors, where appropriate learning new skills.'

## Relevance versus influence

One of the best things I did was pursue an advanced degree in education outside of architecture post registration. I never wanted it to be a career pivot, but rather an opportunity to put my experience through a different perspective. It forced me to have to analyse and explain what and how my design training applies to other realms. Now I use my education degree in my practice to work with academic clients … I received great advice early in my career to actively work towards opportunities that provided outside recognition of my expertise through writing and speaking. While not easy at first, I now reap the benefits of this. One article turns into a seminar which turns into a networking opportunity.
– Emily Grandstaff-Rice

A natural part of being in a technology team is the need to maintain a continuous curiosity, and to keep learning. It can be such a fast-paced field that if you don't do this, you risk being outstripped; you by your peers, and your practice by your competitors. This is something that we maintain at Grimshaw by having both an internal training agenda and also a budget for all staff to seek training externally where appropriate. Personally, I undertake multiple short courses each year, regularly attend industry events and am toying with the notion of additional degrees in the future; probably an MBA and then perhaps a PhD further down the line.
– Andy Watts

It's hard to seek and gain attention over the clamour of the news, social media and all of the shiny new objects people have at their disposal. News cycles are getting shorter, ever more frequently demanding our attention. What in the past were weekly or daily crises seem now to be happening hourly. And this doesn't even include the attention our family, friends, neighbours and work colleagues require of us. How, amid all of this, are architects expected to call attention to themselves? This isn't a specious question – it's an existential one. People – clients – only need an architect when they need an architect. The rest of the time architects reside somewhere in the back of their consciousness, and perhaps once a year among their collection of holiday cards.

One's relevance is not an assured thing, nor is it guaranteed; it has to be earned. And as with reputation and trust, relevance can take years to acquire and with one wrong move or word – even forgetting to send a holiday card – it can disappear in a flash. Today such a misplaced move or poor choice of words is all the easier to accomplish with the advent of social media. However ill-advised, the temptation to go off-brand and wing it is always present.

With all of this to contend with, why focus on relevance? Why not focus on influence? With architects getting a smaller and smaller slice of the attention pie, and often with an inability to succinctly state their value proposition, relevance is key. But so is its corollary: impact and influence.

The advice here is clear. To remain relevant, counter being comfortable with your situation or current level of knowledge; expose yourself to what others are doing in your area of interest; keep expanding outward while investing inward in yourself. What you choose to focus on – where you put your attention – needs to be of value (embraced) by your firm and the outside world. Don't focus your time and attention exclusively on what will directly benefit you or your career; select topics you really care about and are passionate and enthusiastic about. By doing so, you will be much more likely to remain engaged and persevere.

Being able to build an online platform and attract and engage with followers not only improves your influence, but getting your name out there could translate into bringing in a steady stream of talent or even clients and work into the office, not to mention influence on the wider community.

## What anchors the mid-career architect?

It is hard to be nakedly opportunistic [for] a whole career. It takes a toll, and being nimble means being on alert at all times, which is not sustainable. You can't get a job if no one is hiring. And the stakes get higher as we have families, college tuitions, mortgages, and as we progress up the pyramid, as our salaries get higher and the air rarefied.
– Rob Rothblatt

The profession is our anchor and offers architects fellowship, regardless of age or ability. The ability to design is every architect's 'special power'. Architects are also uniquely able to take many paths in life outside of conventional consultancy – similar to engineers. This autonomy is a great asset.
– Alison Brooks

School and licensure not only launch but anchor early-career professionals, who have youth, energy and often optimism (or at least naivety and beginner's mind) on their side. Fellowship, leadership, an encore career and retirement anchor late-career professionals, who often have wealth, wisdom, a loyal network and wherewithal on their side. But what, if anything, anchors the mid-career architect?

The stakes are higher in mid-career: from raising a family to taking on more responsibility at work. Your salary is higher, but that can put a target on your back as younger architects – especially young people with promise (YPWP), who may be able to do some of what you do and learn the rest – are less expensive to the firm and, importantly, to clients. Besides, it's your charge to teach them everything you know (it's an architect's ethical obligation) so, in time, they can replace you – which happened to me in 2010. Today I make my living giving away what I know full-time as a professor.

Most architects arrive at the ten-year point of their career with some significant wins under their belt. Perhaps they've recently become licensed or registered, or are studying for the exam. Perhaps they have settled on one firm, and their efforts have been recognised with a promotion, and with it, a salary increase. But not all who arrive at mid-career feel anchored. 'Perhaps this feeling of a lack of anchoring comes from the newfound freedom of this career stage,' says associate principal at GBBN Angela Mazzi FAIA. 'This is the luxury of mid-career – this freedom to "specialise" yourself.'

Early career and mid-career mirror the main difference between undergraduate and postgraduate education: by the time you reach postgraduate level, you ought to have some idea of what to focus on or specialise in, and you are given some freedom to explore this in depth. 'In the early part of career, you need to build experience; late in [your] career, you are defined by what you did or didn't do,' explains Mazzi. 'Mid-career is that very unique chance to edit and distil what you do, to finally take complete control of your career path. For the first time, you have the leverage of experience! One thing that often disillusions those at mid-career is feeling they haven't "made it", and perhaps now it is too late. This often happens because you are holding on to expectations about what you think you "should" be doing. Realise that you've already proven yourself, and give yourself permission instead to enjoy the freedom you have earned and really get in touch with what you love and start making choices that are in total alignment with that.'

'There are anchors at the beginning and end of one's career,' says Trina Sandschafer. 'I do not think all those in the middle are adrift. The middle is for taking risks. The middle is where you work to build something big. You do that by reflecting on what area of your work brings you joy and what areas you are passionate about. Then, you find a way to do that.' Sandschafer adds, 'A big key to achieving this is reflection on where you have been, and forward thinking on where you ought to go. Mentorship can provide a great deal of clarity or a springboard for these thoughts. I am of the belief that I do not want to look back on my career with regret for what could have been. Take the chance; it will not come along again. Learn from it. Lean into it. Grow into the architect you wanted to be when you were twenty-five.'

*adrift*  *anchored*  *buoyed*

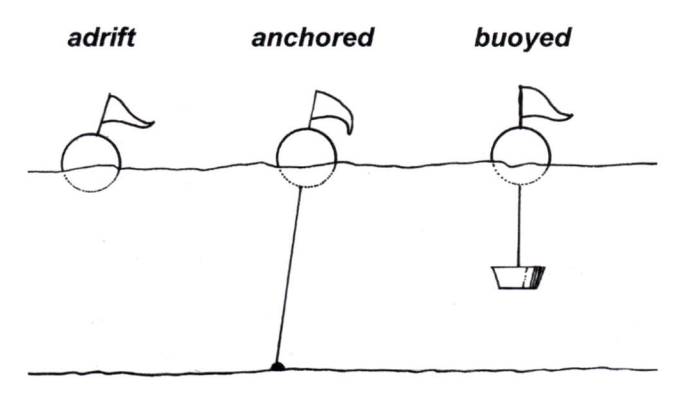

Fig 1.9: Some architects at mid-career feel adrift and look for something to anchor them. Others feel buoyed by their newfound freedom

## Anchored versus buoyed

Anchors are who you are serving, why you are serving them, and who is with you while doing that. What anchors mid-career professionals is the notion that they are building something – not just a portfolio, but a life.
– Diane Reicher Jacobs

There is a lot to be said for the energy and optimism of youth and the wisdom of experience. Mid-career professionals possess some of each.
– Justin Martinkovic

'An important thing that can anchor a mid-career architect is their larger network of professionals and clients that they have met along the way – their peers as well as people they have met [through] professional organisations like AIA, NCARB and others,' says Sara Beardsley. 'A "network" is a very powerful thing, and I recall as a mid-career professional I actually found that I was offered many more opportunities than a newer professional once I began to widely network with others who had similar expertise or interests.'

Beardsley continues: 'Another important thing is their experience and expertise that can be coupled with continued value in terms of being able to use the software and do production work. During a downturn, firms do keep the people who have flexible skillsets, show promise and are of long-term value to the firm. Mid-career professionals do have an advantage over late-career professionals in that perceived potential to be an integral part of the firm, after the downturn – whereas some early-career professionals can be viewed as "replaceable", and some late-career professionals can be viewed as overly costly or as nearing retirement.'

Some didn't care for the term 'anchor' in that it implied being held down or, worse, held back. 'There needs to be some credence [given] to individual experience,' explains Danei Cesario. 'There are late-career professionals with energy and optimism, just as there are embittered, unmotivated early-career professionals. My experience as a mid-career professional has included being buoyed (as opposed to "anchored") by my involvement in leadership, which had built on my professional wisdom, wealth and wherewithal. What buoys a mid-career professional is curiosity, resilience and perseverance. For me, it has meant creating the career I want by surrounding myself with early- and late-career professionals with these admirable traits, and learning from them.'

'The mid-career architect, to me, is the centre of a project. Possibly the centre of the practice,' says John Gresko. 'There is also a shortage of mid-career architects today, which to me makes them highly sought-after and valuable. The mid-career architect's fee rate is lower than senior staff, and [they] are the ones more consistently running and managing projects. Our field is too competitive to keep senior staff entirely billable to projects. Mid-career architects, I have found, are still more open to new ideas and collaborating than senior architects. Most senior architects have found their niche and have excelled in it.'

## ASK THIS

Mid-career architects should, with support of their practices, have set themselves achievable and realistic goals. This is where self-reflection is important – to look inwardly to your own strengths and weaknesses and consider the future. Where are you? Where do you want to be? How do you get there? Personal development plans (PDPs) should not be a HR box-ticking exercise but a fundamental part of any staff members career development to ensure they achieve their fullest potential. **[Philip Twiss]**

## TRY THIS

When seeking credentials to add to your education, how do you decide what to get certified in? Don't just strategically chose those that you feel will benefit your career. Instead select those you care about, are passionate about, or are enthusiastic about. You will be more likely to remain engaged.

## TRY THIS

The aim is to first become, then remain, relevant. But how do you continue? One way is to keep up with what is happening in the world around you. For example, each morning I wake up to a daily dose of Google alerts. Google will send you the top headlines, stories and posts on any topic you request. I am who I am today and have accomplished what I have accomplished in large part due to this simple, free service that not enough of us make use of. You can tweak the settings so each time your client is mentioned online, you are notified immediately or at a set time of day. You can then fire off a quick text or email to your client congratulating them on the news, leveraging what you learn in your next meeting – or better yet, informing them of an industry insight you were just made aware of. On social media, we are all publishers. It's no longer hard to be the first to break a leading story – if it is a story or topic you follow and is meaningful to the work that you do. Google will notify you of this, too, and you can post on it almost as soon as the story appears, or the event occurs. You will become known for sharing vital information with your network or community, who in time will deem you relevant to their interests and concerns. It works. Make it a habit to ask and find out what is important to others, even if not of utmost importance to you. Your client, employer and colleagues will thank you.

## TRY THIS

One of the main values of an architect is to solve problems that users and clients don't always see that they have, creating spaces in which to live, work and play that are inclusive of the community at large and inviting to all. To do this effectively, it means, we must already be in the community, helping our neighbours, volunteering with community organisations and using our talents. Through these informal relationships, we can show our value and knowledge, creating relevance for ourselves within the community by providing value.
**[Lora Teagarden]**

## TRY THIS

To become relevant in your practice, you need to be engaged. Ask questions. Learn. Contribute. Do that consistently. You remain relevant by remaining engaged. We are a product of what we do consistently.
**[Trina Sandschafer]**

## TRY THIS

It is critical to spend time really thinking about your purpose and point of view. This can and will evolve, but you should be able to find a common thread that is your truth, which will naturally lead to relevance. However, the idea of proving oneself can undermine all that good work. Wanting to prove yourself creates expectations and a pushing energy. Sometimes we want it too much and can be aggressive in our need to be seen or heard. I've learned that being an influencer is far more important than simply being a thought leader. Share your passions and let go of what you think should happen or how others should react to you. What good is your point of view or body of work if no one else is adopting it and it's not making a difference? **[Angela Mazzi]**

## TRY THIS

How you find peace with yourself at the mid-stage of your career, while at the same time leveraging those strengths to stretch and have more impact, is the question. Many of us, including myself, used certain skillsets and traits to become recognised. For me it was design, and the ability to apply uncommon design skill to a segment of the market that had been long overlooked: healthcare, education and so on.
This gave me relevance in the marketplace without people having to know me personally. But it is the quality of the relationships you build while achieving relevance that are the true test. Generally, people hire you because they like you, they trust you, or you have a particularly interesting point of view. Having all three certainly increases your odds of being relevant. **[Randy Guillot]**

# 2: Remain

Fig 2.1: Just staying on track in the profession and industry can be fraught – filled with challenges and unexpected obstacles

# Staying can be difficult, filled with challenges and unexpected obstacles.

**If the difficulty is in working with the people around you, I would suggest focusing on building up your soft skills. Effective communication, empathy for others and social IQ will fuel success in any human endeavour that can't be done alone.
– Justin Martinkovic**

**An architect who can work on design stages as well as deliver projects on site is always going to be relevant and handy for the business. If you have worked on several different building typologies, such as residential units, retail and commercial offices, then you are much more useful than someone who has just done retail.
– Stephen Drew**

Why a chapter just on what it takes to remain in the field? Because just staying can be difficult, filled with challenges and unexpected obstacles.

So, what advice is there for a mid-career architect who would like to stay in the profession but is finding it increasingly difficult to do so? What can they do now to assure their career longevity and survival? And are there multiple paths to career longevity? 'There are so many diverse avenues in the profession now, and architecture is a recent profession, comparatively, evolving, [so] that none of us see all the dimensions,' says Rob Rothblatt. The son of a historian, reared in the 20th century, having attended a British boarding school, a small Midwest liberal arts college and a Northeast graduate architecture school, Rothblatt understands himself to be a product of his time. 'We wanted to design great buildings, worthy of the ones we studied in the history books,' says Rothblatt. 'We were products of Le Corbusier, Wright, Aalto, Kahn, Mies, Cubism, *et al*. We were taught in a Bauhaus-derived curriculum, which is being correctly challenged in academia today. Talented designers, some of the most brutal and unsavoury types, were our heroes: not construction managers or project managers or evidence-based experts. We worshipped great ideas, singular intellectual solutions which moved building types forward, which won design awards, which were worthy of going into history books (a largely self-serving endeavour), and we measured others by that same standard. The review system of architectural schools is part Hollywood pitch, part boarding school inquisition, and we loved it! A great project – that's all we wanted to do. Like many designers, when I see a marvellous work which has risen to art, I say, "I want to do it, too. Let me at it."'

By his own assessment, Rothblatt's career path is 'bent and crooked', and his overall career bittersweet. 'In retrospect, I have been blessed, having worked on seminal projects and leading teams towards the holy grail of architecture,' says Rothblatt, 'but I have also paid a steep price for a single-minded purpose, and I am perhaps, in the end, a cautionary tale of adapting or failing to adapt – like an architect!'

At the age of 58, by starting his own practice Rothblatt is slowly beginning a third chapter in his career, 'which is as uncertain and nascent as many who are at the near-beginnings of their career', he says. 'I have only one true love – sensational buildings, uncompromised, abounding in imagination, and ideas. Really, nothing else compares and nothing else brings that sense of satisfaction.'

## Where is the difficulty?

Remember why you started, reflect on what you have achieved, try to rehabilitate yourself as to why you fell in love or wanted to start in the first place … or sometimes it really is about doing something different and taking our architecture skills elsewhere.
– Zoe Hooton

I told my daughter that all my heroes have been eviscerated by the #metoo movement, and she said 'get new heroes'!
– Rob Rothblatt

The singular approach to a career – where mental health and wellbeing are based on certain, specific outcomes – can be fraught. Who doesn't want to design exceptional projects? How do you respond to someone in this situation? Someone who has given their all, but through no fault of their own isn't seeing signs telling them to continue on their current path? You want to be encouraging without resorting to platitudes. And yet, you don't want to give them unrealistic expectations.

Part of the issue might be connecting your happiness and contentment with outcomes not within your control. There are so many factors that architects must contend with – the economy, client whims, public taste, politicians, bank interest rates or the ability to raise the required funds – that expecting each project to result in prize-winning, capital-A Architecture is unreasonable at best, and at worst unrealistic or even futile. And yet it remains a worthy pursuit – the very reason many continue to enter the field of architecture, however unlikely they may be to attain the outcome they want once, let alone on a regular basis.

The tempering of expectations is an excellent place to start. 'First, of course, is to recognise where the difficulty lies,' suggests Joe Cliggott. 'Is it something that can be addressed through learning, experience, or a change in role within a project or studio? Is the difficulty forcing an examination of the current firm or even the path within a traditional architecture firm versus career alternatives? Separate from the work environment, there are the outside influences of family and financial pressures that may also help drive out mid-career architects. There may also need to be a tempering of expectations about salary, titles and bonus if there is an assumption that these "benefits" are how one defines a career.'

Fig 2.2: Architects engaged in discussion at principal Angela Watson's firm, Shepley Bulfinch

To get to the bottom of why it is becoming increasingly difficult to stay in the profession, start by asking yourself a series of questions, starting with 'why?' 'That really depends on why they are finding it difficult to stay,' acknowledges Angela Watson. 'If it's difficult to stay because of a lack of fulfilment, there is likely not a reason to stay at all. If it's difficult to stay because of limited growth paths, then there may be a reason to look at a different organisation, where those paths might be more open and more flexible. If it's difficult to stay because of compensation, we may be facing a broader issue, one that our profession has not been able to really address very well and may not be able to in the coming years. Architecture is not among the highest-compensated professions when compared to the amount of time and money architects spend on education before they start their career path. My advice in this instance is to decide whether architecture is a job or a passion. If design and creative thinking are something that you really enjoy, decide if it is worth the potential financial trade-off.'

## Plan financially

Remain relevant. All of us must continue to have understanding of the needs of our community, awareness of the political, legal and financial world, and of course, the latest in construction technologies, both the built and digital.
– Joe Cliggott

The key is to find not only what you are particularly good at in the profession, but keep enhancing knowledge of what differentiates you from the crowd.
– David Swain

When mid-career architects serve as mentors, they're often asked for career advice. Based on what they've achieved and experienced along the way, what advice would they give to their former selves?

Questions like this have to do with career longevity. 'The longevity of a career is not a very good metric,' says associate principal and architect at Ayers Saint Gross Duane Carter. 'Focus on staying engaged and finding things that are interesting to you and contributing something to the profession. Young architects should plan financially as if they were going to have a "short" career. This is challenging now, because architecture salaries continue to be relatively low and jobs are in areas with high cost of living expenses. However, aggressive savings and lowering expenses early on could lead to financial independence later. This gives you flexibility in your mid-career – you don't have to be trapped at a job you don't like, you can weather a downturn, or you can even take some time off to refresh. It still doesn't rule out a "long" career.'

Before we even start considering the steps we can each take now to futureproof ourselves and ensure our continued relevance and career longevity, according to Emily Grandstaff-Rice we must consider how schools educate us, how firms provide us with opportunities for growth but also personal wellbeing, how individual architects and the collective field are regulated, how our professional organisations set their members up for success. 'First off, get good at finances,' advises Grandstaff-Rice. 'Seriously. You need to be able to understand the business of architecture, as well as the practice. This will provide you [with] the ability to negotiate for fair wages, structure profitable work, leverage your value with clients, and finance opportunities for the really fun projects. You cannot survive without the ability to be financially sustainable.'

The biggest thing we can do to ensure our careers have longevity, according to real-estate project executive at Google Oscia Wilson, is to advocate for the architecture profession and industry to evolve. 'The practice of architecture is so fundamentally flawed that it cannot serve us well,' says Wilson. 'Put plainly, the industry needs to find a way to make a lot more money without charging clients more. Regular architects (not the few starchitects) need to make more money and work fewer hours so that they don't get burned out after a few decades.'

Surveys attest that upwards of 80% of employees would prefer benefits such as flexitime and additional holiday over increased salary.[20] Wilson advocates for embracing an alternative model to full-time employment, one that would benefit all architects, no matter their career stage. 'Part-time employment with benefits needs to become an accepted norm,' says Wilson. 'This would allow older architects the grace to slow down and enjoy the fruits of their labours while still contributing their hard-earned wisdom to the industry. It would also be key to retaining women during the childbearing years that so often lead them to leave the industry. It would allow new fathers to share parenting responsibilities, advancing gender equity in the world. It would support people going back to school part time for advanced training. It would support people caring for elderly parents (again, [work] typically falling on women's shoulders). It would support, in fact, anyone of any age who might want to choose less pay in return for more time to enjoy hobbies and a slower pace of life. We do such a disservice to our industry and society by leaving part-time employment models to the realm of low-skill, low-pay status.'

Wilson believes in the idea of flexitime and work-life balance to such an extent that prior to joining Google she launched and ran an architecture firm for five years where she and her partners met once a week in person, but on the remaining days texted, Skyped, talked and sketched together in real time using Internet-based design tools.[21] This model supported the ideal that architects can be married to their spouse, not just to the profession.

Fig 2.3: Danei Cesario at Hudson Yards in New York City. As a result of the success of their firm round table on Diversity + Inclusion, WALLEN + daub presented a workshop at the request of New York Building Congress to representatives from a wide range of notable New York City architecture and construction firms

Early in one's career, according to Danei Cesario, there is the effort to become a qualified architect in the UK, and fervour to fulfil the AXP (former IDP) experience requirement in the US and study to complete the Architect Registration Examination (also in the US). 'Once you have completed that goal of becoming a licensed or qualified architect, what's next?' asks Cesario. 'I had that sentiment when I finally finished my 20-year quest to become licensed. It is really simple to take a moment to breathe that swiftly becomes months, years ... I realised early on how imperative it was for my creativity to remain inspired. So, I started volunteering at my local AIA chapter. The decision evolved into five years and counting of inspiration, education and collaboration with the finest minds in our industry. It allowed me to work on skills that I was able to bring back to the job, and meet people who created new opportunities for me.'

One controversial piece of advice that has been debated in recent years is whether it makes sense to follow your passion or emphasise employable skills. Passion took a beating after the 2008 recession, but I am a firm believer in the passion side of the equation – the *do what you love and the money will follow* philosophy – for having lived it. The idea of following your interests and passions makes little sense to most rational types (or their parents), but careers are long, and after passing the exam and reaching other milestones, there has to be something besides grit that will help you persevere both with projects and in your career – the two don't need to be diametrically opposed. At mid-career there can be a synergy between what you enjoy and what you are good at, what the world needs and what the world is willing to pay for.

*what you're passionate about* — *what you're good at*

passion / competence / relevance / needs / valued

*what the world needs* — *what the world is willing to pay for*

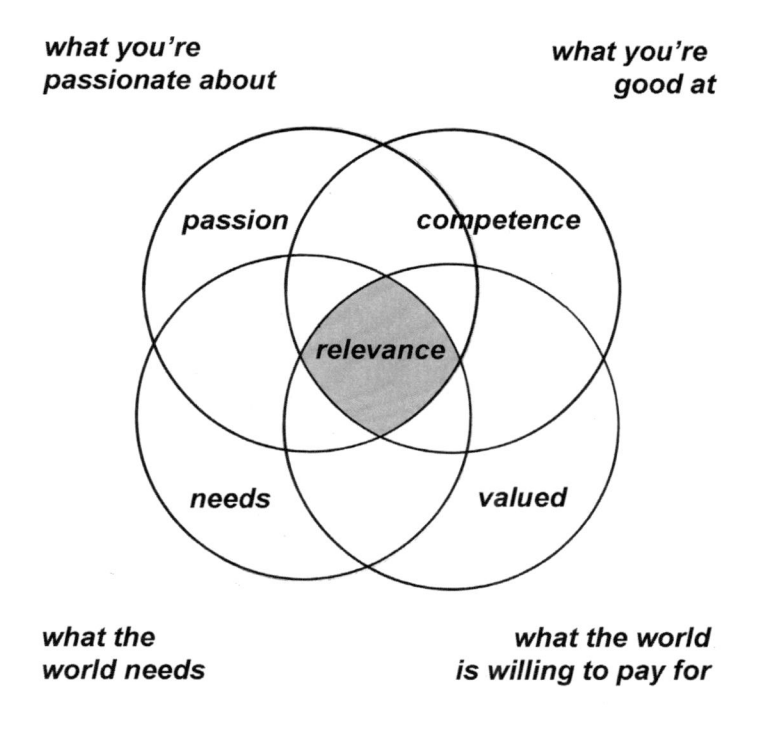

Fig 2.4: To remain relevant, you need to address all four circles. Your career sweet spot is where the four circles overlap

People pick up on your enthusiasm for what you are working on. 'Do something you enjoy, that gets you excited about your work,' suggests director of design technology at Grimshaw Andy Watts. 'This may be perfecting a specific skillset – your art – or it could be to never stop learning new things and broadening your horizons. This latter point may in turn lead to changes in your career along the way, either as minor course-corrections or full-blown career changes, but at least they will be changes caused by passion, not necessity.' While necessity alone may be able to carry a full-time job, it isn't enough to fuel a fulfilling and rewarding career.

## Think outside boundaries

**Evolve. While careers are getting longer, people are not afraid of change. The traditional approach leading to principal has slowly transitioned to working on projects with people that you admire and value. Collaboration and diversification will offer more value and meaning to our careers than excelling in compartmentalised roles.
– Meghana Joshi**

**Know that the profession is a small world. Embrace the opportunities to learn carelessly, freely and abundantly, because you won't realise how liberating that can be until it's constrained. The lessons forced on me by tutors at postgraduate level never made sense at the time, but years later that penny dropped and I'd like to shake the 20-something me into the frame of mind of not taking myself so seriously.
– Zoe Hooton**

I am writing this book not only in the midst of a global pandemic and economic recession, but also during the worldwide Black Lives Matter protests and civil unrest in response to the death of George Floyd. No matter what one was working on at the time of his death – which coincided with a halting end to pandemic-related lockdowns and a hopeful return to some semblance of normality – it was all but impossible not to turn away, however fleetingly, from whatever one was focused on and toward the historic events all around. As devastating as the events that led to this uprising were, the near-universal reaction was swift and inspiring.

One major shift we experience at mid-career, especially once we've achieved a few career milestones such as becoming licensed, registered or qualified, is to turn our attention to others. It's part of the profession's ethical code that architects devote at least part of their time and attention to helping future generations achieve some of the success they may have enjoyed by this point in their career. 'Be willing to adapt. Embrace change,' advises Justin Martinkovic. 'Help advance positive change that improves the lives of the inhabitants of our environments. Think outside of our typical boundaries. Pay close attention to your soft skills. Social intelligence, empathy for others and being able to communicate well with the people around you is critically important. Working productively with your collaborators inside and outside the firm is essential. Focus on the success of the people around you above your own success. Remember that when they win, you will win. Find inspiration and challenges in your work. Don't become complacent.'

This shift often entails a reframing of what one is currently doing. 'At mid-career,' says design principal at HDR Architecture Tom Lee, 'our focus should shift from not only investing in ourselves, but also investing in those around us, especially the younger generations. I've found that giving back and seeing others grow in their careers gives me great joy and can be both fulfilling and sustaining in a career.'

## Lifelong learning

Learn how to code. Computers, AI, prefabrication and robotics are here; they will be improving, becoming more frequently used, and I predict they will become a staple of our industry. To remain relevant you need to look for opportunities to use these technologies and improve the modernity of our industry.
– Michael Riley

Learning all along one's career is key. This can be done in many ways; one is through belonging to a network of people one shares interests with. Building a network of caring people one can exchange ideas with is getting more and more important with career longevity. People skills and ability to learn are key skillsets for career longevity.
– Aurélie de Boissieu

Those born in the 2000s will live long lives; careers are long, and getting longer. What advice do mid-career architects have for those just starting out to ensure that they arrive where the mid-career architects find themselves today? 'The one thing that architects, as well as many other professions, are realising is that you have to become a lifelong learner,' says senior associate and technical principal at WSP Built Ecology Elliot Glassman. 'It used to be that your education would prepare you for your entire career. But performance requirements, standards, and design and fabrication technology are evolving at such a fast pace that we have to constantly be re-educating ourselves to keep up. That is easier said than done, with the demands of increasing levels of project responsibility and mid-life pressures. Technological changes are also difficult for more seasoned practitioners to keep up with. The ability to lead, draw out the perspectives of, and learn from each of the members of a team is critical to maintaining longevity even when it is impossible to stay up on everything yourself.'

What should they learn next? 'Find things that you're interested in,' advises Angela Watson. 'They don't all have to be the same things and they don't have to last your entire career. Even linear careers need milestones where we learn new things, where we master new skills, and where we encounter new challenges. It is recognising those challenges that I think is the key to career longevity and survival.'

One question that comes up again and again is whether it is better for an architect at mid-career to be a generalist or specialist. 'Be a generalist,' says John Gresko. 'That's probably the opposite of what many architects are told. I started designing before licensure. I craved design. Then I was hungry to learn absolutely everything about production. I worked my way up to technical lead in a large company. Then at my 18-year mark, I became a manager and then a lead design architect and soon afterwards an office leader. I learned the basics first and didn't rush into management. Fortunately, I was at a company that told me I could be successful and make just as much money going any route: design, production or management.

I have seen specialists be the first ones out of work when the economy changes.'

At the other extreme, if you decide to be a specialist, strive to be good at a few things. 'If you can be the voice of the industry around a particular topic, or an in-house expert at something (like spec writing or exterior skins), you increase your value to your current employer as well as to future employers,' says Angela Mazzi. 'In today's credential-heavy environment, it also helps you to target which credentials are most meaningful for you.'

The answer is probably a combination of each. As the impact of and response to the COVID-19 pandemic has shown, architects need to be resilient, agile and prepared. 'As architects we need to be keeping abreast of macro and micro trends affecting the profession and sectors where we operate,' says Philip Twiss. 'Engage widely with the profession, listen to peers and professional bodies, understand the challenges we face. You have to understand the sector that you are in; it's often considered dull, but undertaking continuous professional development (CPD) is essential; learn a language, learn new software, innovate and look for missed opportunities and opportunities where can you become a thought leader and voice for the profession and sector where you operate.'

Fig 2.5: Diane Reicher Jacobs of Holly Street Studio presenting the masterplan for Arizona State University's Creative Futures Laboratory + Plaza at Mesa City Center at a public workshop, with Mesa stakeholders, AIA spring 2019

How have mid-career architects identified areas of confidence and strength in order to capitalise on their career development? Diane Reicher Jacobs has learned to be comfortable with what she does not know so that she can learn new things quickly in real time. 'I am learning to prioritise what I need to accomplish the most for the long term rather than the short term, which is at times unpopular among close colleagues,' she admits. 'Without exception these have been good moves, so I need to move more boldly in that direction – reorganising office systems, creating a strategic plan, formal employee reviews, office purge, learning new software or techniques, attending conferences, meeting with community leaders.'

Jacobs continues: 'I also need to continue to build strength enough to go against typical schedules (another pandemic silver-lining), like work time away from the office, seeking broad advice from colleagues, and honest dialogue with clients about the big picture related to their strategic goals – something I find is often forgotten the bigger the project gets. I have found that connecting with others beyond the task at hand has been invaluable in solving what are seemingly impossible problems. I still struggle with confidence, though. Every single day.'

'The more entrepreneurial an architect can become, the better,' says John Gresko. 'In much the same way a musician spends years learning music theory, practising scales and modes over and over again until their fingers know where to go subconsciously, then one day starts riffing and soloing without thinking where my next note should be … That's the same for architects. Learn as much as you can as early as possible about everything design, practice and construction, and start riffing earlier. Learn the basics and improvise like a musician in a jam session. No one knows where the industry will be in 25 years. But the more independent and well-rounded an architect can become, even if working in a company, the better off that architect will be.'

## Multiple paths to career longevity

It is really important that professionals understand there are multiple routes within any career, sometimes leaving and returning at different stages. Actually, seeing the process from a different perspective will help, and there are architects who have come from a furniture, boat-building or building background, which informs their practice.
– Allister Lewis

I am a broadly focused architect in terms of big-picture thinking and firmwide leadership. However, I focus much of those efforts on design-related aspects. I am also greatly drawn to our people – both staff and clients – and how we help them tell their story and reach their potential. I think these have been my lifelong natural tendencies. I was not shy about talking about them in reviews, in asking mentors their take, and in developing my vision for the career I intended to have.
– Trina Sandschafer

There are multiple paths and multiple outcomes which are dependent on personal experience and skills as well as opportunity and the occasional bit of luck, says Philip Twiss. 'The advantage of a single career path is that through specialisation you can rapidly become a subject matter expert (SME) in a chosen field; the disadvantage of this is the additional risk that comes with it. It is widely acknowledged that construction and therefore architecture are first in and hopefully first out of recession. Resilience requires agility to respond to rapidly changing socioeconomic and cultural influences, and specialisation can potentially limit the ability to adapt effectively.'

Twiss continues: 'The notion of honest self-reflection is imperative; you have to undertake SWOT analysis, and honestly analyse your own strengths and weaknesses, and the associated opportunities and threats. Are the strengths relevant, how do you capitalise on them, and do you need to evolve and adapt them to ensure relevance and optimum performance; and are your weaknesses something that you can address by additional learning/training (not always the case), and if not how do you fill the gaps? Can you simply bolster your team or employ someone to do the things you can't, or do you need to develop a role that doesn't require you to focus on your weaker areas?'

Fig 2.6 and Fig 2.7: In-progress hand-drawing at senior associate and design director Philip Twiss's firm, Gensler

'In the past, when one thought of an architect they were often considered a jack-of-all-trades but master of none,' says design principal at Perkins & Will Tom Mozina. 'I'm not sure if this was a good or bad characterisation, but I think the days where an architect had a general proficiency with most or all tasks is slipping. I see a lot more specialised talents and more focused interests. There seem to be a lot more lanes for people to take their career. The job titles seem to be growing. Much like cable TV, there appears to be multiple paths where one can make a meaningful contribution to a project or the profession without falling under a handful of old labels.'

Professionals need different career paths at different times to stay engaged. Virginia E Marquardt reminds us that one's path at mid-career can continue on into an encore career. 'For now, my career path is private practice through a firm,' says Marquardt. 'However, I have been thinking about maybe working for a school district in the future as a facilities director. And when I retire, will most likely be a consultant, as an education planner/expert.' For Marquardt the advantages and disadvantages of having a singular career path are clear. 'Advantages: allows an individual to hone their craft and experience the different roles and responsibilities through that path. Disadvantages: to stay engaged, we need different opportunities and we need to continue to strengthen ourselves, [and] learn new things in order to grow.'

'There are definitely multiple paths to longevity,' says Sara Beardsley, 'and I have seen many people be able to redefine their careers along the way. A disadvantage of a singular path is perhaps being so focused on one specialism that it is hard to change to other building typologies when needed due to economic drivers. But this can also be a strength, as one has increased expertise in one area which is valued. Along the way, peers and mentors have helped me to pinpoint my strengths and that has helped the overall trajectory.'

'The disadvantage of the straight-line path is that you can have huge gaps,' Duane Carter concedes. 'I worked under someone who became a principal at a very early age – it was embarrassing sometimes how little they knew about very important parts of our industry. They had a very successful career because of strengths in other areas, so you could argue that it didn't matter, but they could have done more and been a much better manager if they had been more mature as an architect.'

'I find that my ability to make connections across disciplines has been essential to my leadership,' says Emily Grandstaff-Rice. 'I credit my work with the AIA with providing exposure to higher-level activities much earlier in my career. A lot of these activities I pursued on my own as a distraction from some negativity or boredom in my position. Over the years, it has grown to be an essential element of being a multi-faceted professional.'

No matter your path, for career longevity resilience is critical. But it turns out some paths are more resilient than others. 'A singular career path allows you to become an expert in a project type, project phase or business sector, giving you opportunities to bring work to your firm as a thought leader,' says project designer at RATIO Lora Teagarden AIA, 'but it also likely prevents you from being resilient to economic and professional trend shifts as the world advances and adapts. Resilience comes from diverse experiences, skills and strengths that give you the knowledge to work on different project types or project phases. Time and trial-and-error have given me confidence in different skillsets in my life or allow me to continue to gain and grow confidence and skills.'

Most cannot stress enough the importance of failing fast and having the freedom and trust to make mistakes. Handled right, both can lead to resilience in one's career. 'I don't believe that there is a singular career path, even if one is born into a situation to inherit a firm. In any profession, and throughout a career, there are moments that challenge, that push, that help us grow,' says Joe Cliggott. 'We don't know how we will react to a situation until we are there. We don't always know if we will be successful. That is reality. Until we are tested, and given the opportunity to be tested, we simply won't know. It is through these tests and trials that we learn our true strengths and weaknesses. The "path" should provide a balance between new challenges and those that celebrate one's strengths. We rely on our own instincts, awareness and the feedback of others to help guide us on the path.'

In Angela Watson's career she learned both from self-observation and from conversations with mentors. 'Mostly I learned by being thrown into the deep end early and making mistakes,' says Watson. 'In many ways it's those things that I did not do perfectly that stick in my mind and that have helped me grow and adapt. I built a successful career on making mistakes, learning from them, and getting better. This has a lot to do with the confidence and strength that I have now in dealing with unforeseen situations. You can't really practise for how your career is going to go. Things are going to happen; the world and our profession are going to change. Being able to understand what's at the core of your strength and how to leverage that in a changing world is probably the most important thing you can do.'

'There are multiple paths, and being myopic about any one of them is limiting,' concludes Angela Mazzi. 'The capacity to adapt comes from having varied interests and abilities – sometimes the most unrelated skillsets help bring innovation to an old problem or allow you to deal with unexpected circumstances.'

## ASK THIS

If the difficulty is feeling as though the industry as a whole is lacking something, I would suggest asking yourself some key questions. What do you really want to do? What inspires you? What excites and motivates you? Can you expand the bounds of architecture with the ideas and work that really excites you and generate something valuable? Can you bring something new and innovative to the market that will benefit the lives of people? **[Justin Martinkovic]**

## ASK THIS

I would investigate why it is so increasingly difficult to stay. Is it firm related? Process related? Are you loving what you're doing but not loving the people you're working with? Are you loving the people you're working with but not loving what you're doing? That requires a little more soul-searching to understand what levers are creating the difficulties to really clear the path. **[Evelyn Lee]**

## ASK THIS

If you are currently employed but finding it hard to show up to work every day, take time to take stock and consider why. Are you burned out? Are you not engaged/being challenged at work? Is your project type not something you're passionate about? **[Lora Teagarden]**

## ASK THIS

They have to be self-reflective and recognise why it is that they are finding it difficult. Is the sector where they operate no longer relevant? Has the competition caught up with them; either from within the practice within which they work or practices against whom they compete? Have they failed to develop themselves adequately? Look at what worked for them previously; what enabled them to get where they are and what is holding them back? Where are they now, and where do they want to get to? Are they simply not enjoying it any more? Then they can understand what they need to do to adapt, either by changing their outlook, learning new skills, changing sector focus or by moving practice or possibly even changing profession. It's not entirely surprising that a number of architects move client- and contractor-side, working as development managers and design managers. **[Philip Twiss]**

## ASK THIS

If someone is asking themselves how to grow within the profession, or thinking if architecture is for them, I would ask … What's your why? What gets you up in the morning? Do you want a career or a job? If you want a career, what do you want from it? **[Virginia E Marquardt]**

## ASK THIS

The world and profession are constantly changing, and so are we as architects. It's critical to make sure we evolve with respect to the profession, the world around us, and our own changing interests. For me, I am constantly evaluating my career on a few metrics: am I being challenged, am I learning, and am I enjoying it? Knowing that my answers might change on any given day, if the answer is consistently 'no' to any of the above, then I know I need to make a change, from simply working on a different project in the firm to perhaps working at a different firm altogether. **[Tom Lee]**

## ASK THIS

Practice leaders must surround themselves with talented, ambitious and highly ethical architects whom they can wholly trust and who they want to invest in. Be open to bringing fresh skills and perspectives and technologies into your practice. Hire students and paid interns. Participate in public or industry-wide campaigns to better our profession and inspire your staff: campaign for gender-equal pay, for low-carbon technologies and ethical construction practices.
**[Alison Brooks]**

## TRY THIS

Keep reading, researching and understanding how change is affecting the construction industry. Continual professional development is a somewhat tired term, as in the UK it has come to mean listening to suppliers selling products. However, true professional development could include new qualifications, exploring MSc-level specialist interests, teaching, research and development, engaging with the industry through professional organisations, exploring networks and local groups. This continual learning will be required, with those who are comfortable with continual professional development being able to thrive and also develop specialist skills that keep their interest within the profession they have chosen. **[Allister Lewis]**

## TRY THIS

Create a presence for yourself as an individual. Position yourself as an expert in whatever you do. Even if there are other experts in your field, you'll be able to lift one another up. Being able to position yourself as an expert, using the knowledge and work you have done until now and constantly finding a way to leverage that, will determine how much control you have in the firm you are in. Especially if you are not in a principal or decision-making position. Continuously position yourself as an expert within the public view. Don't be afraid to put yourself out there. When I first started getting paid to write a blog, mostly on the topic of sustainability, I discovered that I was never going to be the sustainable architect who got really passionate about the technical side of sustainability. So my point of view has changed over time. But writing on sustainability helped build my credibility and helped with my career arc. How I position myself as an expert has changed over time. Position yourself, and if it changes, it's OK. **[Evelyn Lee]**

## TRY THIS

A long career is likely defined by how engaged you are in your practice. Do you feel engaged at work? Are you passionate about what you do? If the answer is no, it will be a short career (or a long, boring one.) I have challenged those I know to find the part of their career that brings purpose and passion. That is how to ensure you are working towards a fulfilling, and lengthy, career. **[Trina Sandschafer]**

## TRY THIS

Focus on your experience and expertise and find ways to leverage that. If it requires learning a technology, then do that, but recognise it is difficult to keep up with those that are younger; your advantage will be an understanding of the technology combined with insight that experience brings. This is lacking in our industry and I think those that can bring those things together are particularly valuable. **[Duane Carter]**

## TRY THIS

I would challenge that person to reflect on why they find it difficult to stay in the profession. Is it a lack of path forward? Is it a challenge to stay up to speed with technology? Is it outside pressures? Is it a lack of passion? If given the freedom to examine these, or other factors, there may be a way to remove those obstacles and move forward.
**[Trina Sandschafer]**

## TRY THIS

There are so many paths that an architect can take. If traditional architecture is not working for you, you could consider a related field or a related role.

- Related fields can include working for a contractor, developer or interior designer; or becoming an architecture or design instructor.
- A related role within your firm could include becoming a project manager, team leader or marketing principal.
- A change of role would likely necessitate taking classes in project management, leadership, marketing, business or construction management.
- Seek out a mentor within your firm or through your professional organisation.
- Take time to test-drive your related field or role by job-shadowing or conducting interviews with people in your network.

**[Mary Shaffer]**

> **TRY THIS**
>
> You need to work out why it is becoming more difficult for you. Is it because of your experience? What gaps are you missing? Develop a strong relationship with your clients, the developer. A client-facing person who develops rapport and generates business will always have a job. Be critical of yourself. Have you worked several years behind the scenes for a large, famous architecture practice, working on one or two packages for a large aviation scheme? Well, yeah, you are going to be forgotten, and I question your long-term value in the industry. Challenge yourself, quit your job – go find a small architecture practice doing residential, learn new skills and take a pay cut. Sounds uncomfortable? Yes, absolutely, however you are now not an airport man, you are a more fully fledged architect, and you have a ballsy story to tell someone when you have a beer how you changed the course of your career.
> **[Stephen Drew]**

# 3: Rebound

Fig 3.1: There are as many career paths and ways to become resilient as there are unexpected bumps along the road

# Cope with, adapt to and recover from whatever life throws your way.

*Learn and keep up on new building technologies. Always be able to offer a new and educated 'take' on what are considered accepted standards.*
**– David Swain**

*A key element to resilience is the development of new knowledge through research and training. I am always seeking out learning opportunities and ways to make new connections. When situations get rough, it is my laying the foundation that allows me to pivot well.*
**– Emily Grandstaff-Rice**

When jazz musicians are playing and one hits a wrong chord, some others will not just adjust by playing a solo around them, but will turn a bad situation into great music – and do it without getting upset about a mistake that can be seen as just another part of the process. They are able to turn the situation around to something positive in part because they believe in their own abilities, especially under pressure.[22] Jazz musicians and improv performers must perform under pressure nightly; adapt to changing situations, new information and evolving circumstances; and are accountable to their clients – the audiences for whom they perform.[23]

This is of course true of architects as well. To persevere in your career you need to be resilient to the inevitable yet hard-to-predict challenges that arise along the way. Some mid-career architects have been slow to adapt to the reality that the technical prowess which served them early in their career won't carry them to the next stage, and the stage beyond that. In other words, what served them well as emerging professionals – in particular, perhaps, their comfort working with digital tools – needs to evolve, with less of an emphasis on technology and a greater emphasis on people.

The evidence for this is plentiful, in that mid-career architects increasingly take on managerial roles and responsibilities that are people-intensive. Often – but not always – they leave the more technical tasks for those that report to them. However, there remain those who rise within the profession, in the wider industry as well as their specific organisations, who prefer to keep one hand on the wheel, staying involved with the hands-on drawing, drafting, detailing and modelling that are part of the process of bringing buildings into being.

What have architects put in place in their careers to remain resilient through all the ups and downs? What role does natural talent play versus hard work in determining achievement of ambitions and goals? How important is it in one's career to be able to anticipate what is on the horizon? If it is important, how does one go about gazing into the crystal ball? How important is strategic foresight for the work architects do? Adaptability is a form of survival, as the tactics covered in this chapter – *resilience, perseverance, brilliance, prescience* – affirm. Let's look at each in turn.

## Resilience

To remain resilient, you have to have something to escape to. An activity or place that switches off your brain. I find open water swimming brilliant for this.
– Zoe Hooton

Relationships. A solid portfolio. A strong voice in the community. Maintain friendships and support colleagues, even if you are competitors on occasion. A healthy, supportive architectural community is good for all of us, clients and public included.
– Diane Reicher Jacobs

The second part of the book explores options for switching, reinventing and pivoting. Here, resilience is about having what it takes – including the mindset and attitude – to enable you to withstand the negative forces you will encounter in your career. It's a term borrowed from engineering: the ability to bounce back and bounce forward; the capacity of a system to recover. Simply, resilience is the ability to cope – to speedily adapt and recover from whatever life throws your way.

My current architecture students have in their short time on this planet experienced the repercussions of 9/11, the 2008 recession, the pandemic and the subsequent economic recession of 2020. Challenges that we can predict and those, like the pandemic, that few saw coming are all par for the course. Resilience is about what we do in the face of these challenges. If what you do is stay or remain and manage to thrive while doing so, you likely have done so in part because you have worked hard, and because you possess resolve, no small amount of luck and also a fair share of resilience.

Just staying in the profession is an accomplishment in its own right. Sticking it out has become increasingly difficult for many, and is far from a foregone conclusion or a given. Remaining an architect has become the exception – not the rule.

Were there times in Trina Sandschafer's career where being an architect was hard? 'Of course,' says Sandschafer. 'Did I ever think about quitting architecture? No. Not once. I love being an architect. There were challenges in the economy. There were challenging projects. Sometimes challenging leaders. There were personal challenges. I never once thought of leaving architecture. Each challenge taught me something. It is hard to know that in the midst of the challenge, but each one makes you smarter, stronger and tougher – more resilient. I try to focus my thoughts on what I am going to learn in those challenging times. That is a helpful perspective.'

It begins with surrounding yourself with the right people, says Justin Martinkovic, who by his own estimation has a great business partner, a supportive wife and family, and smart and caring friends he can turn to for advice. Martinkovic's definition of right people includes those who may not be alive today. 'I look to some of my heroes from history – Ulysses S Grant and Winston Churchill to name a couple. I look at what they faced and how they endured. I know my problems aren't as big as theirs, and yet they got through.' It is for this same reason that I recommend people to read biographies and memoirs of music legends – Bob Dylan's *Chronicles Volume I,* Keith Richards's *Life,* Carrie Brownstein's *Hunger Makes Me a Modern Girl,* among many others – for their wisdom on career longevity, and for inspiration on how many times a person can reinvent themselves.

'We've tried to hedge against market swings with our choice of markets we engage, although I'll be the first to say that is only a small hedge when large economic disruptions occur,' continues Martinkovic. 'Resilience comes from within. Know that we all have doubts, sometimes very large and consequential doubts. The will and fortitude to just take one more step forward, and then one more, and then one more is what is called for in these moments. Things do get better, the outlook will get sunnier, and you will gain momentum and optimism.'

We'll discuss the importance of having parallel roles as a means to bolster your resilience in the next part of this book. Here, though, is an instance where becoming more resilient involved diversification. Rather than have a single professional or project outlet, Andy Watts made a conscious decision to have more than one thing on at any given time, including his work at Grimshaw, teaching where he can, and volunteer work. 'Even within my main role at Grimshaw, I work across a range of different strategic initiatives that feed into our overarching technology agenda,' says Watts. 'In doing so it means any downs in a certain area can be balanced out by progress – or the ups – of another.'

Another way to achieve diversification is to maintain a list of plan Bs. Architecture department manager at Mead & Hunt Mary Shaffer AIA keeps a running list of things she does well and things she loves to do, at one point calling the list 'potential alternate careers if architecture doesn't work out'. 'But honestly, that ship has sailed!' says Shaffer. 'Some things on the list are kind of silly, like "party planner" (I do plan really fun parties!) and some are more professional, like "networking and connecting people" or "designing spaces that make people happy". It's a good list to go to when I want to remember where I find my joy, and to check in on my current situation to see if I need to make any adjustments to stay on the right track.'

One way to diversify is by writing books, from which you can reap bountiful rewards, not least of which is helping others in the profession. Director of digital practice, associate principal and architect Evan Troxel has done this with his book, *A.R.E. Hacks,* as has Lora Teagarden with her volumes of books, *ARE Sketches.* 'My books offer me a meagre amount each month in way of royalties,' explains Teagarden. 'The passive income isn't enough to cover expenses each month, but it's income that I no longer have to put out specific effort [for] to receive a return. They also positioned me to be a leader in visualising study material and architectural concepts, which has opened doors to me in different professional opportunities or contract projects. More importantly, it allows me to make sure that my knowledge of the profession and the built environment is constantly refreshed and evolving.'

Career ups and downs are inevitable. How are you going to respond to them when they occur is the tougher question. Trina Sandschafer focuses on having a growth mindset to weather ups and downs. 'Ups are much easier to handle than downs, but each one can teach you something,' assures Sandschafer. 'Someone once told me that the valleys of your career are hard, but the valley is also where the nutrients are. That was good advice. Fuel up for the climb ahead. The longer you work, the more peaks and valleys you find. It helps to keep focused on the long-term goal and not be swayed too much by the highs and lows.' This is a great strategy for building a career that's both resilient and adaptable.

## Perseverance

By far the most important thing is also having a support network for yourself, whether that be a partner or a good friend. Those university peers understand your journey and your dilemmas; for me they are a brilliant sounding block.
– Zoe Hooton

Simply caring about the work deeply. Caring for my colleagues and their growth. Caring for my clients and caring for their projects. Bringing passion, energy and experience to make all of the above better.
– Joe Cliggott

With so many possible challenges to your career longevity, it seems that the only evidence of perseverance is – having persevered! Principal and creative director at Alison Brooks Architects Alison Brooks has based her practice, and architectural approach, on a certain set of social, architectural and intellectual ideals. 'The mission to achieve one or all of these ideals drives every project – "impossible" quests are behind every leap in human culture,' says Brooks.

Fig 3.2: All projects at Alison Brooks Architects are developed from early stages using building information modelling (BIM)

'I am here. Plain and simple,' says Emily Grandstaff-Rice. 'As a female architect with 20 years of experience, just staying in the profession is an accomplishment that is rarely recognised. I was told to leave architecture in school by a professor; I was told to leave architecture by an employer. If I had listened to this well-meaning advice, I would not have the ability to do the work I undertake today. While no one tells me to leave any more, I worry about how statements like this affect emerging professionals, especially from people in power. Perhaps in my early career, I did not fit the mould of what they expected. It reminds me that I need to be patient and open to emerging professionals I work with today. Every architect is unique, and for the profession to grow, we need to encourage opportunity for many.'

Lora Teagarden graduated into the last recession and married a military officer, which meant she ended up moving every year. 'As a newly graduated, not yet licensed or registered, military spouse required to move frequently,' says Teagarden, 'I was basically the least hirable person in the profession. Ironically, years later during my divorce I found stability professionally and was able to begin professional growth that I would never have been able to imagine or plan for. Had I not persevered, none of it would have happened, because there's no way I would have known to work toward or plan for some of the events that I now consider successes along my career path: publishing multiple books, owning my own business, serving at a national level in the AIA. Stick it out and be true to your passions. You're worth it.'

## Work ethic

While talent is discussed next at greater length, the theme that runs through many of the conversations on perseverance is plain hard work. 'You do have to be good at your job and work hard,' says Philip Twiss. 'Just "doing your job" may not be enough to progress your career, as you need to demonstrate your ambition and you get involved with the business. If not, there will be someone younger and fresher on your tail who will. You need to be responsible, be a leader, be an ambassador and exemplar for the firm, but [you] also need to be prepared to fight for recognition and not be afraid to have an opinion, to stand up and be counted (although you do have to be aware of office and corporate politics!).'

Elliot Glassman, who leads WSP's computational efforts nationally, developed his skillset to match what he thought were important directions in the industry – computational design and sustainability – and combined them to position himself where he anticipated they were taking the industry. 'I don't have any unique insight,' admits Glassman. 'There are many others who saw these changes coming as well, and did the same. But perseverance, despite whatever discouragement I received from clients or those within my organisation, has led to some measure of validation years later when the dedication to a direction paid off. That perseverance and grit served me in some ways, but sometimes I wonder if there weren't times where I should have given up on approaches or situations that weren't working earlier, and tried a different tack instead of exerting a lot of energy [and] brute force to

Fig 3.3: There are a variety of informal and formal meeting spaces at the London office of senior associate and design director Philip Twiss's firm, Gensler

make it work. The difference between those that are truly successful and those that are not is [knowing] when to stick it out and when to reconsider.'

In addition to hard work, Glassman believes another important factor is knowing how to leverage the folks around you for support and guidance. 'I realise that I am so willing to make time for informational interviews to talk with students or early practitioners in case any of my experiences are helpful to them, but I am reluctant to ask the same of others to benefit myself,' says Glassman. 'It would have helped me over the course of my development to be more open to seeking advice instead of going it alone as much as I have.'

Fig 3.4: Architects engaged in discussion at principal Angela Watson's firm, Shepley Bulfinch

Perseverance is one of the top ingredients in a successful career, says Angela Watson. 'Talent is only a baseline from which we can work, but determination is the willingness to stay with it and commit to finding a solution,' adds Watson. 'Perseverance means working through different scenarios and talking to others. It means finding inspiration in other viewpoints. It also means that you might not find a solution on the first try.

Perseverance is about letting the problem settle in your brain a little and then approaching it again from a different angle the next day.' Interestingly, that's also how Watson thinks of design. 'Hard design problems are those that don't have an easy and immediate solution. They tend to be complex problems that need some time to understand. Perseverance is critical to that process,' says Watson.

John Gresko attributes his perseverance to his work ethic. 'I am competitive by nature and always look to design, produce and manage to the best of my abilities,' says Gresko. 'I'm trying to find something in every project that's innovative to keep myself interested and drive forward.'

'I have been fortunate that the firms I have been with have experience weathering many ups and downs – and so when a bad time happened, there was always someone there who could share their experience with me of having survived worse,' says Sara Beardsley. 'I have always had a work ethic, to work as hard as I can every day, and in that way have been able to sustain myself in hard times and in good times because I seemed to always have something of value to contribute.'

## The role of others

Architects often attribute their ability to persevere throughout their careers to others – to other people, a network or friends. 'For me, perseverance through challenges has consisted of 1) having smart, caring, generous people around me I can lean on for advice and support, and 2) understanding that, in many cases, the only way out is through,' says Justin Martinkovic. '"Keep buggering on" as Churchill used to say.'

Emily Grandstaff-Rice has a trusted group of friends from different firms that are in similar positions to hers. 'We have been meeting for years through births and deaths of children, job changes, partner changes, leadership transition, starting new firms, and new leadership opportunities,' says Grandstaff-Rice. 'I also have a strong network outside of my firm, which helps me keep perspective.'

Picking people to work with who are a good fit for your goals, and the right firm that matches or at least supports your values, is critical to increasing the odds that you will persevere in your career. What has kept Tom Mozina engaged throughout is the simple fact that he 'got to work with quality clients, on quality projects with some of the most talented and diverse professionals from all over the world. If you can connect with the right firm that values the practice of architecture as an art and is purposeful in the types of projects and clients they choose to pursue, it is easy to stay focused and committed for the long haul. I would find it much harder to be fully invested in a place that didn't share these values. These standards may not apply to everyone, so the bottom line is you need to find the right firm that aligns with your value structure. Once you do that, the rest takes care of itself.'

## The role of focus

The novelist EL Doctorow once likened writing to driving at night in the fog. In making your way through an architectural career you can benefit from a similar approach, where you keep one eye looking ahead and one on the road immediately before you. 'You can only see as far as your headlights, but you can make the whole trip that way,' says Doctorow. To persevere in your career, it helps to keep one eye on your plan and the other on the next step in front of you. 'Maintain a vague idea of the trajectory that you want to set yourself on, and then focus in more clarity on the one or two steps in front of you to achieve that,' advises Andy Watts. 'If you try and achieve the big picture in one fell swoop, you will be continually frustrated.'

And yet, with so many interests, the temptation to look beyond or outside where your headlights shine is a reality most architects must contend with. 'Curiosity is also a driver behind perseverance – each project is an opportunity to learn about new places, from their history, from collective memory or even the absence of collective memory,' explains Alison Brooks. 'These absences are filled by acts of the architect's imagination. This is where we take our biggest creative risks, and where personal value systems rise to the surface.'

## Brilliance

Emotional intelligence is first, then hard work, then talent (whatever that means).
**– Diane Reicher Jacobs**

Hard work and resilience trumps all, but you must still work smart.
**– Justin Martinkovic**

What is talent? Can it be defined? Or, like jazz, do we know it when we see it? John Gresko says that talent is good and can get your foot in the door, 'but talent is not as good as a good attitude and a good work ethic. I'll take work ethic over talent any day. Depending on the goals, if it's long-term, gainful employment in the profession, work ethic and attitude are the key. Talent is fine, but this field is subjective. Art is subjective. Architecture is subjective. Talent is subjective.'

The role talent plays in perseverance is complicated. We have all seen talented architects burn out early in their careers, or jump ship to leverage their talents in another field, for us to never hear from them again. On the other hand, a talent for adapting to changing environments would be a cause for celebration. It is clear: brilliance is overrated. Hard work and putting in the hours levels the playing field, providing opportunity for those who may feel they don't have natural talent.

Architecture has a reputation, starting in architecture school, for overworking its minions. But it's not only a matter of working a lot – but rather working smart.

And it is true: it doesn't feel like overwork if you love what you do. This is easier to say and do when you only have to answer to yourself, though, and not to others and a life beyond the studio.

## Talent versus hard work

*I am not a natural talent but I am resilient. I work hard and deliver. Achieving goals in practice has to be about nurturing both talent and hard work.*
**– Zoe Hooton**

*Talent is only a baseline from which we can work, but determination is the willingness to stay with it and commit to finding a solution.*
**– Angela Watson**

For some architects, talent is a reality, but nothing compensates for hard work – where lifelong learning is the great equaliser. 'Natural talent is a true blessing that some possess, and that talent can certainly take you very far, but I also believe that with great mentorship, hard work and commitment, all aspects of the profession can be learned and mastered,' says Tom Mozina. 'If you are willing to put in the time and effort and align yourself with the right people, there is no reason to limit your goals and aspirations.'

For others, as with resilience, having a strong work ethic and doing the work required are either more important than natural talent or they are complementary. 'Natural talent with a complacent attitude is useless,' says Danei Cesario. 'When natural or practised talent is matched with work ethic you're more equipped to reach and even surpass your goals. Ambition is about looking past where you are and working towards how you want to be.'

Fig 3.5: Danei Cesario at the WALLEN + daub New York Building Congress

What role does natural talent play compared with hard work in determining how far you go in achieving your ambitions and goals? Alison Brooks reminds us that 'there's that famous saying by the golfer Gary Player, "The harder I practise, the luckier I get." And there's another one, "No great art was ever achieved without great suffering." It's the same in every profession. Talent is the product of a feedback loop: ambition, persistent hard work and fundamentally enjoying what you're doing. You have to be able to laugh at yourself, find the humour in the ridiculous things we find ourselves doing sometimes, but also take your work extremely seriously.'

For Sara Beardsley, talent without interpersonal intelligence won't take you as far as having both. 'It is a combination of talent, hard work, perseverance, and also personality,' says Beardsley. 'One has to remember that architects have, and need, very important skills that are not always a prominent part of a traditional architectural education: leadership and interpersonal skills. I have met some very talented people who have not had the right rapport or temperament to succeed, and I have met people who are great at working with others, communicating, selling an idea, leading and negotiating who have been very successful.'

Joe Cliggott agrees. 'Natural talent only goes so far, and actually has the potential to be limiting if you only do the things you are comfortable [with] and good at,' says Cliggott. 'Everyone should be pushed outside of their natural abilities to learn and grow. Hard work is more important than natural talent, in my opinion.'

## You can't teach spark

Hard work does pay off, and I have always tried to 'give my all' to any project I have been tasked with. Just because a project may seem trivial at the time, one has to remember that each project is a step and a learning experience. Communication, relationships and professional activities outside the office are also very important, because it is easier to 'stick it out' when you have peers, mentors and friends to go through the journey with.
– Sara Beardsley

Both [talent and hard work] are important. You can't teach spark. You know if someone has spark. Someone has it or they don't. You can cultivate and grow someone who has natural talent, but you can't give someone that talent. Hard work is available to anyone. It plays a very vital role in getting ahead. Working smart is as important as working hard. Some people are just busy. It is better to be productive.
– Trina Sandschafer

Randy Guillot considers himself one of the few mid- to late-career architects who has spent his entire career thus far in the profession of architecture. 'Many of my colleagues over the years have taken detours out of the profession either by choice or by economic downturn or other unplanned exits,' explains Guillot. 'Most have done just fine for themselves, and in many cases the changes have led to exceptional results for them. I'm quite sure perseverance has had much to do with my longevity. But I've never looked at it that way.'

Guillot continues: 'Part of my passion is teaching. I have the privilege of participating in design and professional practice programmes for students, and they often ask me what is the most important thing they can do. Though I'm sure perseverance is wrapped up in the answer somewhere, my number one piece of advice to them is to work exceptionally hard for people [they] admire at a young age.' He continues: 'There are two pieces to that: the hard work part, and the admiration part. Early in my career I did this, and I truly believe it's served as the foundation for many strong professional relationships I have across the world. I brought hard work and talent into the room and shared it generously because of my admiration for those I was working with. I spend a lot of time with the students I teach, helping them understand that if you can connect your talents and hard work – your exceptionally hard work – with the success of someone you admire, that person will be your advocate for life.'

'Many years ago, I was part of a firm who sold our practice to a larger firm,' says Guillot. 'Although a principal in the organisation, I had just begun my trajectory as an owner and was not part of the negotiations, nor should I have been. One of the senior partners with the firm that was acquiring us was someone I had worked with early in my career, someone I admired, and someone I had worked exceptionally hard for. He told me after negotiations were complete and the firm was sold that his comfort level was, in no small part, due to his knowing that I had, in the past, been a good partner to him and would continue to be.'

Interestingly, Emily Grandstaff-Rice believes that intrinsic motivation is far more important to career longevity and success than either natural talent or hard work. 'Without the desire or interest to grow and explore, it does not matter how fast you are moving,' says Grandstaff-Rice. 'This is also why having multiple interests is critical to going far; it keeps you from becoming burned out or bored.'

## Prescience

We are always looking for the next possible disruptor and planning ahead to hire people with skills and interests that put us in a strong strategic position to weather the next challenge.
– Mary Shaffer

Anticipating the horizon is difficult. It is more important that firms support you and enable you to plan your career long term, and support your development.
– John Edwards

Several architects we have already heard from in this book have anticipated trends – such as computational design and sustainability – got onboard and enabled their firms to be early entrants into new markets and adopters of opportunities.

The pandemic and what comes after is a perfect example, where firms that were prepared – not necessarily for a pandemic, but an economic downturn after a record climb – were better positioned to weather the crisis and come out of it strong. How to anticipate what is on the horizon, how spaces will be used – the exercise of asking *What if …?* – is a necessary skillset.

There is no crystal ball, but planning ahead for potential disruption is essential to the viability of a design firm, says Mary Shaffer. She starts by asking some difficult questions. 'Does your firm have diversity of skills, project typologies and clients? Is there a new market sector that you should consider adding in order to weather an economic downturn in another market sector? Economic downturns tend to happen in cycles of seven to ten years or so. The COVID-19 pandemic accelerated the most recent downturn, and affected the entire world, at a scale unlike anything I have seen in my lifetime,' says Shaffer.

So how did her firm fare? 'Our firm had a strong backlog of civic and government projects going into the shutdown, and was able to continue work on construction, design and bidding services on projects. Healthcare design firms were urgently needed to design pop-up hospitals,' says Shaffer.

The same questions Shaffer asked of firms, she asks of individuals: 'Do you have a variety of diverse skills that add value to your firm's offerings? Are you able to contribute to every aspect of a project, from winning the work to owner-occupancy? Think about where you could add some skills to round out your experience – is there training available to learn that skill?'

Having lived through several economic cycles by the time you reach mid-career ought to help prepare you for the inevitable: ask these questions long before you need answers. 'Although there are other pathways to success, anticipation of what is on the horizon is important and has played a critical role in my career path,' says Elliot Glassman. 'It helped me position myself to be a change agent, and prioritise where to develop my knowledge and experience even though being prescient was sometimes fraught with frustration, given how resistant organisations and our industry are to change.'

Working in a more technology-centric role, Andy Watts believes it is vital to anticipate what is on the horizon. 'This can stem from a number of different influences: the industry and its current trends, what clients are looking for as their briefs evolve, and also beyond the architectural landscape, looking to other fields such as aerospace, IT and even video games to anticipate what new technologies can influence architecture,' says Watts.

## Strategic foresight

As for strategic foresight, you have to have a degree of self-awareness and market awareness; you should not carry on blindly if it's not working. Look for the low-hanging fruit, in the short term, where can you make the most impact in your market in the shortest time.
– Philip Twiss

Strategic foresight is my secret weapon. It allows you to align your day-to-day work with progress towards your goals. I need to be able to anticipate not just where I am today but where I will be next year. Challenging yourself to create multi-year scenarios helps to develop this strategic capability, as well as bouncing these ideas off your network.
– Emily Grandstaff-Rice

Mid-career architects are expected to be able to anticipate what will occur in the future and spend their time, as well as human and other resources, accordingly. Foresight – especially strategic foresight – becomes increasingly important as you grow into mid-career and into a leadership position. 'Here is where tapping into your intuition is vital,' says Danei Cesario. 'If you get a sense that something is off, you have to untangle it. Foresight helps [you] to navigate your roadmap more effectively and personalise your journey.'

Cesario continues: 'Foresight is part of my role at SOM as a project manager. When I write a proposal, it is with the best possible outcome in mind. Still, I have to factor in all outcomes and protect our teams, finances, design and future against the negative ones. Understanding the nature of our client and their goals is key. How I navigate our relationship from the beginning and throughout the project is rooted in strategic foresight for the betterment of our firm. Being mindful and pre-emptive about the future is part of being a PM and an architect. We build for the future and the best possible outcomes, but the time between the ground-breaking and the eventual ribbon-cutting is a different era. For this reason, I believe that being an architect is the ultimate act of optimism.'

'It is important to strategise and anticipate what's on the horizon,' says John Gresko. 'Especially regarding which markets are perhaps more recession-proof, more active and more long-term. Working on projects that are 5–10 years in duration is one way to stay employed for a long time. Working in healthcare, which has been historically one of the most recession-proof markets, could mean long-term employment.'

But how do design professionals go about gazing into the crystal ball? By paying attention to the world around us, says Diane Reicher Jacobs, 'not just project needs. Read the newspaper, participate in the broader conversation. Treat everyone with respect – connect genuinely. You learn a lot by being present, sharing your story, listening to others and treating clients as long-term friends.'

How important is strategic foresight for the work that Jacobs does, much of which is in the public domain? 'Less important,' she admits. 'Our strategic foresight is to be aware, be courageous in connecting with potential clients, and do really good work (both product and process) no matter how big or small the project is. Also – know when to say "no thank you".'

Joe Cliggott believes 'it is critically important to look beyond the simple day-to-day tasks of a job and to understand the arc of a career. It is fundamental to have a destination that is out on the horizon and to take the career steps towards it, all the while knowing that there is much that is beyond our control and unpredictable. No one can anticipate every crisis,' admits Cliggott, 'but we should be prepared to face them when they come. [I'm] not sure that it has been perseverance so much as just [a] lifelong goal to be an architect and work in the profession. [It] would be what I would want to do if I could do anything at all. So, as for advice, simply having a passion and love for what you do is important. If you don't love it, find the thing that you do love. It may even be in associated fields.'

'While we always have to be aware of what is happening in the world around us, there is no crystal ball that will tell us definitively what will happen next,' says Sara Beardsley. 'I do not believe a successful career can be completely planned – it is also a reaction to outside circumstances that exist. One can drive oneself crazy trying to plan everything, especially in a profession as volatile as architecture, where a career is not always completely within one's own control. However, when "bumps" do occur the important thing is how we rebound and move on from those difficult times.'

## ASK THIS

Always ask yourself one question: 'Is what I am doing rewarding and stimulating?' **[John Edwards]**

## TRY THIS

I have thrived in environments where I was not welcomed and sometimes sabotaged. In short, my tips for the long haul would be:

- show up
- always do your best work
- establish trust with everyone you work with
- get outside your comfort zone
- politely stand up for your values and integrity
- keep your cadence, even if you have to hop over a few hurdles in your path
- trust and bet on yourself.

**[Danei Cesario]**

## TRY THIS

When I've had a down day (and over 30 years, there have been a few), I usually will take some time to reflect, and often will journal about the situation, or write a letter (that never gets sent) to the other person telling them exactly how I feel about what happened. While we can't always control situations, we can always choose how we respond to other people's actions. I remind myself that everyone is human, we all make mistakes or errors in judgement, and perhaps the other person had a bad day or something terrible happened in their life, and then I try to find a way to handle the situation with poise and dignity.
**[Mary Shaffer]**

## TRY THIS

Adapt on the fly by using improv techniques; being mindful; being present; and through active listening. Work with others by supporting them, not 'hogging the stage'. Your ultimate goal is to be in a better position to adapt to unexpected changes, changes that can be brought about by any number of forces, such as the fact that you are working with fallible people – including yourself. Try change, improv or adaptability workshops for yourself and key players on your project team.

## TRY THIS

The key is to decide what kind of work you want to do and focus on that culture, or that sector. This has to do with your value system, but also about developing skills that will be relevant for the areas you're interested in. This is where architectural competitions are valuable; they're a form of in-house research and development. Those competition entries become portfolio pieces that demonstrate both your 'ideals' in terms of design approach, but also your ability to conceive of solutions to new problems. Competition proposals for projects outside of your existing portfolio demonstrate agile thinking.
**[Alison Brooks]**

# 4: Flourish

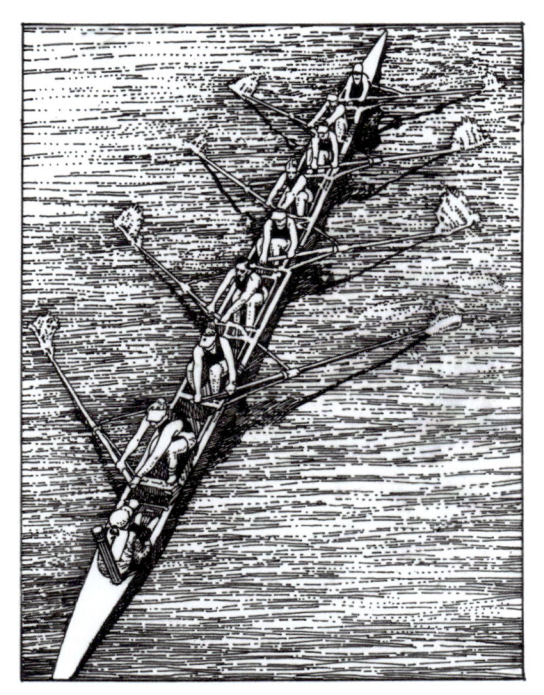

Fig 4.1: Training makes you more adaptable, ensuring your continued relevance

## Show up to your work and be willing to let it change you.

The good news is, you can make this change. I have seen lots of architects move sectors, learn new software and challenge themselves. You are going to need to influence this change; not all employers are going to want you to move between sectors or train new software.
– Stephen Drew

Middle is a very hard place to be, where you can choose to be inspired by what's ahead or be comfortable with what you have. Those who continually challenge themselves, learn and adapt to the changing world, will flourish, while others might become obsolete.
– Meghana Joshi

We've seen that our perseverance can be attributed to our work ethic and network – but how about to our adaptive brains? Our perseverance both as humans and as architects is due in large part to our problem-solving, adaptive and exploratory brains.[24] It's thanks to the adaptive neuroplasticity of our brains that we are able to adjust when new employees join our firm, when there's a new client on the project, when a contractor gets swapped out mid-project, or when we find ourselves working on a new project type or in a new firm.

Adaptation is why intrinsic rewards are so important – why architects can't rely exclusively on titles, promotions, awards or money to carry them through to the career finish line. The effect of extrinsic rewards is fleeting, and we adapt to a baseline level of satisfaction – *hedonic adaptation* – as with those who win the lottery. Because our brains enable us to adapt so readily to external circumstances or rewards, we need an internal compass we can count on – to recognise a job well done, take pride in what we accomplish, or learn on the job. Could this be why some mid-career professionals flourish while others struggle or become obsolete?

### Traversing the mid-career chasm

Randy Guillot has had the pleasure of working in large firms and, as such, has worked with hundreds of mid-career professionals. 'In that time, I have seen traits that seem to be shared by those that have succeeded in traversing the "mid-career chasm",' says Guillot. 'Leading with curiosity and having the perspective and honesty to shape meaningful explorations that engage others around you is key. Knowing how to do something is a short-term win. As we advance in our career, we all know how to do things. Ultimately someone will be able to do it better, but being at the centre of asking important questions that enrol others in your search for meaning in whatever you are doing has the effect of multiplying your impact.'

Guillot continues: 'Others excel because they choose to embrace leadership and the responsibility that comes with it. This doesn't mean you have to have your eyes on becoming president of your organisation or step on the backs of others to move up. Rather, to lean into the opportunities that are created or better yet, that you create. Creating your own opportunities, either through client engagement or industry leadership or whatever your passion is, is key to both real and perceived value. Being a "hunter" when others are "farming" has often reshuffled the deck for mid-career design professionals in their favour.'

Be open to the adventure, advises Guillot. 'Very few things we do today resemble how we were educated to do them. Whether mid-career professionals acknowledge this or not, they have changed, learned and adapted their whole careers. That same spirit of knowing you have a good foundation and can learn and adapt has carried you this far and can carry you into the future.'

## Find the passion within

There are no spectators in architecture. Architecture is a participatory activity, and those who persevere do so in part because of their level of engagement in their projects, with their teams, in their firm, in the larger profession, and in industry and communities. When Ted Hyman thinks about the architects that are successful, they are typically the ones who find the passion within themselves to do great things. 'Those who just want to come in and "watch design happen" tend to move on to related professions, whether it is working as a developer, a builder or other related professions.'

Fig 4.2: Unplanned desk-side discussions can lead to real-time design innovations. Here, a member of a ZGF project design team and the partner-in-charge review a Revit model of a clinical space

Hyman continues: 'We have architects in our firm that are strong conceptual "form-makers", some that are more interested in building performance, and then others who care fervently about the detail of how a building is put together: we need them all. That said, the individuals that are the most valuable in our firm, and I believe in the profession as a whole, are those who are interested in the exploration of innovation: whether it is a new "carbon positive" office development, or a hospital [in which] the planning will help the medical staff save more lives. I recall my very first design professor in college saying, "If you are not passionate about changing the world, you should not waste your time and money becoming an architect." I've tried to live by that philosophy, and it has kept me excited about every project I work on.'

'The leading traits in all professions that indicate a better chance at success still exist in architecture: ambition, willpower, drive and competitiveness,' says John Gresko. 'Many architects are in the right place at the right time for a big opportunity or promotion. Others are persistent; they focus on what they want, and they work methodically to achieve it. Some develop relationships with the right people, and out of luck or persistence or people skills find themselves in positions to be promoted. Most design architects flourish based on talent. Good designers get more work and bad designers get less work.'

Gresko continues: 'There's a focus in architecture school on design. [So] when someone in the office shows signs of being good at sales and business development, they stand out against the crowd. It's really about being a little different than the field around you that could elevate someone. I've seen very diplomatic architects with tremendous leadership abilities and people skills get promoted quickly despite the consensus from their peers that their actual architecture skills were not so great.'

By necessity, in terms of how the structure of most successful businesses work, there are often a diminishing number of opportunities for advancement and growth, according to Joe Cliggott. 'An organisational model is typically a pyramid, not a square! However, one can still flourish within a role without a change in title and responsibility. We can celebrate someone who is a senior project architect when they retire; not everyone needs to be a principal to consider that their career "flourished". Alternatively, if there is a real struggle, this may be a sign for changing organisations or searching for new paths to find a place more suitable and supportive.'

'There are a lot of mid-career (and late-career) architects who are surprisingly one-dimensional and don't flourish,' says Duane Carter. 'One reason is that most firms tend to put people into a specialisation (PM, PD, technical, etc.) early in their careers. However, much of it is because of attitude. Most people, early in their career, know that they have a lot to learn. Then at some point, they stop growing. It could be because they are more focused on things outside of work – which I understand, but with most people they don't seem to have an interest or any joy in learning new things. They also stop listening to others who have different knowledge and skillsets.'

## Employability

Do architecture firms provide architects with opportunities to keep up with advances in the profession, including the use of new tools? Because both the architect and their firm have a responsibility to ensure that while they work in the firm, employees remain employable. 'It's about employability and being able to remain employable,' explains Virginia E Marquardt. 'In the past employees worked for one firm for their entire career; they were faithful to one employer and employers were faithful to their employees. Today it's different. Both employee and employer have a responsibility to ensure that employees can remain employable. We as employees need to be growing our skills and knowledge, and our employers need to mentor, coach and allow us the opportunity attend and participate in outside resources to gain skills and knowledge. In the long run this is of value not only to the employee, but to the employer as well. It's about succession planning, promotions, giving back, whether a direct benefit to the employer or not.' Or, as Richard Branson has said, 'Train people well enough so they can leave; treat them well enough so they don't want to.'

Fig 4.3: HMC principal-in-charge Virginia E Marquardt leading a meeting

Architecture requires of the architect not just continuing education, but continuous learning; being someone – to paraphrase Henry James – on whom nothing is lost, and being motivated by learning. Architecture is a profession that takes in, sorts, analyses and creates design solutions from the information of so many other professions and knowledge topics, says Lora Teagarden. 'The single process of a project requires the understanding of economics and politics of a city (project funding), geography (site location), socioeconomics and cultural history (site location and project priorities), and so much more ... on top of the typical knowledge of materials, spatial design and structure to actually create the building. Many of these topics continue to grow in breadth and depth of available information, so if an architect is not of the mindset that they need to continue to learn throughout their career, they will stagnate while others continue to grow with the profession and the communities they are in. At a micro scale internal to the profession, the same can be said for a willingness to learn and take on new technology.'

How, you might ask. How does one remain employable? It requires risk (you may learn the wrong tool or pigeonhole yourself) and courage (all learning requires change). It is important to continue to grow, adapt, try new things, take risks and expand your network, says chief technology officer and principal at FXCollaborative Alexandra Pollock AIA. 'But this does not come naturally to many in our industry, and change can be intimidating. I would also argue that, as an industry, we would benefit from finding ways to make change easier for mid-career professionals, as they have so much knowledge and skill that can be leveraged. We need to become more comfortable culturally with cross-mentoring, and knowledge that flows in both directions.'

## Attributes of those who flourish

To flourish it is important to stimulate collaborative behaviours. Collaborate with clients to realise their aspirations and be at the cutting edge of research and technology, and improve the likelihood of successful design, manufacture and construction of projects. Key is the ability to develop new skills across disciplines within a firm that is willing to support your development.
– John Edwards

Longevity is more than just attendance; you must show up to your work and be willing to let it change you.
– Emily Grandstaff-Rice

Just as there are qualities we associate with those who struggle – for example signs of burnout associated with stress and resistance – so too there are qualities common to those who flourish. 'First, a common trait I see in those who flourish is a genuine sense of self-awareness and the ability to be honest with themselves,' says Tom Lee. 'As a young architect, we can be passionate about anything and everything, and can be ambitiously working towards learning the necessary skills to fulfil said passion. At mid-career, it's important to begin to acknowledge what our emerging strengths and limitations truly are, and understand that what we are good at and what we are passionate about might be two different things. It doesn't mean we can't learn or pivot mid-career, but architects need to understand that their increasing responsibilities and rising salaries are tied to a developing series of strengths (value), and that can be a great foundation to continue to build a career upon.'

Lee continues: 'Another factor I see in architects who flourish is that they tend to be great managers, regardless of their area of expertise. That said, management and leadership to me are two different things (not everyone is a leader, and that's okay), but in order to advance in a career, the ability to manage projects and people (team members and clients alike) is essential to rising in a practice. Managing the latter seems to come easier for people who have a higher level of emotional intelligence, but just an awareness of how others feel can make a big difference.'

## Sunk costs and complacency

Complacency is fine – if what you're complacent with is excellence, which never seems to go out of fashion. Otherwise, one needs to get comfortable with evolving professionally. Or, comfortable with discomfort – being able to live with challenging yourself, and change and growth; the perpetual marshmallow test (of the ability to delay gratification). Either will work for the mid-career architect. 'There is a moment in your career where you finally have the experience and confidence to feel at ease in your role,' says Danei Cesario. 'The difference between carrying on versus thriving is the former focuses on maintaining, while the latter homes in on challenging your ability.

That discomfort – similar to that of an intern's first few months on the job – allows a mid-career architect to propel themselves forward.'

Fig 4.4: At 2019's AIA Conference on Architecture. WALLEN + daub presented its first live podcast on Planning the Future: Principles, Practice + Purpose

Especially today and in the post-pandemic world, you need adaptability and agility – something our profession in general lacks, says architect and the first-ever senior experience designer at Slack Technologies Evelyn Lee. 'The further you find yourself in this profession, people tend not to want to leave due to all the time they have committed. One way you can look at it is, I've built up all of this experience and am going to continue to struggle because of everything I have put toward this profession. Or you can take more of a business approach – not to cut your losses, but because everything leading up to this point enables you, taught you and built your perspective on the communities you serve and the work you are able to bring to individuals. There's an opportunity to take that knowledge and apply it in a variety of different ways ... And be more agile in times when architects are hit really hard – such as now, or in the future – so architects can thrive, and we can move the mark further for architects.'

## Comfort and complacency

When you fail to recognise the signs of burnout, complacency and groupthink, according to Emily Grandstaff-Rice, they become familiar in pattern. 'That is exactly the point when you need to pivot. A lot of mid-career architects fall into the trap of thinking "if I continue to grind away, it will get better",' says Grandstaff-Rice. 'It may get more familiar, but not necessarily better. That is where I see the struggle. This belief that years at a firm or a job will earn you credibility. Longevity is more than just attendance; you must show up to your work and be willing to let it change you.'

'When it comes to internal motivation, some people lose that over time and become complacent in their jobs,' says Mary Shaffer. 'It takes focused energy to keep learning and growing; it is easier to maintain the status quo and put in your 40 hours and go home than to strive for more. "Worker bees" like that may be technically competent, but they are not going be the innovators or the early adapters to new technology or processes. Sometimes external encouragement can come from a simple gesture. One of the principals in a design firm noticed that I had been working over a weekend, and he left a handwritten thank you note so that I received it right away on Monday morning. I was touched by that; it was really motivating to know that my extra efforts were noticed and valued.'

This relates to how comfortable you get in your position, says Trina Sandschafer. 'There is a danger in becoming too comfortable. Growth happens outside of your comfort zone. You should strive to be growing in your position, in your knowledge and in your influence.'

There are those who do everything they say they're going to do and achieve everything they set out to accomplish – which is great when it happens. But it's hard to maintain over an entire career. 'You've heard it before: you're either progressing or you're dying,' says Evan Troxel. 'Many professionals set goals early on in their careers and achieve them without adjusting those goals higher or differently along the way. I've worked with many people who "made it" and weren't interested in pushing in new ways or stretching different muscles. I think the main topic here is drive – being intrinsically motivated – to help others achieve great things, to work on yourself, the business, the profession, or on a more global scale. The professionals that flourish have that. Intrinsic motivation is hard to come by, and I think more people are extrinsically motivated, but they typically aren't skilled in the art of leadership, and thus aren't seen as "relevant" as others in the field.'

One sign of complacency is when we begin telling ourselves and others that we don't have capacity, as opposed to creating capacity. It's about having an abundance mindset. For example, we don't tell our clients that we just can't fit their gymnasium or auditorium in the floor plan – we keep at it until we find a way to make it work. And it should be the same for ourselves. 'One of the most career-thwarting things I hear people say is "I'm too busy",' says Angela Mazzi. 'Successful people know that deadlines will always be there, and they don't wait to have time to pursue their goals. No matter how eminently competent you are, just responding to your current workload and doing what you know to do won't move the bar.'

Successful people find that the busier they are, the more they can agree to and accomplish, rather than less. There are times when it is important to say no, but there's a reason why, when we have something important to do and can't get to it, we delegate it to the busiest person, not the slowest, because we know they'll cut to the chase and get it done. 'As a species, humans don't like change,' says Philip Twiss. 'We become stuck in our ways and don't want to adapt. We fail to see the trends influencing society and our profession, the business where we work. Sometimes it's easier to accept mediocrity as the norm and stay somewhere in mid-management, or in a firm where "the fit" isn't right, than be self-reflective and accept that where you are is not right, will not provide the career growth and professional opportunities to flourish. We also have to acknowledge that sometimes there are practitioners who simply aren't good enough.'

Fig 4.5: One of a variety of informal and formal meeting spaces at the London office of senior associate and design director Philip Twiss's firm, Gensler

'This is as much about personality and appetite for risk,' suggests Alistair Kell. 'It is easy for individuals to get into comfortable roles that once mastered are relatively easy to maintain as long as they provide value to a business. This suits some people, whereas others continually look to drive into leadership roles, be that at a project or business level. Individuals can tend to settle into what their personality allows. Recognising this can either force people to actively change or allow them to be more relaxed about maintaining the status quo.'

## Fear holding us back

Flourishing is a choice, Angela Mazzi reminds us. 'It requires being exceptionally clear about who you are and where your passions lie,' says Mazzi. 'It also requires that you feel what you do is an authentic expression of who you are – that you are committed to doing this work and making a difference in the world through your efforts. Inspirational, perhaps scary, totally necessary. Those who embrace taking empowered action to advance, will. What holds some people back is fear. Fear of failure. Fear of being seen as too presumptuous in their aspirations. I've seen intelligent designers spin their wheels, constantly second-guessing themselves instead of asking how the project could be a way to explore or advance some aspect of the profession that most excites them. Others are intimidated at the prospect of writing or speaking. They assume that that is something for "the experts" even when they have a great deal of their own expertise.'

One thing you can do positively to advance the likelihood that you will flourish is to counter complacency with continual learning. 'The industry is complex, with programmes of work [that] are becoming shorter,' says associate architect at BDP Michael Riley. 'It appears that people who "stick to what they know" are the ones who struggle to stay relevant. They continue to be good, careful and competent; the breadth of their knowledge, however, stays relatively static. A misguided loyalty to ageing working practices starts to make meeting deadlines more difficult and the quality of work reduces; for example, imagine trying to complete all your drawings on tracing paper – it's an extreme example, but shows how working practices can change dramatically over time. This change away from tracing didn't happen overnight, and if you don't continually improve using incremental small steps then your knowledge needs to suddenly leap forward to keep up to date.'

## Signs of burnout

Just as there are qualities we associate with those who flourish, there are qualities common to those who experience burnout, stress and resistance to what they do. These are important to recognise. Over a long career, even minor but persistent experiences of resistance, of holding your tongue, or suppressing feelings of conflict can wear you down. Or finding yourself doing tasks unrelated to why you went into architecture to begin with, and the constant need to reframe what you are doing in other terms – learning, growth, challenge. All of these can add up to a loss of enthusiasm for your work. 'So many of us entered the profession for a love of design, building and creativity. But as you chase your staff timesheets, sit in a professional indemnity insurance meeting and argue about fees with one of your clients it's hard not to let the business of architecture grind you down,' says Zoe Hooton. 'That's why it's so important to have many generations of architects and students in practice: to boost morale, to shake up your thinking and [help you] rediscover the infectious enthusiasm you forgot you had.'

One of the most rewarding and consistent ways to ensure you will be motivated and energised by your work is to invest in yourself and be motivated by learning. If you are motivated by learning, you will find that a career in architecture is the gift that keeps giving. In terms of flourishing, Oscia Wilson explains that for some, it's because they didn't invest as much in cultivating their people skills as they did in their architectural knowledge. 'For others, it's because they didn't stay curious and keep learning,' says Wilson. 'And we all know it's an exhausting industry rife with burnout, so one can hardly be judged for running out of the energy needed to keep seeking knowledge, decade after decade.'

Related to burnout is mental health, and making it appear that you've got it all together – when you haven't. There are times in our career when we are in trajectory mode – and others where we need to sit out and give our attention to other aspects of our lives. We need to be able to recognise this, and know the difference. 'Even those who carry on and thrive can lose their marbles,' says Emily Grandstaff-Rice. 'We need to let go of the idea that everyone always has it together. A successful career is a juggling act; no one's trajectory is linear. We must be able to recognise when it is time to pick up and leave a bad situation, as well as stay the course for something bigger. Having multiple interests allows you to maintain stability in one area of your life when the rest of it seems to be falling apart.'

## Positioning yourself

Sharing knowledge, with a goal of becoming a thought leader, is for most time well spent. 'A lot of it comes down to attitude and how you position yourself,' says Andy Watts. 'Those who are successful and progress are well aware of the context in which they find themselves. Not to say that it is a case of "playing the game", but rather being conscious of what a team or practice needs to succeed, and how you can contribute to that outcome in a meaningful way. If you can't, there may be a risk of being overlooked.'

People don't come with a 'use-by' date and can peak multiple times throughout their career – and of course have multiple careers. An architecture career is almost never one and done, but a series of experiences. Danei Cesario doesn't believe that people with the ability to create can become obsolete. 'With the ability to make something out of nothing, how is that possible?' asks Cesario. 'Reminding yourself at every step of your career of why you started is vital, especially mid-career.'

Fig 4.6: Informal design discussions between Alison Brooks and project architects

Alison Brooks also doesn't believe anyone ever becomes obsolete. 'Architecture is a highly complex profession,' says Brooks. 'Forces beyond the architect's control can turn a practice, or a life, upside down. Flourishing practices are made of people with expertise, energy, good communication skills and sheer will. Ambition means trying to be the best in your field, or the best at what you enjoy doing most. Some would say today's most successful architects have media-friendly personalities propped up by armies of publicists. Others would say one loved building, a great detail, or generations of architects who have learned from you is a sign of architectural success. Time is the only real judge of architecture and architectural thinking.'

There is a key moment in any professional's career where either one moves forward on an upward track or ends up struggling to just tread water, says senior project leader at Studio Gang David Swain. 'The key is to be recognised by a mentor in the firm who can "pull" you forward up the trajectory you want. It's also important to recognise that at your current position you may never find that mentor, and maybe it's better to change jobs or attempt to become a sole practitioner. Additionally, although maybe it's counterintuitive, sometimes it's not the best to become too skilled in the position you currently have and therefore become pigeonholed. Broadening your knowledge behind what defines your position will help in moving ahead.'

'Self-awareness, and an understanding of one's own strengths and weaknesses, are critical to carrying on and thriving,' says Joe Cliggott. 'Empathy, and a deep understanding of others, and their needs, goals, strengths and weaknesses, is a complement to self-awareness. This impacts a career in being conscious of how one can help others in more senior roles, taking on more of their responsibility and activities, thereby allowing them the time and opportunity to move up themselves, while simultaneously delegating your own responsibilities to more junior colleagues. In this way, everyone moves up the ladder together. Being a mentor and a protégé at the same time.'

### Become a better communicator

The question of why one architect thrives while another becomes obsolete may have something to do with how architecture education works. 'In school we learn to design and to talk about design to each other. We do not learn about communicating our ideas to those that are not architects and not versed in our "language",' says Angela Watson. 'This is sufficient when we are not working in leadership roles and when we communicate only with those inside of our immediate team. Once we enter roles where we need to communicate beyond our team, we need the skills of translating our architecture language to others.'

Fig 4.7: Preliminary design session at Angela Watson's firm, Shepley Bulfinch

Watson continues: 'When we don't have an opportunity to learn those skills and to practise them, we don't learn to effectively communicate with those that actually manage or commission projects. Since this is a vital component of leadership, this may lead to a stagnating career. It's not unlike careers in every business. Some succeed in growing to leadership; others do not. If we are able to communicate effectively with others, we will thrive. If we don't, we will linger. To thrive we need to learn how to put ourselves into the shoes of those that we work with. That could be our clients, or our co-workers, or consultants, or our contractors. We must interact with different people in different positions with different priorities. In order to communicate effectively we must understand what those priorities are. We must be able to communicate in the language of those we wish to influence.'

## How we can be more like those who thrive?

Architects are not just creative individuals; we have a passion that drives that in us ... and pushes us to learn and be curious. And for many of us architecture is a calling ... it's our way of giving back our communities ... a way to better our communities and society.
– Virginia E Marquardt

As hinted at in the title of this publication – adapt. Be open to new ways of working and new knowledge in order to meet the needs of your context.
– Andy Watts

What can mid-career architects do now to be less like those who become obsolete and more like those who carry on and thrive? One suggestion is to look to those who we work or worked with who serve as role models in practice. Stephen Drew recounts a mid-career architect from the perspective of an intern, emerging professional, and associate, finding that what you do and who you are has an impact on those around you, including their own dedication and longevity in the profession, by serving as an example and role model. Drew remembers when he was an architectural assistant working under an associate at the architectural practice where he was working in London. 'He was articulate and the genuine article – a true architect,' says Drew. 'I found it inspiring how he used to freehand sketch, use BIM and most importantly engage the client. He could design and carry projects on site. He went above and beyond; this was 10 years ago ... now this associate is a board director of this top-100 company, and he has gone on to design towers in central London. He gave everything his all, he went above and beyond and lived and breathed architecture. A true director, influencer as well as a mover and shaker.' This role model clearly left a lasting and – importantly – positive impression on the now mid-career Stephen Drew.

Zoe Hooton also looks to her own role models and idols in practice. 'The Sadie Morgans of this world,' says Hooton, 'who continue to challenge and embrace new problems. Her involvement and call to architects to challenge infrastructure is a testament to this. The John Assael, who continues to want to improve his office environment for the wellbeing of staff. Or the Robin

Partington, who in his decision to make APT an employee ownership trust ... made himself dispensable so that he can be challenged again. All of these characters have an infectious enthusiasm, a love for learning and the drive to tackle a challenge.'

And, of course, Stephen and Zoe and the other architects whose voices appear in this book today serve as role models for today's architectural assistants, emerging professionals and future generations. How can we be more like them? We identify them, model ourselves after them, and emulate their behaviour. 'The work of architects can be so demanding and so varied from one office to another, one context to another: it's important to keep one's purpose in mind and make sure we are not losing sight of it,' says associate professor at the University of Liège in Belgium and former London head of BIM at Grimshaw Aurélie de Boissieu PhD. 'Further to purpose, which is an amazing long-term drive, I would not underestimate the importance of simply "having fun" as well. Making our work environment and work community a nice and fun place to spend our working hours should be part of our strategy to thrive. We shouldn't underestimate how supportive (or not) our environment can be, and how much we can participate in it.'

## Getting unstuck

Keep moving, even if that means jogging in place for a minute.
– Danei Cesario

As inherent problem-solvers and optimists, architects have a difficult time walking away when stuck.
– Emily Grandstaff-Rice

There are times when architects realise they may be on a dead-end career path. You might be on a track you are not enjoying, or learning from, or that you feel is taking you away from – not towards – your goals, and you can't get off it of your own volition. Or perhaps you made a deal with the Devil – you agreed to do roll-out stores and be paid handsomely for it – and now you regret that decision. You're stuck: now what do you do?

## Instigate change

Sometimes we find that we just need a push. There have been many times in my career where I felt immobilised, but it turned out that I just needed someone to make a bright suggestion and I was good to go. All the writing in my journal, repeating affirmations or meditating did nothing to help me become unstuck – whereas a conversation with a trusted colleague, friend or mentor did the trick. Start by recognising when you do leave the road – before your career goes too far off-course – but be assured that you might just be feeling the discomfort of the path not taken. 'Being stuck is perhaps the hardest thing in a career,' admits Joe Cliggott. 'On the one hand, it may make sense to double down, work harder to break through a challenge. [To recognise] that the effort and strain will be worth the success. On the other hand, banging one's head against a wall even harder will only result in a headache. You have to be keenly aware how to differentiate between the two opportunities.'

## Be your own advocate

Tom Lee was put on a public project, which was for him really exciting, but the nature of the project and the size of it meant that he'd be looking at a couple of years' worth of paperwork and less drawing in the later phases, and he wasn't looking forward to it. 'I loved the firm and didn't want to leave it,' says Lee, 'but I simply mentioned to colleagues and my mentor my concerns. I was prepared to follow through with the project, but perhaps coincidentally I was reassigned shortly thereafter to a different project more aligned with my interests. All this is to say that patience is a virtue, but it shouldn't be limitless.' It should be apparent that this probably wasn't a coincidence. Because Lee acted as his own best advocate – on his own behalf – he was able to let his concerns be known. So, speak up, have that conversation – just make sure your interests and those of your firm, when possible, are in alignment.

## Talk it out

John Gresko has been stuck a few times in his career. 'Both times I switched jobs,' says Gresko. 'I advise addressing the problem or plateau with a supervisor, and get their or a mentor's advice. In my case, I had neither, and just wanted to do something more challenging or new which wasn't available to me at the time.'

Philip Twiss had worked at his first practice for almost 10 years, having joined as a graduate. 'I lived and breathed the company, the most recently appointed directors were just a year ahead of me, and I had followed immediately behind them in the practice's succession plans as I was promoted through the firm,' says Twiss. 'As I progressed through the practice and got more involved with the management of the company I found myself at variance with the company's culture; I also wanted to experience alternative approaches to design, and considered that the next opportunity for me to succeed to partner would not come within a timescale that I wanted at the time, and so realised that I needed to move practice and I haven't looked back. My advice is don't be scared. The grass is not always greener, but whether it works out or not you will always learn from the experience.'

Sometimes you just have to be patient; good things are around the corner. And then, once the good thing happens, give it 100%. 'There was a point when, after three years in practice and successfully completing my first major project (in Germany) with no work to follow up,' says Alison Brooks, 'I realised that working in Europe, as opposed to London, was a difficult way to build a practice, a clientele. I realised the value of working closer to home. Fortunately, a London client contacted me for a project that became the

VXO House. It completed in 2002, won major awards and was published worldwide; invaluable "free" publicity and credibility. I still give tours of this house to new clients. One good client who trusts you can go a long way towards creating a foundation for practice. The important thing is to treat every project like it will be your last, like your opus magnum. This will stop you from compromising.'

The time Trina Sandschafer felt most stuck was just before she changed roles. 'I was ready to take on a larger leadership role,' explains Sandschafer. 'This was collectively agreed upon and we were moving towards that leadership change over the course of several years. Ultimately, the most senior leader wasn't ready to make the change. I was stuck. I could continue waiting for a change that might never come, or I could be the change. I needed change. I spent a long time thinking about what that role could be like for me if it wasn't where I was. I took that vision for a new role and carried it forward. There were roles out there that were not right for me. Then, when I connected with my current firm, I knew that role was the right one for me and for them. Our goals and visions and timelines aligned. There was an immediate synergy.'

'This Too Shall Pass' has become Diane Reicher Jacobs's personal motto. 'I have it up on my wall. When I see that I realise that being stuck is temporary and that life is long. One of the ways I get unstuck is to take a few of my favourite people – or some that I may not know well but admire – to lunch. Our conversations are not specific, but just breaking bread with someone who might have a different perspective on one or two things – not your life story – can help move things in a better direction.'

### ASK THIS

Architects in the midst of their careers are either expanding or contracting. Like the shark, they must keep moving. There is no stasis or in-between. To be static is to atrophy and fall behind. Does your company give you the opportunity to grow and challenge yourself? Or must you look outside your work – to tutorials and training, and outside groups – for these challenges and opportunities?

### TRY THIS

Find a problem that needs solving and dedicate yourself to it with no expectation of the outcome. Document your journey and share it along the way. People are thirsting for knowledge and insight into how you are doing it, not just the shiny, polished outcome. Sharing your thoughts, your approach, your process and your solution gives insight and can be applied to many other problems in the future. Architects are great problem-solvers – be the one that shares how to do just that; others will notice, and you'll thrive. **[Evan Troxel]**

## TRY THIS

Don't forget about why you chose architecture in the first place. When people feel unsettled or unfulfilled in their jobs, I advise them to think about where they find their joy. Literally make a list of things you love to do, things you dislike doing, tasks you do well, tasks you struggle with. What is it about your current situation that is preventing you from thriving? What needs to change to allow you to thrive? Is this something within your control, or will it necessitate taking another action – even leaving your current job – to make it happen? If you want to stay in your current firm, you can meet with your supervisor to share your goals for thriving there. Are you ready to take on new responsibilities? Are your assignments not challenging enough, and are you ready for something more challenging? If you cannot make a shift within your current firm, you may need to take the courageous step of finding a new job opportunity. **[Mary Shaffer]**

## TRY THIS

Never stop learning. Ever. Read books that may not seem relevant to architecture, because it still tells a story of how people live. Read fiction that lets the creativity muscles in your brain flex as you envision the scenes in the book. Read history to understand how our world was shaped. Read science, equity and political books to understand how we are currently shaping the world and how we can improve. Go to AIA or RIBA events to meet peers and stay up to date on the latest trends and materials in the industry. Get out in your community and meet the people who use the buildings you design. Figure out their needs, what drives them, what they dream of for their future. Be a sponge, and let all of this information influence your design. **[Lora Teagarden]**

## TRY THIS

There are several things that I do when I'm stuck. Most of the time I draw. What I mean by that is that I sketch to visualise the problem. This is not about creating beautiful drawings, but rather about understanding a problem by visualising and reframing it. Looking at it upside down sometimes helps too. I find that my most important tool to get unstuck is talking to others. Questions that come up in conversations often open up new avenues and allow me to take in a different perspective.
**[Angela Watson]**

## TRY THIS

There are many scales at which you can get stuck. If stuck on a project-based item, the best thing you can do is stop working on it for a bit.

Take a coffee break. Go for a walk. Sleep on it. The best ideas will come when you rest. Always. Give it some time and come back to it. If you're working on a project that you do not connect with, focus on what your job is and how you can do it to the best of your abilities, and how that helps move you and your firm forward. If you are in a valley of your career, focus on what you can learn in the valley. That will move you out of that stuck feeling. **[Trina Sandschafer]**

## TRY THIS

I also love to read memoirs and biographies. There is great compatibility and therefore inspiration in other people's stories.
**[Diane Reicher Jacobs]**

# 5: Shift

Fig 5.1: Some adapt to midlife pressures by shifting on their path to career longevity

# Take the path less travelled, differentiate yourself.

You can only control whatever you can control. There is always opportunity to move if you are willing to find it. Even in the worst of times. Your next step may not always be a forward step, but it is a step away from being stuck. That is what is most important.
– Evelyn Lee

The larger question is whether the architect cannot see the path forward or no path exists. Those are two different scenarios. One can be a leader at any time in one's career. There is a misconception that you need a title to lead.
– Emily Grandstaff-Rice

To shift is not the same as to leave. It's a trade-off – between your current firm and another.

A fatal flaw at mid-career in architecture is an inability to adapt. The corollary to this is that you don't need to adapt as an architect as long as you can adapt as an owner's rep, a contractor, a construction manager, an owner – as a former architect. This book focuses on how you can adapt throughout your career while remaining an architect – with an emphasis on the word remain. The crucial question is whether you can adapt and reinvent yourself when necessary to maintain your relevance, impact and effectiveness throughout your career. What advice might there be for a mid-career architect who sees no clear path to leadership within their current organisation? Looking back in years to come, might they have found a move beneficial to their career and wellbeing, and if so, in what ways? If they were to do it today, how would they do things differently, if at all? Sometimes all it takes is a shift.

Recognising one's career path is not just the responsibility of the individual, but also of the company they work for, says Chithra Marsh. 'The responsibility of the individual is to understand what direction they want to pursue in their career and work hard to attain this. They need to consider if their aspirations align with the objectives set within the company's overall business plan. The collaborative efforts between the individual and the company are the keys to success for both. If personal/ethical values and aspirations are not aligned, then the individual should discuss with their senior manager how they can best contribute to enhancing the business plan objectives with their core strengths. Alternatively, if this is not possible then they may need to seek a position at another company that shares similar goals and aspirations. A better fit will breed greater success, and the individual will feel they can genuinely contribute and enhance success for both themselves and the company.'

To shift, it helps to have an abundance mentality. Just as the advantage of having a variety of projects to work on is the opportunity to switch from time to time, it also helps to build relationships within the industry, so you know people at different firms. And switching – whether projects, firms or foods – helps you to adapt better over the long haul.

Did someone say food? It turns out that when a person switches between different foods on their plate during a meal they reduce sensory adaptation, or the likelihood that the food they are eating becomes unappealing.[25] The same is true for having a variety of projects to work on, or teams to work with, or firms at your disposal should the tenure with your current firm not work out. Variety indeed leads towards a rewarding career.

## The firm's responsibility

Justin Martinkovic believes that it is the responsibility of the organisation to provide clear paths for advancement for all employees, mid-career and otherwise. 'Leaders in the firm must challenge their team members to grow, to explore, to push their boundaries, and to find meaning in our work,' says Martinkovic. 'The hard part for me as a leader is finding the sweet spot: pushing and challenging, not too much, and not too little. Indeed, whether explicitly stated or not, most employees want to be appropriately challenged and encouraged to advance. For some, the next challenge may include a position with leadership responsibilities. Others may be less interested in formal roles of leadership and more interested in finding new challenges in other aspects of the profession. Nonetheless, being appropriately challenged, and finding the joys inherent in the hard work to surmount these challenges, is a key aspect of personal fulfilment.'

If a mid-career architect sees no clear path for advancement yet wants to remain within the firm, Martinkovic would first encourage her to speak to her manager or principal and discuss where they might see mutually beneficial opportunities for growth and advancement. 'She should come armed with her own ideas and discuss ways in which her talents and passions are underutilised, and how nurturing these talents may benefit the firm,' says Martinkovic. 'It's critical to position ideas and requests as an all-around win: a win for the employee, for her teammates, for the firm and for the clients. A critical mistake in these interactions is when the employee implies this is "all about me". If after engagement and discussion with firm leaders it is clear there is no fulfilling path to pursue, she should seek challenges, advancement, contribution and fulfilment elsewhere. It is worth mentioning that leadership and title are not necessarily correlated. Some higher-ups are flat-out bad leaders. Some folks lower on the totem pole are exceptional leaders and demonstrate it in their day-to-day work in ways big and small. Each one of us called to a position of leadership can demonstrate it every day if we so choose, regardless of our title.'

'It is a bit disheartening to hear that some organisations' structure is not conducive for growth or leadership opportunities,' says Tom Mozina. 'Having been a part of a large firm for my entire career, I often lose sight of the fact that the majority of architects are still working in much smaller offices where it just might not make sense to expand the ranks of leadership. If this is your situation and achieving equal billing on the marquee is not an option, I would strongly advise you to consider joining a larger practice. Although a perception may exist that at a larger firm it is harder to distinguish yourself,

I have not found that to be the case. In fact, it is just the opposite. Sure, you can blend in if that is your desire, but I'm assuming the question implies that the desire and ambition is alive in the candidate but just not the opportunity at the current firm. Inherent in a big organisation are big structural issues that need to be addressed so the office can function. In our practice we have so many sub-interest groups and knowledge communities that need people to step up and get involved. Everything from technical and design leadership to getting involved in social responsibility initiatives and building office culture. There are just far more opportunities to assert yourself and lighten the load of others in a larger practice. In most large firms, and it is certainly the case in my firm, there is a recognition of the need for succession planning, which is why we have instituted a structured leadership programme that provides tools from presentation training to business 101 to assist in project management as well as hone other skillsets to groom that next tier of future leaders.'

## What is the path? Is there a path? How do you know?

Not seeing a clear path to leadership in an organisation can come from several different directions, says Angela Watson. 'One of them could be that it's just not visible. The path may not be explicitly spelled out. There may be no boxes to check, making the path seem murky and arbitrary. That's not a good situation. There may be hidden paths that can be pursued, but the organisational structure makes it very difficult for objective decisions to be made. There may be a path that is visible but does not have checkboxes. This can be a little bit more difficult for some. In this case it's important to focus on what you're good at, what you want to do, and where you believe you can bring value and leadership to an organisation. It's not about checking someone else's boxes and it's not about fulfilling a path that has been set by the organisation, but rather setting a path that is built on your strengths and your abilities. There are places that do have a very clear path with very clear steps and very clear checkboxes. This may not be for everybody, but some are very comfortable with the predictability and the structure of this kind of a journey. So, consider the situation you're in,' says Watson. 'Consider where you want to lead and then make the decision of staying and taking it on, or moving into a different situation that is a better fit. Some thrive in one firm, others in another – it's not all the same.'

Start by assessing the economy and the firm's situation. Is the economy growing or contracting? How about the business? The firm's situation may have changed since the last time you considered a move. 'This depends highly on the situation, the individual's relationship with the management of the company, and whether they are a good fit for the company overall,' says Sara Beardsley. 'Sometimes, it is simply a matter of being patient and pursuing the right opportunity within the company when it arises. This opportunity can be a new project, a retirement or transition that opens a position, or a project or internal initiative where one has the chance to grow and show one's abilities. It is important to remember that companies go through trends of growth and downturns that can match up with

Fig 5.2: Design meeting at Angela Watson's firm, Shepley Bulfinch

larger downturns in the overall economy or in a certain business sector. Opportunities for promotions or new roles will likely be broader when the overall business is growing. Conversations with management can help individuals to determine the overall picture of the firm, and to determine whether a path to leadership might be more available at some point in the future. It is also worth looking at the current leaders and whether the company likely has a transition or growth plan any time soon, for a role that one is pursuing.'

Consider that things can change: people retire, move firms or shift roles, suggests Duane Carter. 'If you really like an organisation, think about how you could position yourself or learn from those currently in leadership roles, both positively and negatively,' says Carter. 'However, at the point you have learned as much as you can, you need to move on. I've seen scores of mid-career architects make big jumps by switching firms. This could be because there was an opportunity at that firm, but often it's also because they were perceived differently.'

## Your responsibility

Beyond the firm's responsibility is your responsibility. It seems like such an obvious step, but so few consider it until it is too late: talk to your firm's leadership. Tell them about your interests or needs and work out a plan. I cannot tell you how many employers have told me, when I've asked why they didn't hire one of our graduates, 'They didn't ask!' A simple but necessary step, however uncomfortable it is to do: ask. What good could come from talking about it? List the possible outcomes: they are thrilled, or they didn't know. Adjust accordingly – especially if at first, they say no.

Think critically, and anticipate objections – not cynically, but because you want to be prepared. 'There are two main ways out of this,' says Oscia Wilson. 'The first is to explicitly ask for a jump up in responsibility. Remind the powers-that-be of your experiences that have prepared you, and then just ask for the opportunity you think would be a significant step up for you. Whether that's serving as the client-facing project manager or the lead designer or an internal-facing leadership role, name it and ask for it (with all the recommended humility and gratitude, of course).'

Asking is hard because you need to be prepared to hear something you may not want to hear, i.e. the truth. Trina Sandschafer's first recommendation is for you to speak to your current leadership about a path that may be available, and to openly discuss your desire to move forward. 'If, having utilised reviews and made your intention known there is no timeline or path forward, I think that person owes it to themselves to explore finding a role or firm which provides more opportunity to advance,' says Sandschafer.

Get good honest feedback on why you are not being considered, says John Gresko. 'I'd say to the architects that through no fault of their own feel overlooked for a leadership role, to leave if waiting around and building a case isn't an option. Companies change all the time. It goes two ways; [it] has to be a good fit for both employee and company.'

This point – to ask, talk, have a conversation – is almost universal. 'Check in with leadership and have a conversation about mentorship and leadership,' advises Lora Teagarden. 'Emphasise your desire to be helpful to the firm and to grow within; ask what tasks or skills you need to advance to the next level or how to access those opportunities on projects. If leadership can't clearly dictate what's needed for the different management levels or how you fit within the path, consider looking elsewhere for this growth and work in general.'

Elliot Glassman is more hesitant about having the conversation, believing it is first worth evaluating what the blockage is. 'Is it something missing in your skillset, either as a designer or a leader?' asks Glassman. 'These types of internal problems will follow you wherever you go. It is a good practice to schedule regular discussions with your manager or firm leadership (quarterly or even more frequently if possible) about your professional goals, what they see as your strengths and weaknesses, and how they can support you in gaining the experience necessary to develop as a practitioner. If the blockage is something within your organisation that does not offer opportunity for advancement or professional growth, or if the leadership is not interested in helping you develop, then it's probably best to look for a better and more supportive work environment where you can reach your full potential.'

## Demonstrate your value

'The best advice I can give,' says Mary Shaffer, 'is to demonstrate your value and your commitment to the success of your firm, and let your firm leader or direct supervisor know that you are interested in advancement. Some firms have roadmaps that are publicly available and discussed freely. Architects working in those firms know where they sit on the leadership pipeline, and what they need to do to move ahead. Other firms have a culture of mystery and uncertainty around promotions; it is hard to know where you stand in that case. As a mid-career architect, you should be aware of the skills and experience that you bring and, as such, you should be comfortable advocating for your personal advancement in the firm. Ensure that your leaders know you are committed to the success of the firm and that you are interested in growing as a leader in the company. It is important to show your value in order to be promoted – promotion is not an "entitlement" after so many years of experience. Meet with your supervisor or firm leader and talk to them about their succession planning, and what you can focus on today that will be valuable to them in the future. Have them help you map your path to advancement; their investment will likely be their first step in advocacy for your growth.'

To create value for your company, understand the circumstances of the firm and question the timing of your intervention. 'At times the opportunity to advance within a business is entirely down to good timing and a fair degree of luck,' says Alistair Kell. 'There are also on occasion opportunities that may not necessarily seem preferred but can allow growth and development within business. Business running, quality and compliance matters for example are all necessary within any business, and established, more senior staff members are often best placed to take on these roles, but often a step away from project delivery is seen as a risk. In reality these roles can offer growth and career development without the risk of a moving business.'

It may be that firm leaders need to evolve their perception of you. I recall someone inquiring at one firm whether I was a good designer and being told I was a good 'sketcher', and with that response I was pigeonholed and put in a box – one I knew I was better than. I saw that my work was cut out for me to try to communicate my capabilities and brand better – in my case, to someone more receptive, elsewhere. 'It's sometimes the case that people at your firm aren't able to evolve their image of you as quickly as your skills develop,' says Oscia Wilson. 'The result is you find yourself a mid-career architect with deep experience and a licence, being treated like the junior you were when you arrived.'

I tell this to our graduating students: if they accept a full-time job post-graduation from a firm where they interned the summer before, it is best for them to request a job interview and re-interview for the position – even a position that is being handed to them. Why? It will be their only opportunity to sell the firm on what they, as a final-year graduate student, learned in the year since they last worked for the firm; a chance to talk about their career plans and ambitions; to reacquaint the firm with their capabilities but also re-establish what they want from their position; and most importantly, to create a gap between the intern they were and the full-time employee they now are. Interviewing for a job you already have serves a second purpose; instead of being offered a little more salary than what you were offered as an intern – often only a symbolic pay bump – you have a chance to prove your value and your worth. I have seen this work again and again for our students.

That said, be careful what you ask for. As a firm leader, you may miss the relative freedom of not being responsible for clients, budgets, feeding other people and firm outcomes. Ask yourself: is a leadership path really what I want? Or is it something I feel I *should* want? 'The role of architects is not just to design to a client's request but to delve deeper into the question of whether what the client says they want is what they actually need to best serve their goals,' says Donna Sink. 'Likewise, an architect who sees no clear path to leadership needs to first ask if leadership is what they actually want, or not. We are bombarded by professional messages that one needs to excel and elevate oneself constantly, but I believe there is a critical role to be played by those who become excellent in their own niche and maintain it. As Kurt Vonnegut said, "Another flaw in the human character is that everybody wants to build and nobody wants to do maintenance." I have always applied this quote to the architect's desire to build new buildings rather than renovate and maintain existing ones, but it also applies to one's own career. If an architect enjoys being a project manager and has no interest in taking on the billings, staff management and administrative tasks required of being a partner, there is no shame in not wanting to move upward. On the other hand, if one truly wants to be the leader, and a current job has no ability to rise up, then it may be time to move to a different firm or start one's own office.'

## Be a both/and architect

If you feel that the present company you are in is limiting you, stifling your growth, move where you are valued and you can grow. Don't let anyone decide your worth.
**– Meghana Joshi**

It is always essential to learn what you can from each stop along your career path. But if that path hits a dead end, there are options available to take what you've learned and to pivot to a larger firm that will allow you to take on new challenges.
**– Tom Mozina**

Look for an opportunity to shift as a chance to differentiate yourself. One way out of being pigeonholed 'is to switch companies', says Oscia Wilson. 'A fresh set of eyes on your resumé can see your value more clearly. This option also offers you negotiation power, because you can hold out for a company whose offer includes the title/role you're looking to land while continuing at your current company. The other benefit that a few strategic pivots gains you is the resumé appeal of being "this AND that". If you can be an architect and

## 5: Shift

a spec writer, or an architect and have experience working at a construction company, or an architect who spent time at a marketing firm, you will stand out from those without variety.'

The air is thinner and more rarefied at the top where there aren't as many leadership opportunities in terms of title, but there are many other ways to lead within organisations – ways that don't require a title. I recall in the 1990s a major international firm, where previously relatively few were promoted to senior positions, suddenly made dozens of mid-career architects vice-presidents. The one caveat was that within the next year each had to bring in one project. Many VPs who were not able – or who were unwilling – to adapt to this marketing expectation on top of their current roles had left the firm within a year, and in many cases went on to even greater success.

'Model leadership behaviour and assume leadership responsibilities in any way that you can, including firm leadership, project leadership, professional/community leadership and peer leadership,' suggests principal and workplace studio leader at SmithGroup Matt Dumich FAIA. 'Clearly communicate your goals with senior leadership in your firm and other mentors. If it is clear you are not advancing or will not advance in your current firm, seek new opportunities that position you to lead and value your contributions.'

Fig 5.3: Informal meeting at principal and workplace studio leader Matt Dumich's firm, SmithGroup

'Many large practices today suffer from "top-heaviness" – a large number of senior associates and associate directors who are seen as obstacles to upward progression of ambitious younger architects,' says Alison Brooks. 'If your effort to claim that leadership position goes unrecognised, it's time to move to a smaller, growing practice that offers more opportunity (but less comfort), or start your own practice. Entrepreneurial architects are valued in any scale practice and will create their own leadership roles. Rise to the occasion. Spearhead projects, initiatives, competitions that will support the practice's growth. Find new business, go the extra mile so that progression is inevitable.'

Two options are offered by Joe Cliggott. 'First, remaining within [the] current organisation and creating a role that can be recognised, respected and gives self-satisfaction,' says Cliggott. '"Leadership" does not always mean a title. Second, typically there are a diminishing number of role opportunities in an organisation. There are few generals, and a lot of infantry! There may be a point on those diminishing opportunities for roles that leads one to another organisation. That is perfectly okay. I've witnessed numerous examples of colleagues flourishing within the framework of a different organisation.'

There is of course a third option – which is to stay and trailblaze your own path. Take the path less travelled, and by doing so differentiate yourself. 'Think beyond the ideal path that you have envisaged, or that has been prescribed to you,' says Andy Watts. 'If you want to hew closely to the traditional career path of an architect, remember that the majority of your contemporaries will be doing the same. If you find that this is not working for you, my suggestion would be to move away from the traditional route into a specialism where there is less saturation, or create a unique selling proposition (USP) for yourself within the traditional route, something that will make you stand out.'

'Be innovative and open to creating your own path,' says Danei Cesario. 'Everyone has a role to play in every organisation, and the truth is that the best path for you may not be immediately apparent. Do the work to the best of your ability, show up and be strategic. It also helps to have an open mind and patience, because things do not always materialise as fast as you would like them to. Your colleagues will come to admire your diligence and enjoy working with you. Those traits open doors to leadership most effectively.'

## Should I stay or should I go?

Don't be afraid of change; either try to make the change for yourself in the organisation, or go elsewhere. You may never know how much you are appreciated or needed elsewhere.
– Zoe Hooton

I made a major job shift from colleagues I adored in the fall of 2019. Sometimes you have to make moves beyond what is comfortable. It was scary, but worth it. The move has been beneficial to the career I want, now and in the future. Joining an 80-year-old firm with hundreds of global colleagues has challenged me for the best.
– Danei Cesario

Fig 5.4: HMC principal-in-charge Virginia E Marquardt helping lead and facilitate a meeting

Transitions are never easy. Virginia E Marquardt loved where she worked: the people, the clients, the projects. She felt their values aligned with her values. 'However, my husband and I wanted to move back to LA to be closer to family and friends. And I needed a change. I needed a new challenge. Through a lot of self-reflection and conversations with family, friends and mentors, I began asking questions of myself. I made a list of what a dream career move and position would be, and I made the move. It was not an easy decision, and it's one I considered for about two to four years. Even though it was very difficult to make the decision and then actually follow through, it was the right decision and I am very happy.'

The start of our evolution occurred when Africa first experienced drought; the precursor to modern humans didn't adapt to the new conditions, but instead left. Those that remained were captured, and those that adapted were trapped.[26] It helps to think of one's prospective move in terms of both mobility and migration. Both require adaptation. Today, of course, architects don't generally leave their firms due to climate change (though some may). When they switch firms, they do so to take advantage of new opportunities – leaving firms, markets and regions experiencing adversity, economic or otherwise, for more promising prospects.[27] To stay or leave? Making a shift can be scary.

Switching raises questions of our ability to cope and adapt to new situations and environments. There is the potential for us not fitting in, being seen as an outcast. It is not for nothing that so many architects decide to stay in a lesser situation: where the proverb 'better the devil you know than the devil you don't' speaks to our aversion to ambiguity. And we're architects, supposedly comparatively comfortable with ambiguity and uncertainty!

About six years ago, Tom Lee made the switch from a design-led firm of eight people to a firm of 10,000 doing very complex, programme-driven buildings where performance comes first, and design was steadily rising in importance and quality. 'I realised things were different when I first discovered that we had more digits in our job numbers than colleagues at my previous firm,' says Lee. 'As a matrix organisation with a robust corporate structure, we have a lot of policies and protocols, but they enable an incredible array of resources that support us both at work and at home, as well as subject matter experts in every facet of architecture and engineering. At the small firm, which I loved, I naturally had to be a generalist and try to be good at all facets of the design and construction process, but it was becoming clear that my value was really at the front end of the design process. Moving to a larger practice where my role is elevating design has really allowed me to focus while also learning new facets of practice that I wouldn't have otherwise been exposed to if not at a larger firm. With international colleagues and projects, I've also been fortunate to be able to travel and see the world, and that has really helped to define who I am as an architect today.'

Trina Sandschafer switched firms this year, leaving a boutique design firm she had been at more than a decade. 'That firm had my fingerprint on so much of the ethos and the work,' says Sandschafer. 'But I was outgrowing it. My future was not there.' She joined a 125-person firm to lead a new office expansion as a design principal and vice-president. 'I have never felt more alive in my career. My new position has everything I am passionate about – design leadership, crafting a firm design framework, building and mentoring a team, shaping a firm culture, telling our story, cultivating strong business relationships, promoting research and thought leadership. There is a lot to do. Each day we work hard. Each day we make progress on our goals. Each day we move forward. That is very rewarding. We are building something very big. That's exciting.'

Eight years ago, having been laid off for the fifth time in his career (three times in LA, twice in New York), Rob Rothblatt joined AECOM as the design lead of the NY office. 'It was the second time that I joined a firm to help build a design practice – the first time being part of the original architectural group at Gensler NY in 1995,' says Rothblatt. 'Although AECOM had collected a number of past firms of some note (Ellerbe, DMJM, Spillis Candela), they first had turned more and more to exploring the wide range of design, alternative delivery, construction, but had a wealth of obscure resources. Mostly, though, I was attracted by the less patrician, more ecumenical atmosphere, and the diversity a major corporation promised. While it lasted six years (until financial difficulties killed the balance sheet and killed many of our jobs), it was a glorious experiment. I don't regret it for a second.'

There are many reasons for switching: as we saw in the previous section, for more money, opportunity, family reasons, a change in location, or because there is no clear path within your current organisation. We've seen how the firm you are with will determine whether you stay relevant. While ultimately your relevance is up to you, if your firm doesn't provide opportunities, leveraging advanced tools, the onus will be on you to evolve.

In 2020, senior project manager at Little Diversified Meghana Joshi transitioned to her current firm from another traditional architecture firm in Orange County, California. For Joshi, the biggest motivation for the change was adapting to technology. 'I wanted to be with a firm that valued industry's advances in building design and design tools,' says Joshi. 'It's been a great transition, especially during the COVID quarantine period, to have the privilege of remote working and [a] cloud server.'

Duane Carter switched two years ago because of a family move. 'I'm still not sure if it is going to work out,' says Carter. 'The biggest impact has been changing cities. I had lived in Chicago for about 30 years, so I had a huge network of former colleagues and contacts. At this point in my career it's very difficult to start at zero. Going into a new firm where no one knows you or knows about the work of the previous firm means you aren't going to come with automatic credibility or respect. It has been challenging to find ways to bring in that experience without turning people off.'

Fig 5.5: A ZGF project's design team and partner-in-charge work closely with a graphic designer to reach a consensus on materials for a client presentation

John Gresko not only switched firms less than five years ago, but he moved thousands of miles away for a new job, too. In general, he says it's been a great move. 'I'd never say that I am totally adjusted, as the difference in the way architecture is practiced in Chicago, where I am from, and southern California, where I practise now, is very different,' admits Gresko. 'Different cultures, different clients, different industry partners, different delivery methods. It took about three years for me to be acclimated to the new market. At first, as the new guy, the experience was wonderful; because just like in grade school, the new kids are popular. After a while, the contrast in how I was accustomed to working and how things are done in SoCal was highlighted – and it becomes part of how people see me: good, bad or indifferent. The move has proven (at the time of this writing) to be beneficial. I was promoted to office leader. I don't regret [it] nor would I change things if I could do it all over again.'

Some are inevitably held back due to fear – fear of making a next step, of the unknown, or of ambiguity aversion – and, looking back, consider they should have acted earlier. 'I should have switched sooner, but I was too scared,' admits Emily Grandstaff-Rice. 'I feared being obsolete. I feared starting over. I did not realise how powerful the experience of reinventing myself would be. My greatest regret was the missed time of not leaving sooner. I had been at a firm for over a decade and during that time you internalise a lot of the culture and behaviour of that place. In many ways, I will always have that legacy with me. Now that I am at a different firm, I realise both how wonderful and limited that culture was. It provides me [with] an opportunity and perspective to apply to the new firm setting in which I work now. I am so grateful for that perspective. If I had to switch firms today, I would have taken more time to observe the power differentials before diving right in.'

## When you have the opportunity to switch and you don't

Elliot Glassman recently had the opposite experience, where he was being pursued by four or five firms simultaneously and decided to stay where he was. 'I usually get recruiters contacting me every once in a while, but usually with opportunities that don't match my experience or interests, so they are easy to ignore,' says Glassman. 'In this case, there were two firms that really had compelling offers that caused me to consider leaving my current position. One was similar to the role I have now but more senior, and the other was a different career track but one I think I may be interested in pursuing one day. In the end, I stayed where I was because my current firm offered more support for my computational design initiatives, and I wanted to see through some of the work and projects I had already put much of my blood, sweat and tears into.'

Glassman continues: 'Every time there is a bump in the road since then, it is easy to wonder if one of those other opportunities would not have offered a smoother and more supported path, but I know the grass always only seems greener on the other side. The COVID situation has also made some of the initiatives we had planned more difficult and shifted priorities. So only time will tell if choosing to stay was the right move, and if I may have wanted to do things differently in retrospect.'

## It's all a learning opportunity

We learn about ourselves – our preferences and dislikes – with every career move. It's healthy to use each shift or switch as a chance to learn about yourself, your likes, interests, passions – even when you discover a firm is a mismatch. 'With all due respect to the practice, I landed what I thought was my dream job designing speculative mixed-use high rises and developments,' says Tom Lee. 'A few months into it I realised the work wasn't very fulfilling and perhaps was contributing to cities in different ways than I had envisioned, and I discovered that the type of work I was passionate about wasn't the same type of work the firm did. It was no fault of the firm – it was a great practice, but I was a young architect trying to find my path forward. I left the practice and joined a very different one, because it became really hard to reconcile the long hours and personal sacrifices I was making to do unfulfilling work, and I knew it was time to move on.'

Perhaps the ultimate switch is to your own firm. Since starting in architecture school, John Gresko's goal had been to start his own company. 'I remember my very first week of work after graduating from school, a smug principal of the firm asked me what my five-year goal was, and my answer was to have my own company,' says Gresko. 'He actually looked up to make eye contact for the first time since I had been in the room to smirk and say, "Why? Just so you can have your own name on the header?" I admit I said that because he would not look at me in the discourse that led up to that question. There was truth to my answer, though. I have approached every moment of my career as a learning experience. I always had in the back of mind an idea to have my own firm. I don't think that will ever happen, but the mindset is good. It is good in that I looked at everything good, bad or otherwise as a lesson. I didn't live in the moment but used whatever was in the moment to help me.'

### ASK THIS

Ask. The path may indeed exist, but it may just be vague or the expectation is that a true leader would define their own path. I would follow up, too, with some other questions to ask yourself: What do you bring to the practice that doesn't currently exist in established leadership? Do you genuinely share the guiding principles of the practice? And to be brutally honest, do you truly deserve the position you are seeking, and are you an effective leader? Not everyone is, and that's okay. That said, sometimes great leaders just need to find the right practice where their specific leadership style and talents are of value, and can thus thrive. **[Tom Lee]**

## ASK THIS

They need to ask themselves: Would they like to be a specialist in a certain field of architecture? Or, would they prefer to be a general practitioner and work in a number of areas? Perhaps it's a drive to strive for a senior management role? Or, take on other areas of expertise that help to make a business successful? This could be softer supporting skills such as business development, marketing or PR, or more technically creative such as an expertise in BIM, 3D visualisation and modelling or VR, or anything in between. **[Chithra Marsh]**

## ASK THIS

They have to be self-reflective and recognise why it is that they are finding it difficult. Is the sector where they operate no longer relevant? Has the competition caught up with them; either from the practice within which they work or practices against which they compete? Have they failed to develop themselves adequately? Look at what worked for them previously; what [will] enable them to get where they are, and what is holding them back? Where are they now, and where do they want to get to? Then they can understand what they need to do to adapt, either by changing their outlook [or] learning new skills. Set SMART goals and talk, constructively and honestly, to their peers and line managers. The grass is not always greener. **[Philip Twiss]**

Fig 5.6: Hands-on, interactive work sessions with the contractor, design (ZGF), subcontractor, and consultant teams all in one room help further the development of smart solutions in real time

## ASK THIS

Ask yourself many types of questions:

1. Is your firm growing or promoting new leaders at this time? If not, why not? What is the firm's succession plan? What economic factors may be affecting whether the firm is growing, shrinking or staying the same? If there are outside factors affecting opportunity, are they particular to this firm, or are they more global issues that will change with the ebbs and flows of the economy, and are affecting all (or most) firms in a particular sector of work at once?
2. If there are new leaders emerging in your firm – who are they, and what qualities do they have that made them a good choice for promotion? What are the criteria for promotion? And have you talked with management about your desire to move up in the firm? If you are not moving up – is it because you are not a good fit for the firm, or because of other factors that may change in the future?
3. What opportunities are there, not involving a formal 'promotion', that could allow you to prove your worth? Are there areas the firm needs help on where you can contribute? Are there certain projects that may have roles that need filling that would allow you to grow, and have you expressed interest in them? Is there work that you can bring into the office by being a part of business development strategies?

**[Sara Beardsley]**

## TRY THIS

Formulate an exit vision. Early in my career I was unhappy working in a particular office. It was clearly a bread-and-butter kind of job. One day my boss, who could tell I was not happy, said to me, 'You know, this will not last forever.' Although I knew that, it weirdly gave me great relief. I realised that I was not thinking beyond the moment and had not yet formulated an 'exit vision', something another friend told me about years later. **[Diane Reicher Jacobs]**

## TRY THIS

The best advice I could give to someone on how to approach finding their path to leadership, is not to focus on the path at all. Way too often I hear from individuals during reviews, 'I want to be a leader, how do I get on the partnership track?' and when you ask why, the answer is usually akin to 'that's what I want to be'. The first thing if you want a leadership role is you need to think about what you want to gain from being a leader: is it power, money, or is it about elevating the quality of a project or helping the people around you to excel? If it's about the first two, I am not sure they are in the right place and I suggest they really think about what they want out of their career. If it's the latter, then my question to those individuals is 'what is stopping you from doing that right now?' The interesting thing is when people focus on the value they can bring to their job, the money comes, and if it doesn't they certainly will be able to go to a place where their value is recognised. **[Ted Hyman]**

### TRY THIS

First, you have to decouple being a leader from a title. I would recommend that they focus on doing work they are passionate about doing and relentlessly providing leadership both internally and externally around that passion. Become recognised as a thought leader and a mentor. When your work is getting attention and your co-workers are referencing you to leadership, you will get noticed and be offered opportunities to lead. This might not look like a partnership offer, or director-of-something kind of promotion. You have to be okay with that, but also be clear about your non-negotiables. If you get to pursue work you love and get the support (and the compensation) you need to do it, then this other stuff becomes irrelevant. After all, you might find that getting that sought-after promotion pivoted you to responsibilities you don't really want and took away from the work you love. **[Angela Mazzi]**

### TRY THIS

Identify problems that cause issues in your organisation. Solve this problem that the business recognises but old working practices can't resolve. Make sure it is simple, easy to understand and creates value. **[Michael Riley]**

### TRY THIS

Look around. Chart your own [path]. If this is impossible in your current position – rethink your chart or consider making a move. Also, interview at least five or maybe ten people informally. Never make a decision in a vacuum; open your eyes, mind and heart to understand the possibilities out there. So many people forget to do their homework on this stuff. **[Diane Reicher Jacobs]**

### TRY THIS

When there is no clear path to leadership, even when times are good/a firm is growing, it is also important for mid-career professionals to assess, within themselves, whether the current organisation is the right fit in the long term. This can be done through an assessment of long-term goals and priorities, and can often be helped by having

conversations with other professionals at the same level who may be facing similar challenges or are on the cusp of new opportunities.
**[Sara Beardsley]**

## TRY THIS
It may be time for you to look. Before looking elsewhere, write a pros/cons list – reasons in favour of switching firms on one side, reasons for staying (or against switching) on the other. If one list is twice as long as the other, consider your decision made.

# PART II

# 6: Pivot

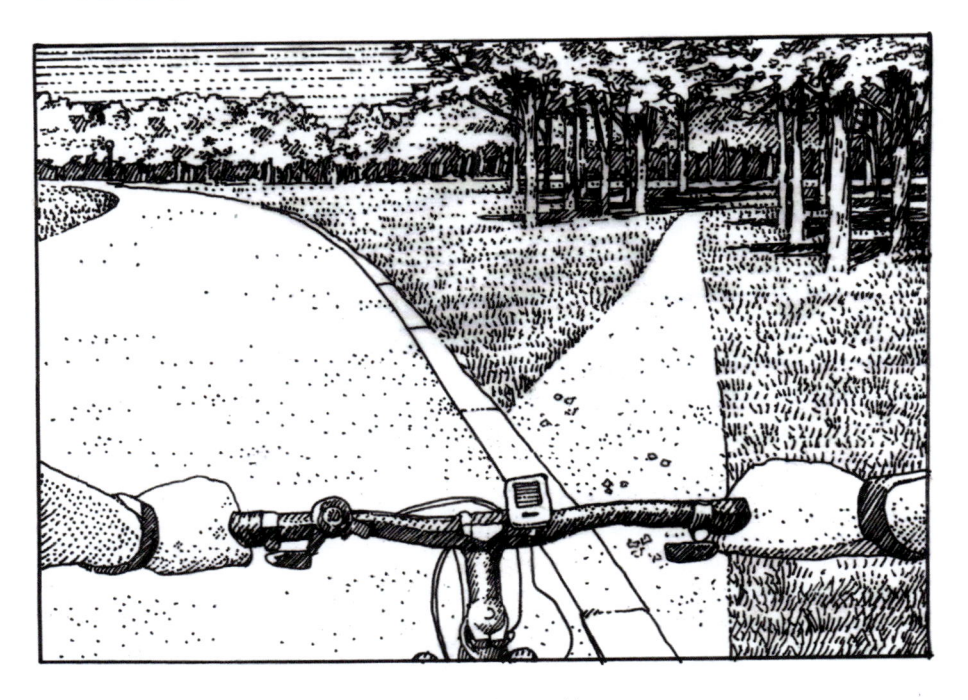

Fig 6.1: Some architects adapt by pivoting to a different role or position

**Not all pivots occur in mid-career, but many mid-career architects do what they do today as a result of an earlier career pivot.**

**Sometimes moving up the career ladder involves moving laterally or sometimes a step back.**
**– Stephen Drew**

**There was a time where I was being given much of the responsibility of running a firm, without the final title or autonomy to make the decisions that needed to be made. There was not adequate compensation for this role. It became clear that I needed to explore a role and a firm that would help me do all of this and solve those problems. This was a big decision, and one that I did not make lightly. I knew there was more for me in so many ways. I pursued that choice. The outcome was very favourable.**
**– Trina Sandschafer**

You've attempted adapting, proven your relevance, tried remaining, built up your resilience, considered a shift, done what you can to flourish in place – and it is still not enough?

It may be time for a reboot.

By renewing ourselves, changing our environment or location, our circumstances or situation, we give ourselves another chance. It might take a backwards or sideways move – but it will ultimately lead us forward.

The second half of the book – the last five chapters – are premised on major career redirection. A career pivot: taking on parallel roles, wholesale reinvention, rewiring yourself – through mentoring and training, rebalancing work and family, and re-evaluating where you end up, with a goal to thrive both in your career and in life.

A career inflection point can be internal or external to the person it impacts. It might be brought about by an external event or circumstance that is out of your control, or it might be triggered by something you are experiencing. Inflection points are times in your career that represent a significant change or a turning point, professionally or personally. They might impact your role within an organisation or the profession, and your resolve to remain – in your firm, or in architecture. So how do architects turn inflection points into positive outcomes, and what advice would mid-career architects give to enable others to do the same? What are the commonalities between instances in architects' careers where they pivoted from one role to another? Who or what brought it about (architect, firm, circumstances), what was the outcome, and what advice would they have for others facing a similar situation?

Elliot Glassman finished his BArch in 2005, a few years before the 2008 recession. Given the academic work he had produced, his professors encouraged him to go on and pursue a master's or a doctorate. 'But I felt that I had already had five years of intense design study, and I wanted to begin my professional career,' says Glassman. 'I interviewed at many types of firms and turned down the larger firms I got offers from because I (rightly or wrongly) was worried about becoming just a cog in the machine. I instead went to work for a smaller design studio, where I got exposure to a lot of different aspects of the profession sooner than I might have otherwise, although the trade-off professionally was that there were smaller-scale projects and less support for my career development outside of direct experience. Because of the interest I had in sustainability, I became the expert in sustainable design and LEED for the office.'

Glassman continues: 'A couple years in, and the recession hit. Work slowed down and we began taking on any kind of project to keep the lights on, including simple DOB [Department of Buildings] filings. The firm's struggles left me wondering what my options were in the current environment. Simultaneously, I also was realising that there was a technical limitation to what I could offer in leading our firm's sustainability efforts. I could recite the LEED checklist backwards and forwards, and I knew generally what the passive design strategies were, but how to correctly design to these principles and measure the impact was beyond me.'

'So, in 2010, I decided to go back to school to pursue a master's, but in a programme that focused on sustainable design. I attended Harvard GSD, where the programme gave me more than I had hoped for; not just exposing me to sustainable design ideas but also how to leverage computational design to study building performance as an integral part of the design process. This approach was just emerging at the time, and really has come to define my career since I graduated,' says Glassman. 'Reflecting on this path, I realise the recession was an inflection point that caused me to make a major readjustment to my trajectory. To this day, I don't know if I made the right decision on how to start my career, but certainly the economic conditions led me to go back to school at a critical time and upskill in a couple of ways that are becoming increasingly relevant to the profession. The timing may have been serendipitous, but the general advice I can offer is to try to turn every uncontrollable setback into a way to come out stronger than you were before.'

By definition, recessions and now pandemics are external events that can bring about career inflection points. As major readjustments to your career trajectory, inflection points are ideally your choice and not dependent on outside events or other's decisions. It's what you do with it that's important. Glassman's transition has all the hallmarks of a career inflection point, having both outside and inside forces and opportunities. Inflection points can occur when recognising your own limitations, or that you've arrived at a jumping-off point; a sense that you are ready for another challenge. Use the inflection point as an opportunity to become an expert at something just as demand is rising in the industry.

An example brought about by external factors, Sara Beardsley's career inflection point came early on. As a recent graduate, she joined a firm that, after less than a year, ended up downsizing and later relocating. It was not too long after the 9/11 terrorist attacks, and the economy was still feeling the effects of this. 'This first job full-time that I chose, out of several opportunities

Fig 6.2: Adrian Smith + Gordon Gill director Sara Beardsley at a construction site

I had at the time, was at a very small firm because I felt as an early-career professional, I would learn the most in that role,' explains Beardsley. 'While at the time it was a great personal challenge to change jobs (and actually change to a different sector of work within architecture) after only a short time out of school, it taught me that factors far beyond oneself can affect a career path, and that we have to be able to rebound and move on. It led to quickly learning how to network, capitalising on previous experience, and to securing a long-term position at a very different type of firm that was actually a better fit for me. I was able to use all the skills I had learned at the previous job in order to move on successfully to that next step. Looking back, if this inflection point had not happened, I would have likely had a very different career path.'

The impact of internal factors on your career could be within your firm – recognising if where you work is a good fit – or even internal to the person who is experiencing the inflection point, especially when brought about by factors beyond your control. An example would be where you find yourself in the wrong location or firm at the wrong time – even though you thought it was what you always wanted. The forces you're up against could include sunk costs and buyer's remorse. Before Tom Lee started his undergraduate coursework, he interned for a couple of summers at a prominent architect's firm that specialised in high rises and airports, which he found exciting and rewarding as a high-school student. 'So, I spent my entire academic career studying the tall building, which drove not only the classes I took, but the professors I sought out, research I conducted and internships I pursued,' says Lee. 'After graduate school, I was fortunate enough to land a job at a firm as a project designer working on high rises, and quickly realised that it wasn't nearly as fulfilling as I thought it would be. I struggled because I was questioning whether I had wasted all this time and money on my education, and questioned my choice of profession. After 18 months, I joined a smaller practice as a project architect instead. I took a significant pay cut and was working on much smaller projects while under a great mentor at the time and I loved architecture all over again. Looking back, moving from large-scale buildings in a larger firm to smaller-scale projects in a boutique practice really helped me today, where I enjoy overseeing design on projects that range significantly in scale from small fit-outs to much larger, complex buildings.'

Tom Lee advises others approaching a similar inflection point to have the courage to trust their own judgement, and not to be afraid of changing course or taking a risk. 'Failure is nothing to be afraid of – it only makes you better and helps define focus in a career,' says Lee. This speaks to the importance of building up resilience and an ability to rebound or bounce back when you realise you've made a wrong turn.

Inflection points can involve moving to another city and accepting a new role or position. In 2007, Joe Cliggott was offered a position entailing a move from the US to the UK, and leaving a firm where he had been planning to stay for the rest of his career. 'The real catch was that it was also a move to the client side,' says Cliggott. 'The ability to work internationally on projects plus the exposure to another perspective in the process was extremely intriguing. That one decision to accept this position has changed the course of my career ever since. One can never totally predict what will happen, and where the adventure may take you. Having both an open mind to adapt as well as the strength to remain persistent on a path is critical.'

This is the very definition of an inflection point – where one decision can impact the trajectory of your career well into the future. Responding to the call of a career inflection point requires a combination of adaptability and persistence. Beyond moving to another city, inflection points can come about in reaction to external events such as recessions and pandemics.

## Inflection points as moments of growth

One such moment of growth for many architects involves an opportunity to work on large projects in construction administration. 'In retrospect, I probably was not ready at the time, but I approached the experience with the skillset that I had and a humility that I had a lot to learn,' says Emily Grandstaff-Rice. 'I learned more in those experiences than I likely did [in] three times [as] long sitting at a desk. It provided me [with] an opportunity to expand my personal leadership on a job site in a way I was not getting in the office. After those experiences, I have used them to provide the same opportunity to emerging professionals as they approach their own early pivot points. I encourage them to seek job site experiences along with the assurance that I will be their safety net if they feel like they are [in] over their heads.'

Not being ready and making the leap anyway can therefore lead to a career-changing inflection point. In a sink-or-swim situation, it helps to know your firm won't let you sink. It also helps to approach such a new role with humility and an openness to learn.

There is always some risk when change is involved, and the pay-offs and outcomes of answering career inflection-point opportunities are not guaranteed. Making such career transitions will test your comfort with risk as well as your intestinal fortitude. For Andy Watts, at this point in his career his inflection point was his transition from façade designer to computational specialist via an aspiration to be a traditional architect. 'The outcome has definitely been positive for me, and has set me on a path I enjoy immensely, but it was never a certain thing,' says Watts. 'Especially as the role at Grimshaw was a pilot … it was never a sure thing that the job would exist 12 months later – it required perseverance to make it work. It paid off, though. We went from a global design technology team of five to over 40 in the space of four years.'

For Danei Cesario, her career inflection point came about when a few years back she followed her strong interest in the business of architecture and the approaches firms take to remain relevant while staying profitable. 'My experience at that point allowed me to understand that the design of architecture – the product – cannot flourish without an infrastructure of business development, data analytics, marketing and accounting,' acknowledges Cesario. 'I knew then that I wanted to move into project management.'

Fig 6.3: Danei Cesario's role as chair of the Diversity + Inclusion Committee encompassed engagement through creating interesting programming – here celebrating Black History Month

Inflection points don't even have to be positive experiences to have a lasting impact. For me, one memorable inflection point occurred as a result of my second KA Connect[28] talk nearly a decade ago in San Francisco. My first in Chicago had been a hit. The second time around, the format for my talk was the relentless PechaKucha[29] style, and I made the mistake of trying to memorise the script. It was the last presentation of a long day and, as I am a morning person, the result was that in front of 300 VIP attendees I literally blanked out and left the stage mid-presentation.

What happened next changed my life. Immediately after the debacle, I picked myself up and participated on the panel as though nothing had happened. It had of course happened, but that was then (five minutes earlier) and – I told myself – this was now: a new moment and opportunity. What followed was unexpected and transformed my career for the next decade for the better. People approached me afterwards to introduce themselves (or express empathy), which led to great long-term friendships, annual teaching work at Harvard GSD Executive Education, invitations to contribute to others' books and publications, lucrative consulting gigs, international keynote invitations, and an invitation to speak again at KA Connect – all despite (or because of?) having bombed on stage.

Inflection points can come about through a new role, self-reinvention or by focusing on other aspects of the profession. Having worked for about 25 years in a few organisations, Randy Guillot separated from the firm for which he was a design partner, which gave him some time to think about what he wanted to do next. 'Up to that point I had built my career exclusively along the trajectory of design,' says Guillot. 'Working my way up from junior designer to design partner, even being recognised with an AIA Fellowship in Design. I decided that after years of charging straight ahead down the design path I wanted to expand my view of the profession, but also challenge myself to see if any of the skills I had learned could translate into other parts of the profession. I joined a new firm with a role still grounded in design excellence, but with an added focus on building business in industries such as healthcare, education and sciences, which they had not yet been fully pursuing. The challenge of understanding how to build teams around the country and grow our client base challenged me in ways that the pure design track never would have – taking design and design thinking into how we build our business. What I learned, and continue to learn, is the amount of discipline, vision and hard work it takes to build a business. It has given me a newfound appreciation of the many talents and skillsets of the team it takes to produce great work.'

## Pivoting roles

Six years ago, I had two children in schools/daycare, and had just started the licensure process. As much as I wanted to be in a leadership role, and work on award-winning projects, I was limited in my contributions and opportunities. But that didn't stop me from seeking challenges. I was told not to rock the boat in a closed-door meeting, but I rocked it anyway. It led to award-winning projects and promotions, and my motherhood didn't come in the way of my professional commitment like my leader led me to believe. My advice is, if you strongly believe that you are capable of being more, and doing more, go ahead and do it. Don't let anyone tell you otherwise.
– **Meghana Joshi**

**I became the third-generation of director at my practice, which has been running for 40 years. The step up to director from architect at a young age has often left me conflicted. It's been a role I've had to grow into in my own time and find my own way, especially as it is within an established business. My advice to others would be that pivoting from one role to another is challenging – you can't change the world in one day – but persevere.
– Zoe Hooton**

Chithra Marsh's pivotal moment occurred relatively early in her career. She entered professional practice as a RIBA Part 1 student ready and willing to learn as much as she could. 'I wasn't sure at that point where to position myself within the industry, but I got my first insight into what being an architect meant,' says Marsh. 'I had a fantastic mentor who encouraged me to build my network and trusted me to run my own projects. He taught me that architecture was as much about personality and building solid relationships as it was about being a skilled designer. It was then that I knew I could use my passion for people to enhance my career path and find joy in what I do.'

Some pivotal moments occur earlier in one's career than others. Not all pivots occur in mid-career, but many mid-career architects do what they do today as a result of an earlier career pivot, and share their advice. 'A few years later, just after I had fully qualified, came the biggest opportunity of all,' says Marsh. 'My husband and I were invited to relocate from London, setting up and running a new office in Manchester for a large international practice. We relocated over 20 years ago and the city is now most definitely home for us. Having that early responsibility and accelerated learning gave me an insight into developing a business. The management skills I gained were invaluable alongside honing my skills as a newly qualified architect.'

Marsh continues: 'Since then I have always held a senior management position and have played my part in developing the business for the practices I have worked for. I have gained trusted friends and colleagues along the way. This has helped me build my network and win new business. Sharpening my skills over many years, I now hold a board position as an associate director at Buttress Architects. I recognise that the opportunities offered to me so early in my career were a real privilege, so I make sure I say "yes" as often as I can. My advice to anyone taking on a pivotal change in their career: be brave and take on new challenges. You never know what direction it may take you.'

The difference between a switch and a pivot is subtle: switching implies that you leave one firm for another, whereas a pivot – which can take place within your firm or involve a firm change – leverages what you do to something similar. The different pivot types – strategic, opportunistic and happenstance – can only really be understood by looking back.

Joe Cliggott had multiple opportunities in his career to pivot roles. 'Sometimes these have been strategic, some purely opportunistic, and still others are simply happenstance, where the impact is only understood in retrospect,' says Cliggott. 'There are lots of things that occur beyond one's control. The challenge is when you reach a decision point, choosing between options, [so] that you can confidently, and without regret, decide between path A and path B. In my own career, and specifically within my mid-career, I've accepted opportunities to move to the client side, to move overseas to the UK, to move back again to the US. In addition, every time that I have accepted a new role at a new firm, it has represented a pivot in my career. Each of those steps has afforded [me] the opportunity to continue my growth and education.'

To misquote Shakespeare: *Some are born to pivot, some achieve a pivot, and some have pivots thrust upon them.* 'I sometimes pivot in my role daily,' says Angela Watson. 'Currently I'm a principal, and an owner in a medium-to-large architecture firm. I'm also a board member and currently the chair of the board. All these roles require a very different focus. When I became a principal about 16 years ago, I remember thinking: "Wow, now that I'm in this position, am I going to be doing the same thing for the next 30 years?" I remember being a bit terrified by that. Then I remembered that I've always found new things to work on, new problems to solve, and new challenges to overcome. To me that's what keeps me motivated. I'm really interested in exploring new things, finding out if they can be done, and enjoying the learning process that goes with it. For me, inhabiting new roles every now and then is a really great thing.'

## Pivot to firm leadership

When I asked Ted Hyman if he can think of an instance in his career where he pivoted from one role to another, he responded, 'Which time?' He wasn't kidding! Hyman spent the first five years of his career as a young designer, working on a broad range of projects in three very different firms for a year each. The first was an eight-person office doing residential homes and condos, then he moved to an interior firm of about 20 people and worked on corporate interiors projects. The third was a startup office for a very large firm working on commercial developments. 'My boss and mentor there decided it wasn't the right place for either of us, so he took me with him to ZGF, where we have worked together for the last 30-plus years,' says Hyman. 'In the end, I realised that rather than being a "designer" focusing on the conceptual parts of a project, I really wanted to be a whole architect, and transitioned into a project leadership role.'

Hyman's architectural education had a strong foundation in engineering and putting buildings together. 'So, I was in a great position to lead teams working on complex projects including laboratories and hospitals; they call it project management, but it is more than just making sure projects are on budget,' he explains. 'I've always hated maths and have never had a business class in my life. For me, I framed the role more about leading teams in design and building performance, where my passion for solving issues like climate change has really been valuable.'

126　**Adapt as an Architect**

Fig 6.4: ZGF partners and design team leads review an
early-stage model of a proposed building design

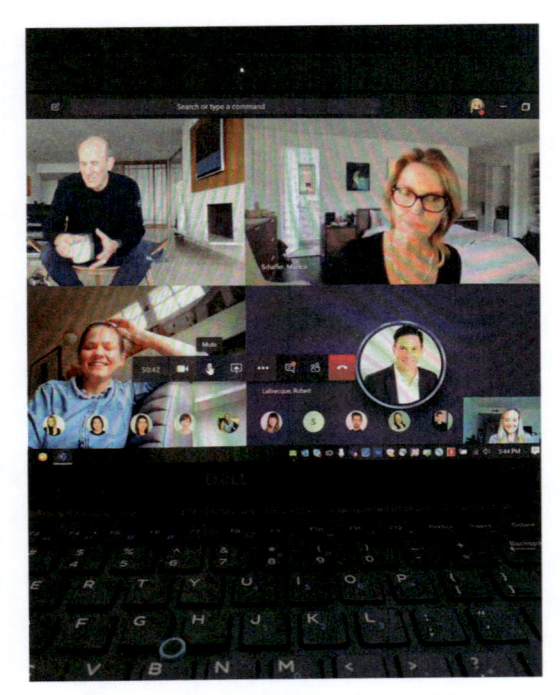

Fig 6.5: Even when the whole team is working remotely,
informal meetings are still possible. Here, ZGF's managing
partner Ted Hyman, project design team leaders and
communications team leaders came together
for a casual brainstorming session

Hyman continues: 'The biggest "pivot" in my career came years later when our firm transitioned the senior leadership in a single day. I was asked to become the managing partner of the entire firm, all 700-plus people in six offices. The truth was, I had no formal training or mentorship as a managing partner or even a clear understanding of what the role of the "managing partner" should be. I was terrified and overwhelmed. That has all slowly transitioned to a place where I am today and listening to my own advice: "If you want to be a leader, why don't you just do it?" I am more and more confident that the decisions and leadership approach, all on my own terms and in my own way, have set the stage for the next generation of leaders in the firm, because in the end that is all we really have as a legacy.'

## Pivoting during a brisk walk to the train

Why pivot? As we've seen, one reason is to focus on a particular part of architecture. 'I pivoted during a brisk walk to the train station,' says Danei Cesario. 'I wanted to understand the infrastructure around what we do as architects, so in my annual review, I planned on expressing this to my supervisor. He was notoriously busy; during my review he mentioned that he had to leave to catch a train. I told him I would walk with him so we could finish my review. On our brisk walk from Park Avenue to Penn Station, I shared my interest in transitioning from project architect to project manager, the responsibilities I had already taken on, and a corresponding raise.'

Cesario continues: 'I think he respected my tenacity for making sure we had the conversation, regardless of the setting. We came up with a transition plan on that walk. Within three months, I was training on PM tools, working closely with the marketing team and firm leadership to strategise our business development in my new role as a project manager. I would encourage mid-career professionals to pursue what piques their interest and let leadership know. Firms are not necessarily known for "bringing" new roles to their staff, particularly if they are in the earlier part of their career. However, initiative and interest go a long way. You have to take ownership of where your career goes, even if it means being insistent and walking seven long blocks in peak August humidity.'

'I am likely in the fifth or sixth of my nine lives in architecture,' says Emily Grandstaff-Rice. 'I spent over a decade in a firm that celebrated generalists. Their philosophy is that specialist expertise is just as valuable as the ability to translate it to another discipline. It was a wonderful exposure to different building types, project roles and design practices. What I learned from this experience is that building your base skills of communication, research and work ethic is just as important as the specialist knowledge you will develop throughout your career. My first major pivot was completing construction administration on a major project in Boston. I had the theoretical skills as an architect, but what I learned through that role was negotiation, collaboration and client communication far beyond what I could have encountered just in the office. My advice for others is to try the pivot on like a new coat. It may suit you – it may not. It is not permanent, but you may learn something about yourself in wearing this role, and most likely it is preparing you for an even better one in the future.'

## Segue to technology

About eight years into her career Alexandra Pollock made the pivot to focus solely on design technology. Previously, she was spending about 80% of her time on project-specific work, with the other 20% focused on firm-wide technology initiatives. 'The opportunity to direct design technology at FXCollaborative came through a reference who recommended me for the role,' says Pollock. 'It felt a little intimidating to make that leap, but it was where my passion was – and the opportunity to focus solely on it was a big draw. I also felt confident with career experiences to that point, as I had worked in all phases of many projects of different scales. That early experience has been an immense asset to my specialised role and allows me to provide thought-through and tested technology strategies for projects.'

Evan Troxel has always been a proponent of us designing our own future rather than waiting around for someone else to come along and tell us how it should be done. 'So please excuse the really bad pun,' says Troxel, 'but I architected a new role for myself just a few years ago. I saw the need for our practice to go through a digital transformation, and the role to lead that transition in our firm simply didn't exist. There were no leaders in place who could effectively make it happen. I've made my career in design, and this problem was really no different – instead of working in the business, I'm now working on the business. I designed a new role for myself, of designing how our practice would work in the future, and am carrying out that plan today. My advice is to look for opportunities to design your own path that may not fit the current matrix of positions in the firm you're working at. If you can spot those opportunities, you probably have more insight than others into how to tackle the problems you see that need solving. Start solving them, and show your work. If it's valuable, you will be recognised for it, and you just might create something new that no one had ever thought of before.'

A pivot can be an opportunity to stand out and differentiate yourself. Andy Watts experienced a pivot brought about very much by circumstance. Having trained as an architect, he worked in a small façade design firm for a long time. 'When I left that practice, having never properly applied my qualifications as a registered architect, I sought to align myself back to the traditional architecture route and applied for a number of firms including Grimshaw,' says Watts. 'While I applied for an architect position, it was also at a time where they were looking to expand their technology team beyond BIM to include a dedicated computational design specialist role, and so I was asked to interview for that. It aligned well with my own aspirations – using my skillset and not being tied to a single piece of work for years and years – and so I leapt at the opportunity. That would be my advice – if an opportunity crops up, just jump at it. I had originally thought that it would be a temporary move, but found that it opened up a host of further opportunities for me.'

A number of respondents found they were pigeonholed working on a part of a project – for example building envelopes – and felt a need to pivot away from that. A few years after postgraduate education, Matt Dumich was working as a technical architect on the type of complex, mixed-use projects that he enjoyed, and felt extremely fortunate that the projects he worked on were getting built around Chicago. 'In each project I found an innovative material, system or detail that I was excited about exploring,' explains Dumich. 'This was formative experience, but it was limited, primarily to exterior enclosure systems. I eventually felt like I needed to seek new opportunities to become a more well-rounded architect. I joined a new firm with a good balance of design quality, office culture and a more diverse portfolio. There, every project was a new, unique design problem, and team members were generalists who could contribute in a variety of roles. My first project was a high-rise hotel, to be located just a few blocks from our office. I was the project architect through design and documentation for the base building, and worked on the interior design for the hotel common areas. When our project manager was on maternity leave, I assumed her role early in the construction phase – until construction stopped after the structure topped out in 2008. As the recession decimated our profession and most of my colleagues', I was fortunate to stay employed by being a nimble generalist. I eventually had the opportunity to lead a large building renovation/addition project that was supported by tax incentives for energy savings. I remain convinced that those incentives made the project viable and kept me employed.'

## Pivot to firm ownership

Others pivot in order to open their own firm. When Oscia Wilson had seven years of experience, she caught the entrepreneurial bug. 'At that point in my career I had a raging intellectual curiosity I needed to follow, that outpaced the opportunities I was able to tap through traditional employment,' says Wilson. 'I pursued an MBA on nights and weekends while continuing to work full-time for a year, and then quit my job to start my own little architecture firm while still studying business.'

There are two elements to this story that Wilson would not recommend to others. 'First, it was too early in my career – mainly because I lacked the network to bring in high-value work,' says Wilson. 'Second, despite the pervasive myth of scrappy entrepreneurship that people love to tell, if you start a company without capital it will fail. This is true even for professional services companies. The reason is that you can't do it alone; you need other people with expertise, and that requires money to pay those people. Even if you're a very well-rounded architect who can do everything from closing the deal to design to construction documents yourself, it's unlikely you also have expertise in bookkeeping, HR, taxes, websites and lead generation. It's even less likely that you have time to do all those roles and do them well. Revenues from an up-and-running firm will cover all this overhead, but you need enough capital to get fully up and running.'

Wilson continues: 'I did manage to string together five years on this journey, through sheer hustle and leadership charisma. Those five years were incredible, if not profitable in the traditional sense. The connections I made and the knowledge I gained forever changed my career path. The employees who agreed to take a chance on my idea and work for less money than they could make elsewhere will always hold my respect and gratitude. This pivotal time in my career shifted my perspective away from individual projects and on to the bigger picture of how a company is run and how the industry works. Focusing on the architecture firm as a business model captured my imagination in a way that made it impossible to go back to working as an "individual contributor" architect.'

If she could do it over, what would Oscia Wilson do differently? 'I would be smarter about protecting myself financially,' says Wilson. 'I might have continued working longer before launching. I might have waited to launch until I could capture a major client. I might have found a co-founder investor or started a design-oriented design–build firm. There are many ways I could have done it smarter, but being willing to follow my intellectual curiosity is not something I would change. It led to so many wonderful experiences, and set me up for a mid-career reinvention.' And this is the subject of the next chapter.

When co-directors at Harrison Stringfellow Architects Sarah Harrison and Su Stringfellow set up their firm, they were at a tipping point, ready to step up the career ladder. Sarah was an associate at a medium-sized commercial firm (the only female in the senior management team, in fact the only female architect in the firm) and had hit the glass ceiling. 'Su had just won numerous plaudits for the Midland Hotel, for which she was the project architect, started a family, and got made redundant after her maternity leave,' says Sarah Harrison. 'This created a perfect storm of discontent in the way our previous practices ran in terms of HR and practice management, and gave us the impetus to start a practice on our own terms.'

After ten years at a firm Donna Sink loved, doing good work and enjoying her co-workers, she had the opportunity to move to a new city to join a friend from college in starting their own firm. 'Coincidentally, a co-worker who had started a couple of weeks before me at the traditional firm also received an opportunity to move on,' says Sink. 'I chose to leave, the co-worker chose to stay. My former co-worker is now a partner in the same firm, happy and justifiably proud of the work they have done; staying was the right choice for them. I chose to leave, and it was the right choice for me! Several years after leaving I found that I did have a voice in architecture that was informed by my previous firm, but was also one I would not have found if I had stayed there. "Leaving the nest", as it were, was a necessary step in my own professional development. I learned from my former bosses so much about how to run a firm, both financially and ethically, and I could apply those lessons as I found my own path in being a firm owner.'

## 6: Pivot

Some people will warn you that once you open your own office it is difficult to go back to working for someone else. After several years, Donna Sink was starting to tire of the financial instability and 24/7 hours that are part of being a business owner. 'I did a project as a consultant for the local art museum (Indianapolis Museum of Art), which led to them offering me a full-time position in their facilities department,' says Sink. 'At the time my husband's job had changed and we no longer had employer-sponsored health insurance, plus I was exhausted from running my own firm, and my child had started public school, with its regular schedule leading to more predictability in my day-to-day. I accepted the offer and became not only a full-time employee again but was not in the role of architect: I was on the client side of the table! I held that position for five years and learned so much about being a building owner. I definitely feel that I'm a better architect [for] having had the experience of operating and maintaining a public facility.'

The biggest pivot for Justin Martinkovic came at the age of 25. He had been working for a firm for two and a half years after graduating from architecture school, had brought projects into the office and was performing the work. 'I really enjoyed the firm I was working for and the people there,' says Martinkovic. 'They were very good to me, and I reciprocated and did good work for them. But I was ready for something more. I decided in 2001, in the midst of a recession, to start my own firm. It wasn't too hard a choice. I was single with no kids, no one else depended on me, and I had backup plans. As a plan B, I believed I could get a job if things didn't work out. And should that fail too, I had a plan C: my last $300 was set aside for a flight home to live with my parents.'

Martinkovic continues: 'Having backup plans was important; it gave me options. If this leap was all-or-nothing it would have been much harder. Yet I also made sure the leap into the unknown was truly a leap and not a half-measure. I "burned the ships", so to speak: I resigned my job and surrendered my salary, and I had very little savings. To others considering a pivot like this I'd say first and foremost, know what you want. This is hard; it may take time to figure it out. Talk it out with friends, write essays to explore it, read books by luminaries, find inspiration and be brutally honest with yourself. Explore what success means and what failure means. And put failure in its proper place: if you fail, you can live with it, and I guarantee you'll learn and grow from it.'

'Then find the courage to make [the] change,' says Martinkovic. 'You can approach this like a design problem. Find your safety nets by designing a workable plan B and plan C. Sketch out what degree of "uncomfortable" you can tolerate in service of your higher goal. Finally, figure out how you'll "burn the ships" so that you'll be well motivated. Then take the plunge and don't look back. Look at change as an incredible and exciting opportunity, and get comfortable with a certain degree of discomfort, especially in the beginning. Nothing worth doing comes easy. Fulfilment requires difficult challenges.'

Pivoting out of a recession into an architecture-adjacent role is a skillset worth acquiring. During the last recession, Lora Teagarden graduated from her master's programmme into a dismal job market. She spent years searching for work in the profession: full-time, part-time or contract. 'An architecture-adjacent role I took on during this time was as a building plan reviewer for the State of Indiana,' says Teagarden. 'I was studying for my licensure tests at the time, and this role not only gave me steady, albeit meagre, income, but it also taught me the nuances of the building code and ADA requirements that are traditionally hard to learn in a standard firm hierarchy. As the economy improved, I was able to highlight this experience as a skill that not many young professionals have: both the knowledge of the national and local code, and also the permitting process for our state and local jurisdictions. Architecture-adjacent work can open you up to new lessons and insights into the profession. It helps you grow in ways your peers might not, and can set you up for future opportunities by putting new skills in your toolbox.'

There will be times when the pivot you need to make isn't entirely your choice. Tom Lee was recently asked by a colleague to temporarily step into more of a management role in their practice to allow him to turn his attention to delivering a large, complex project that needed his expertise. To date, Tom was leading the practice from a design perspective, which entails management to a degree, 'but this temporary role exposed me to more of the operations side of the practice,' says Lee. 'Truth be told, operations isn't an interest or strength of mine, but I was happy to take it on to help out and I learned quite a bit in the process. I am now returning to my role as a designer but with a newfound appreciation for it, and with a better understanding of how our business is run. I'd encourage others to approach changing roles while being mindful of your own career goals, but with an open mind because someone else might think that you have other strengths that may not be obvious to you, and that might bring added value to the practice and your career in the long run. Embrace change when it feels right.' Knowing how to pivot back is a must-have skillset when you are asked to do a reconnaissance or mission, ideally noting what you learned from having temporarily pivoted and applying that to your previous role.

## TRY THIS

Su Stringfellow helped to set up a social enterprise, Growing Sudley, which in turn has become a job in the office and led to lots of other similar projects for social enterprises and people employing them based on social value. Within the Growing Sudley project they helped set up a forest school in response to a local need for quality childcare (a need they also had themselves, so it solved their own problem). Children play outdoors, den-making, using tools and cooking round the campfire. They send their junior staff members to volunteer and help with the den-building. Harrison and Stringfellow also accessed a business grant through the Local Enterprise Partnership to refurbish the shop/

office they purchased on Penny Lane and saw an opportunity with the flat above, which they turned into an Airbnb, providing them with vital cashflow. Both of these other small enterprises have helped advertise their services to a wider audience. As a result of thinking like this, during the COVID-19 pandemic they were able to adapt quickly, as they were used to having to juggle childcare and be agile. They quickly got their cashflow in order to protect jobs and respond to new enquiries, rotating staff so there was always someone working (albeit from home), and keeping the work they had going.

# 7:
# Reinvent

Fig 7.1: Some architects adapt by pulling away from the crowd and reinventing themselves at a career inflection point

## Pull away from the crowd, reinvent yourself.

*Transitioning to a new role and leading a team was definitely self-disruptive. It takes some adjusting for your colleagues, who are comfortable in interacting with you in your former role, to update their expectations in your new role. I do not miss my role as project architect, but I know my years in that capacity made me a better project manager. I understand the schedule and resources that our projects require for optimal design. As a PM, I have more input on how we can best support the team, client and project.*
*– Danei Cesario*

*Recently I took on a position as a technical mentor on multiple projects in my new office. The role is both rewarding and confounding, since it takes patience in working with younger architects who have yet to learn some of the hard lessons of what it takes to make buildings. I do often miss my former role, where I had more direct client, consultant and contractor contact.*
*– David Swain*

## What else have you got?

It may seem to outsiders – to those not doing the reinventing themselves – that it happens suddenly, unannounced, out of the blue. But most career reinventions have multiple stages and take time, often unfolding over a year or more. What seems like a sudden change might be based on years of adaptive activity.

Here's how I reinvented myself at mid-career – a career that can be split cleanly into two halves.

In the first half I practised as an architect, designed over 100 large-scale projects, and eventually ran my own office. I served on AIA Chicago's board and as an officer, taught as an adjunct at University of Illinois Chicago (UIC), and received the AIA Chicago Young Architect Award.

In the first half of my career I became eligible to pursue Fellowship in the AIA, but was strongly advised against it. I was told I hadn't achieved anything yet – and they weren't wrong – so I let it go.

In 2010, in a restaurant with my family, I celebrated 25 years in the profession without being made redundant. The next week, wouldn't you know, I was unemployed.

So began the second half of my career. And my education in career reinvention.

I found myself at mid-career jobless for the first time, and noticed that while there was a great deal of information for students, emerging professionals and senior architects, there was a dearth of information and resources available on the middle decades of one's career.

I told myself I could either improve at Revit and find another job doing what I was doing, or see what I could do in the face of new technologies, threats to our relevance and increased marginalisation to help advance the profession, the industry and a new crop of students. I chose the latter.

So, I turned the former adjunct teaching position at UIC into a tenure-track position at University of Illinois at Urbana-Champaign (UIUC, where I teach to this day), teaching professional practice, design studio, building technology and digital technology, while innovating in the online teaching space, and serving as associate director until 2019.

Instead of building buildings, I built an online platform, turning one follower – my wife – into 12,000 on Twitter and LinkedIn, where I continue to spend inordinate amounts of time, sharing industry information. I started – and am paid generously – to coordinate social media for various schools.

I turned a couple of blogs into a book deal. Which became two, then four, and now with the one you are reading, six books. Then I started getting invited to write book chapters, forewords and blurbs for other people's books, including *The Architect's Handbook for Professional Practice*. My books were translated into other languages and recommended as study guides for the ARE licensing exam.

In high school, instead of having classmates sign my yearbook, one year I had them sign a world atlas. Ms Skobel wrote in it, 'The world is your oyster!' – so I made that my mission. In the second half of my career I started speaking locally, regionally and nationally, then with a single well-timed tweet was invited to keynote at the Palazzo Medici in Florence, Italy, then throughout Italy, multiple times in China, Australia, the UK, Finland and Spain.

While I never attended Harvard GSD, I was invited to lead an Executive Education course there each summer, and in 2018 invited to speak at the GSD and to serve on *ARCHITECT* magazine's R+D awards jury, among others.

Despite all I had accomplished since being made redundant in 2010, in 2016 my university (where I continue to teach) denied me tenure.

Time to reinvent!

Speaking and writing – as they are wont to do – led to consulting gigs with architecture firms, engineers, construction companies and verticals, manufacturers, owners, venture capitalists and software developers, regulation boards and universities, conducting workshops and leading roundtable discussions that engage the built environment community to start a conversation about how they can together help transform their teams, practices, firms, boards and the industry to prevail in the future. Which led to an opportunity to serve as a grant-supported researcher working towards the creation of the nation's first AI institute for design and construction.

Still eligible to pursue Fellowship in the AIA, I was again told I hadn't achieved anything yet – only this time I ignored their well-intended advice, and in 2020, during the pandemic, I was elevated to Fellowship in the American Institute of Architects (FAIA) and to Senior Fellowship in the Design Futures Council.

## Self-disruption

Architects soon find that they are never done reinventing. How have architects experienced mid-career reinvention, self-disruption or self-transformation in their role? How has it worked out for them? Do they miss their former role?

There are a lot of ways to disrupt yourself. One involves leaving your own firm to return to traditional architectural practice (with a twist). Recall in the last chapter how Oscia Wilson started her own firm, spending years 8–13 of her career founding and running a small five-person architecture firm. That shifted her role from architect to business owner or entrepreneur. What followed that period was another seismic shift, prompted by her becoming a parent. 'When I became a mother, two important things happened that changed me,' says Wilson. 'First, I was utterly exhausted. Creating a human will do that to you. So will running a small business. There wasn't enough coffee in the world to fuel me to do both. The second thing was that my career focus shifted from valuing the pursuit of intellectual curiosity above all, to valuing stability and work-life balance above all. I knew I had to leave the entrepreneurial world behind and find a traditional job.'

Wilson had three criteria for her next position:

- it had to be a fun place to work,
- she had to make at least as much money as she'd been making running her business, and
- she wanted to work somewhere that provided lunch (remember, she was exhausted).

'The idea that someone would make lunch for me just tickled my imagination in a way you can't understand unless you've fed a child in the middle of the night for a few months,' says Wilson.

Since she lives in San Francisco, she figured the tech world would probably meet these criteria. 'I began interviewing and found that all the large tech companies were building enough to justify full-time staff to administer those projects,' continues Wilson. 'My architectural background combined with my experience speaking and writing about project delivery approaches and the MBA got me a job at Google. Now I am the client at the OAC [owner, architect, contractor] meetings, making the decisions about scope, schedule and budget. It's a fun place to work. I instantly doubled my salary. Four years later I'm still tickled pink that they make me lunch.'

## A chance to give back

Chithra Marsh's mid-career was largely spent juggling both her commitments at work and raising a family – as many do – but she felt there was more that she could do. She wanted a chance to give back. 'I loved being creative, but something was missing,' says Marsh. 'I took charge of my career, while continuing to build my network and finding new opportunities. I sought to build on my passion for encouraging more people into the industry and sharing my knowledge. As a volunteer ambassador, I joined an amazing social enterprise, PLACED, that is still to this day devoted to promoting design in the built environment to both primary and secondary school students. Learning through workshop settings, the children get the opportunity to learn about placemaking and architecture first-hand. Taking part in these gave me an opportunity to inspire the next generation of creators. Over recent years, this social enterprise has expanded to consultation and engagement with local communities and a much wider audience. They offer them a say in how they see their neighbourhoods developing. I get to be a part of genuine social value programmes that make a positive change in people's lives. I am now a strategic ambassador for PLACED. The course of my career has changed for the better, adding more variety into my day-to-day activities.'

Marsh continues: 'People are at the heart of architecture and design. There is now a greater emphasis on putting communities at the centre of their environments. Genuine engagement and consultation have become a necessity within the design process, not a nice-to-have, and rightly so.'

Buttress Architects has a company ethos that architecture is as much about people as buildings, and that buildings should be shaped by their surroundings, their role and the people who'll use them, explains Marsh. 'I joined Buttress just over two years ago, and from the outset our ambitions and goals were completely aligned. My role has now expanded to leading our Social Value programme, working externally to enhance our architectural service and also internally with the health and wellbeing of our staff. Since joining I feel I have found my place. No longer a square peg, but very much a round peg in a round hole.'

## Rebranding yourself

Architects can find themselves put into one of three boxes – design, technical or management – on their way to becoming project designers, project architects or project managers. One way to break out of the one you've been placed into is to rebrand yourself.

A few years into my career I was promoted to associate as a technical architect at the successor to Mies van der Rohe's office, and while I valued technology (and to this day teach the subject) it's hard to change perceptions, so I left that firm, going to another more design-oriented firm to rebrand myself as a designer. While I knew if I got to design I would be happy, I wasn't married to the result (which is often out of your hands, impacted by the local community, economics, regulations, politics and client whims). Even if I wasn't always designing, the association with that firm led to my working with the Rolling Stones and Disney, among others. To make this move I had to take a pay cut (I recommend telling your spouse first), and when I eventually left that firm I was seen as a design leader for the rest of my career.

John Gresko always believed he had talent as a designer. 'For whatever reason, in big companies, people are often pigeonholed into three categories: design, production and management,' says Gresko. 'I was a project architect for most of my career because that is what the position called for when I was originally hired. It's hard to change perceptions after one is hired. Typically, if one is hired to be a project architect, it's very hard to become a designer, and vice versa. This to me seems unnatural for an architect. Mastering technical skills makes one a better designer, and mastering design makes one a better technical architect. Managing and management is a skill that applies to all positions in a company. Changing companies, states and starting over gave me a chance to rebrand myself. I showed my boss some ideas for a proposal we were working on, and offered to be the designer since we didn't have one. He liked what I had done, and soon I was leading the design of a near billion-dollar project. I was a senior project manager when I became the lead designer for our office. My experience, resumé and willpower helped me transform my career. I would never go back to my former position.'

Sometimes, due to division of labour or the aforementioned pigeonholing, changing roles precludes you from being who you are and doing what you do best. Arising from this is the need to reinvent your role, or the definition of your role, to form a hybrid. Emily Grandstaff-Rice recently fell into the project management role which she feels in some ways suits her, but has a tough time when it forces her to relinquish input on design. 'There tends to be a false dichotomy among architecture firms that you are either design or technical; project management or production; creative or analytical,' says Grandstaff-Rice. 'This works against getting the best out of all architects. I find the boundaries of a specific role difficult to stay within, with the greatest pressure coming among other professionals. We are best when we are able to think and be exposed to all elements of the process. Each contributor has their own skills, but for us to grow as professionals exposure to all of the roles is necessary to facilitate collaboration and innovation.'

As Randy Guillot has grown in his career, he has spent more time developing younger design talent around him. 'The perspective I bring to the overall trajectory of the work and the client insights around the particular kind of work we are doing have ultimately become more valuable than my ability to produce the work,' says Guillot. 'This is a natural progression, and ultimately, I truly believe I will be judged by how I have supported and grown the people around me. At times, I do miss the singular focus, the exhilaration of working through the detail until it was perfectly resolved, or that aha! moment that comes only after dozens of iterations on a scheme. The ability to spend all of your time thinking about one aspect of a project, as we did early in our careers, was a gift. The balance of where I spend my time, how to have the most impact and the most influence with limited time and many more clients, is a daily struggle. The days never have enough hours in them to do all I want to do, or to have all the conversations I want to have. This yearning for more is how I know I am still a designer and always will be.'

## Paths to reinvention

I do admire those that stop, change careers and forge a new path. The training of an architect can be a brilliant grounding for so many other professions and careers. I also believe that those entering the profession who have had life experience in other professions are a vital part of the profession and should be encouraged and better supported in their architectural training.
– Zoe Hooton

Maybe an external observer could see my career as disrupted (from academia to R&D to practice to academia again), but for me it all makes sense as the continuity of my purpose (empowering people with design technologies). The continuity I see in it is actually pretty clear, and helped me build confidence reinventing myself. And transforming my roles has definitely helped me in my career, and I don't regret the costs it came with.
– Aurélie de Boissieu

Mary Shaffer was working as a project manager (she had been a project manager for about half of her 22-year career) and team leader for a major retailer that was building stores across the US and starting to expand internationally. 'I learned of an architecture school that offered an online "distance" Master of Architecture degree, and having always wanted to get my advanced degree, I applied and was accepted,' says Shaffer. 'After two years of working full-time while going to school full-time, and giving up everything fun in my personal life, I obtained my MArch degree! I knew that degree would initiate a major shift in my career, but that was not my goal going in. During my two years in the programme, I learned how to apply design thinking to every situation; new ways to frame questions and new ways to solve problems; new design software and new ways to present my ideas. Once I finished that programme, I began to feel restless in my job, and decided to seek a new growth opportunity. My degree enabled me to apply for positions that were not previously available to me, and ultimately led me on the path to becoming a department leader today. I missed project management for a few years when I was in a department director role; at my current firm, I have the opportunity to lead both projects and people; leading projects keeps me grounded in our processes and allows me to be a better resource to the project managers on my team.'

## Reinvent by starting your own company

Andy Watts has seen this approach work for others on a number of occasions, particularly through observing those who define their own ways of working by creating their own companies. 'Of particular note are three former employees of Grimshaw,' says Watts. 'Having led fantastic careers in our design technology team, they sought to move away from a singular practice model. Two of them went on to found – and a make a huge success of – designtech.io, a computational BIM consultancy, before being joined by the third. The three of them have now gone on to co-found matterlab, an AEC [architecture, engineering and construction] technology and innovation lab. Watching this evolution unfold has been fantastic, as they have embraced new ways of working at every turn, giving more innovative approaches back to the industry.'

## Treat your reinvention as a design challenge

Evan Troxel's mid-career transformation is working out well. 'Moving from being a designer on projects to leading the digital transformation in our company has been the biggest design challenge I've ever undertaken,' says Troxel. 'And because I view my work as a design problem, I still feel like I'm designing on a daily basis, albeit not on architecture per se. I feel like I'm doing more meaningful work now than I've ever done before because it's for the people I work with and know very well, and it's for our future together. I love the people I work with, so it's gratifying to serve them in this way. On some days, when I participate in design reviews on projects, I do miss the role I used to be in. Designing the built environment and the experiences people have in it has been my lifelong passion. But now I feel like I'm enabling others to make an even bigger impact than I ever could with the way we are moving into the future of practice, and I find that to fulfil me in ways my old role never did.'

Zaha Hadid Architects' Henry David Louth reinvented himself from project architect to computational designer and researcher. 'As a computational designer I now ask, "What if this were a façade system?" not "Which façade system should I use?"' explains Luoth. 'This is one of the fundamental shifts between the two roles, and on research-based practice in general. I approach design through a series of open-ended, constraint-based problems for which there are many solution sets, each demonstrating a varied degree of usefulness toward the initial problem (fitness). As a design researcher, I often do not have a direct application for a technique, process or simulation method. This can be frightening at times! Working open-ended with boundaries (a lot like bowling with the kids' rails up) is not for everyone. I "fail" often; it can be trying at times. It takes focus, independence, a responsibility to argue for your actions, and a confidence in yourself to know you are asking the right questions, even if the answers remain elusive.'

## Reinvent yourself over and over

Career reinvention doesn't have to be a one-time thing. At the 12-year mark of his career, we saw how Joe Cliggott accepted a position to move internationally, switch to the client side, and even became the client contact for his previous firm. When that office closed, Cliggott took on a project management role within the London studio of a world-class design practice.

'A project opportunity back in Chicago allowed our family to move back home, and a few years later in 2013, now with over 18 years of experience, I reinvented myself again to manage an entire office,' says Cliggott. 'This constant evolution has continued, as nine months ago I accepted a national position within my current company. Each role has represented different challenges and opportunities, and each help to add a complete picture of a career.'

'While, according to the definition of this book, I may only just be entering the mid-career phase, there is definitely a theme of further self-transformation that should be recognised,' says Andy Watts. 'For me, there have been moves from project digital support, to a slightly more strategic look at project digital transformation, to a much more strategic look at firmwide digital transformation and innovation. While all are interrelated, there is a change in the approach, interface and skills required for each change. While there is often a nostalgic tint to previous roles, each change brings its own challenges that I relish each time.'

## Reinvent how you run your business

Three years ago, Justin Martinkovic and his business partner felt that their practice was being held back by them, the two principals. 'We both work incredibly well together, and we were both effectively wearing all hats at all times,' says Martinkovic. 'We had our hands in every project, and we both had responsibilities in marketing, design, client communications, finance, HR and everything else. At 20 employees we simply topped out on what each of us could handle. The business was constrained by the bottleneck at the top. My business partner Brian suggested we pivot roles toward our natural strengths. He loves the craft of architecture, so we appointed him the director of design. I love thinking about the future, and I'm pretty good at marketing. I was bestowed with the unofficial title of "visionary" and took on the responsibility of sales. We'd have loved to hire out a director of finance and director of HR, but we could not afford those non-billable positions, so we split those roles while employing great people to do the day-to-day work.'

Martinkovic continues: 'It was a little scary. We had operated as jacks of all trades for so long, to reshuffle the deck and narrow our individual focus was daunting. It felt like the scene in *Indiana Jones and the Last Crusade* where Indy comes to the rocky precipice and, hoping there is solid ground over the abyss, he takes a step off. It was a leap of faith for us, but it paid off. Our roles gave us clear silos of responsibility within our personal strengths and took other less appealing responsibilities off our shoulders. Being ordained director of architecture let Brian firmly take the helm, coach staff and manage workflow. Being titled "visionary" emboldened me to try to experiment with new ideas, and being director of sales made it clear that if our sales were lagging, it was my job to fix it. Neither of us have any inclination to revert to our former roles; we only wish we had made the change a year or two sooner.'

## Reinvent yourself as a large firm leader

Tom Lee had a job he loved at a small design firm working on great projects with people he admired, when he was presented with an opportunity to join a much larger practice with a challenge to come in and elevate design. 'I was very sceptical at first and considered they might need someone with more experience, but after several very honest discussions with leadership, I realised my intuitive approach to the situation was ideally suited to the challenge, and leadership was committed to helping me grow into the role,' says Lee. 'It was a huge risk for me and the firm, but it has truly been a privilege to have the freedom to work intuitively, trusting my own judgement in a practice where we do very meaningful work for society, and I feel I have the full support of leadership. The joy of seeing colleagues rise in their careers, seeing our work win design awards, and together understanding the positive impact we've had on lives is a reward that I wasn't expecting. There are times I do miss my former role, but I am blessed to love my current one just as much, but in very different ways.'

## Parallel roles

*If your profession acknowledges your work with awards and recognition, I believe you have a duty to give back. Like offering my wisdom to this publication and the architects who might benefit from it!*
– Alison Brooks

*I fundamentally believe that parallel roles make us all better architects and leaders. I encourage all architects, but particularly young architects, to find a passion outside the office, dabble in new things, and invest in relationships.*
– Matt Dumich

One tested means to reinvent yourself mid-career is to take on parallel roles both inside and outside your organisation. The thought of taking on more may be discouraging for those who already feel over-burdened, but in my experience, and that of others, it is clear that wearing multiple hats and having parallel career tracks not only enriches but can advance your career. Indeed, it is through parallel roles that I met many of the architects whose voices fill this volume. Are there any parallel roles that they have played – such as leadership positions in industry organisations, or running for office – that influenced or informed their primary role, and if so, how?

After licensure, Virginia E Marquardt wasn't quite sure of her next step. Through her local and regional AIA components she learned about AIA's Young Architect Forum (YAF), and over the next 10 years she was highly involved in the YAF at a local, state, regional and national level, leading her local YAF group, then serving as regional young architect director (YARD), and the last five years serving on the National Advisory Committee as the community director, vice-chair, 2015 chair and past chair. 'The YAF allowed me grow and hone my leadership and soft skills in a supportive environment

Fig 7.2: Internal meeting at principal and workplace studio leader Matt Dumich's firm, SmithGroup

with others that were going through similar shared experiences, including how to work with individuals remotely, individual offices across the nation with different perspectives and viewpoints, and virtually,' says Marquardt. 'It was the best experience and I recommend it to everyone. Not only did I develop leadership and soft skills, I've met some incredible individuals, peers, mentors [and] experts that I call friends today, and [who] I continue to keep in touch with and learn from. Additionally, another value I bring to my firm is my relationships with these individuals for their expertise, knowledge, networking opportunities, and as potential partners on projects and as clients.' She's also had the opportunity to be part of committees and boards, gaining a seat at the table to envision and shape our profession's future – a perfect example of a parallel career track.

Matt Dumich found early in his career that the American Institute of Architects (AIA) was his tribe. 'As a graduate student at UW-Milwaukee, I was selected to serve on the AIA Wisconsin Board of Directors as the associate representative,' says Dumich. 'There I found a group of firm leaders committed to advancing the profession. They treated me as a peer and became early mentors. They instilled in me the value of service and leadership in our firms and communities. I have gone on to serve the profession in a variety of roles at the local, regional and national levels of the AIA. Recently, I had the honour of serving as 2017 AIA Chicago president and just finished my term on the board of trustees for the Chicago Architecture Center, formerly Chicago Architecture Foundation. I am currently leading the AIA National Emerging Professional Task Force, focused on supporting the next generation of architects. My service provided leadership opportunities and soft skill development I was not yet getting from my firm early in my career. Today, I continue to be inspired and learn from my professional colleagues. I always gain broader leadership perspective while staying connected with the profession and the next generation.'

Danei Cesario served as chair of AIA New York's Diversity and Inclusion Committee for over five years while working full-time. 'During that half-decade, I created, moderated and served on panels, curated an exhibit, and met so many talented people who actively push our profession forward,' says Cesario. 'Currently, I continue my servant leadership on the AIA New York State Board, representing nearly 10,000 members across 13 chapters. I am still a contributor and ambassador to organisations such as the United Nations, the Beverly Willis Architecture Foundation, Parlour, Stephen Lawrence Charitable Trust and nycobaNOMA Executive Board. As a core member of these groups, I am dedicated to fostering mentorship, sponsorship and leadership among the diverse design community as they navigate their careers within architecture and beyond.'

Fig 7.3: Danei Cesario delivering her keynote at the AIA Student Conference in Seattle on the ways ethics and advocacy can positively engage and 'infringe' on the norms of architecture

This excellent example of a parallel track doesn't end there. 'I founded WALLEN + daub to expand on these principles,' says Cesario. 'WALLEN + daub was born one late night during my education at City College of New York, studying architecture. I wanted to create a space in support of the brilliant contributors of architecture, STEM industries and design. This would be a space to educate through shared information and experiences, share their diverse stories to empower others, help to retain talent through engagement and encourage cross-pollination for expansion across our creative industries. The idea evolved at every step of my career and has made me a better leader in my professional life.'

Donna Sink is someone who does so much for the industry and is involved in so many ways. Among many other roles she has been a board member of the non-profit People for Urban Progress for almost 10 years, and considers it a parallel role to her profession. 'Board membership has exposed me to collaborating with people from widely different backgrounds (law, healthcare, tech, marketing, community development and many others) and helped me understand that the ways that architects collaborate with one another depends on an internally understood vocabulary and process – a shorthand

– that other professions don't share,' says Sink. 'This helps me communicate better with clients, and also have more empathy for the skills required to manage a business and run an organisation of employees. I have also served as a board member in our local AIA chapter, which has exposed me to lots of different kinds of firms and their concerns within our profession. By connecting with so many others in our discipline and community I've been able to become a very well-rounded architect, even while working within a fairly small subset of building project types. On the more practical side: board membership and work with AIA are fantastic networking arenas.'

Angela Mazzi has always been involved in professional organisations. 'In the early years of my career I lived in Phoenix and got very involved in the ways that urban design and housing impacts the health and wellbeing of a community,' says Mazzi. 'I was on the Housing Commission, the board of a nonprofit called Arizona Forward, and the board of a local community development corporation. It was very rewarding to see first-hand how being an architect could make a difference, especially since architects don't often serve in organisations like this and our point of view isn't informing decisions. Later in my career, I moved to Cleveland and became involved in the government affairs committee of the local AIA chapter, and also became a member of the education committee for ACHA. ACHA was the first time I had been involved in a national organisation, and it was a great opportunity to meet other colleagues involved in healthcare design and think outside of the everyday issues of my projects. Now, in Cincinnati, I have continued to raise awareness on the importance of the built environment in shaping wellbeing. I'm on the board of ACHA and will be its president in 2021. I've had the opportunity to lead several committees and help reshape our organisation, including our value proposition and having our certification recognised by clients. I've continued to be active with AIA, including helping to plan a regional convention in 2019 themed around wellness, and am on the current board of the Cincinnati chapter.' Another parallel role Mazzi has played is through her website, The Patron Saint of Architecture, through which she has been able to help many architects and designers move forward purposefully in their careers.

## Where a parallel track becomes a way of life

I am currently regional chair for my local RIBA region (West Midlands) and an elected member of the RIBA's council representing the West Midlands. I saw it as an opportunity to get involved with the direction of the profession, [and] raise my personal profile and therefore that of the firm in the region.
– Philip Twiss

Multiple or parallel roles (team leadership, commercial, mentoring and technical) have enabled me to consider projects holistically and call in additional expertise as required, [and] set the overall direction, even if [I am] not always involved in the detailed execution, [and this] has enabled me to be seen as a source of technical knowledge.
– John Edwards

**7: Reinvent**

For most of her career Trina Sandschafer has worn multiple hats. 'I am a design leader,' begins Sandschafer. 'I have also served on executive leadership and strategic planning teams. I have been leading talent acquisition for over a decade. I play a key role in business development. I help tell our story. I help our clients tell their story. Each of these appointments helps me see a bigger part of our profession. Outside of the office, I have been unofficially and officially involved with my alma mater for 14 years. I find it extremely rewarding to spend time with the next group of future architects. We have a large mentorship role to play as leaders in our profession.'

There are two parallel areas that have had positive impacts for Alexandra Pollock. The first is her involvement in academia. 'Whether I am teaching a full course, lecturing or being a guest critic, the energy and innovation that comes from students can be incredible,' says Pollock. 'There is a great transfer of knowledge in both directions. The second area is my involvement in industry. I co-chaired our local AIANY Technology Committee for five years, and in that time, I met so many amazing people who inspired me and also have remained an important part of my network.'

Fig 7.4: Informal discussion at Angela Watson's firm, Shepley Bulfinch

Angela Watson has played and continues to play many parallel roles. In her firm she's a principal, a board member and board chair. 'I also participate in several organisations that bring many professionals together to talk about ideas,' says Watson. 'I present at events and conferences and have moderated national events. I am a member of several councils at institutions of higher education. I've organised symposia and roundtable events, and I have taught.'

## The benefits of parallel roles

*My involvement in the AIA has been essential for my sanity. In many ways it provided me [with] leadership training early in my career that I did not get in entry-level roles. I find that it keeps me connected to the larger realm of the profession. It has challenged me to push beyond my day-to-day work and create the connection to the larger community.*
– Emily Grandstaff-Rice

*At AIA Orange County, California I am a board member, as well as director for equity, diversity and inclusion. This role outside of work has given me an awareness and insight on the state of diversity within our chapter/county, as well as inspiration to work towards an equitable future.*
– Meghana Joshi

Having parallel roles in one's career can have lasting, tangible benefits. It emphasises that there are multiple versions of you, and provides an opportunity for giving back. 'All those roles and activities have broadened my horizon,' says Angela Watson. 'They have broadened my understanding of the perspectives that others have that might be different from mine. Maybe most importantly those roles have required me to think about questions and problems differently from different vantage points, and they have required me to imagine solutions to problems that I had not previously dealt with. All these experiences have become a backdrop for how I do my work every day, giving me a much wider-angle lens on what I do.'

After winning three major RIBA awards in 2006, 2007 and 2008, Alison Brooks was asked to serve on the RIBA Awards jury. She did this for about five years. 'Every shortlisted building is visited, across the UK and Europe,' explains Brooks. 'It's a significant time commitment but a fantastic learning experience. New buildings are rarely as great as they appear in photographs. But it's always wonderful to meet architects from around the world who in my experience are universally friendly, welcoming and generous. I see architecture as a fellowship of professionals with shared experience and a common cause regardless of nation, race or religion: to better our built environment, for everyone.'

Brooks continues: 'I taught a diploma unit at the AA for two years and a year at Harvard GSD. Teaching is critical to distilling and focusing one's position as an architect. I stopped because of pressures of practice. The business model of winning work through competitions makes teaching difficult, but I continue to give public and academic lectures around the world. For many years I was an external examiner at the AA and several other UK schools of architecture. I'm currently a design advocate for the Mayor of London, and serve as a trustee for Open City, the architectural education and outreach charity that kickstarted the world-famous concept of "Open House".'

In addition to running her firm, Diane Reicher Jacobs has served as president of AIA Arizona, founder of the Women's Leadership Group, member of various committees both locally and nationally, and in advisory roles at both the University of Arizona and Arizona State University. 'These efforts have had a great deal of influence on my primary role. These efforts have allowed me to give of my time and talent in a shorter timespan. Buildings we work on are two-year endeavours. It is satisfying to work with like-minded people who struggle and get joy out of the same things and promote the profession I love so much. They balance the at-times myopic focus on the day's issues with a broader perspective of our work. I have also learned techniques for motivating and gelling teams.'

These and other career reinventions may have taken dedication, time and not a little risk, but all would agree that it was well worth the effort required.

# 8: Rewire

Fig 8.1: Adapting throughout your career requires you to navigate the near-constant equivalent of whitewater conditions

# Mid-career architects: the bridge between generations

The architecture profession is changing, widening, and with new models of practice. The old blue-chip firms will probably exist side by side with more firms involved in fabrication, robotics, prefabrication. Corporations have joined the mix, offering construction, many ideas of alternate delivery, and of course the profession has widened to provide other "architectural services", often for business, which have made the megaliths – architecture firms on a scale the world has never known. Many will be tried – some will fail, but there WILL be a continual evolution of new practice models for the next generation to consider.
– Rob Rothblatt

Technology and architecture are finally at a point where they are merging in design development rather than being limited to design tools. Post-COVID, the way we live will require a careful integration of the sciences in architecture to provide a safe and comfortable space for all.
– Meghana Joshi

Withdrawing from the world has an evolutionary purpose, in that it gives us time to heal and reflect productively on what went wrong so we won't repeat the behaviour. And yet there is little point in going over and over what went wrong – whether with the economy, the world health situation, race relations or climate. Studies show that mentally we're better off coping with bad fortune by distracting ourselves, rather than brooding, pondering or ruminating over the situation.[30] Though we may catch ourselves doing it, there's no point in catastrophising the future.

Better than either ruminating or distracting ourselves by binge-watching whatever happens to be streaming is being able to adapt quickly in times of crisis through the practice of scenario planning and simulating future scenarios.[31] This chapter won't solve the problems that face all of us, but aims to provide an opportunity to consider future scenarios based on impending change. Do architects believe the profession is in the midst of change? If yes, how so?

While Angela Watson believes this to be true, she says 'it will remain to be seen how drastic the change will be, and if we will see a difference in how we work together after we have experienced working with each other virtually. Generally speaking, the entire building and construction industry has to become more collaborative. If we continue to work in silos we will continue to be inefficient, and we will continue to be adversaries with our construction partners and sometimes our clients. It's important that we recognise the leadership position that we can take. I don't mean leadership in the form of directing. I mean leadership in terms of our ability to facilitate discussion, so that we can all deliver projects that are financially successful and have a positive impact on our changing world.'

## The role of the architect is changing

One way in which we are seeing change is in the role of the architect. 'I see our profession undergoing a fundamental shift, or perhaps a split, between the familiar premise of the architect as "design consultant" to the architect's work as an integrated part of the construction supply chain: design for manufacture and assembly, or DfMA,' says Alison Brooks. 'We're currently producing construction information for our precast concrete and brick tower in King's Cross with fully 3D native files and scripts that feed directly into the contractor's digital manufacturing processes. Using traditional 2D construction documents, a contractor will typically double the amount of material under the assumption that 50% of construction materials go to waste on site. BIM combined with DfMA is about removing those unknowns: de-risking the construction process, reducing costs and, most important, reducing carbon miles and construction waste. However, there's an equivalent exponential increase in the architect's work – both in the amount of information and the time it takes to produce. Current professional appointment documents don't fully recognise that architect's native 3D and 4D digital files are now feeding directly into a digital and robotic manufacturing supply chain. Our profession must urgently address this radically important role of the architect as both creative author and integral part of a digital manufacturing industry.'

Fig 8.2: Alison Brooks' light-filled studio in a converted industrial workplace, overlooking Camden in north London

## Slow to change

Change is constant and the profession is always changing – and yet this time feels different. 'The profession is always in the midst of change, which is necessary to staying relevant, though I can't remember a time in my career when there were more changes occurring simultaneously: the maturation of BIM, 3D printing, proliferation of data, rise of artificial intelligence, and perhaps most urgently, the need to combat climate change, to name a few,' says Tom Lee. To Lee, this is a signal that though the art of architecture has always been important, the focus is shifting to the science of architecture, which means there is a lot more to know as an architect. 'Not to mention that the role of the architect is evolving as project delivery methods and programme managers intercept the client–architect relationship, complicating the design and procurement process. As I've experienced, this will lead to a growing number of specialists/consultants who will all have a voice in the design, putting architects at risk of simply managing the design process rather than leading it.'

*new technology*

*internal*            *external*

*transformation*     *disruption*

*work processes*

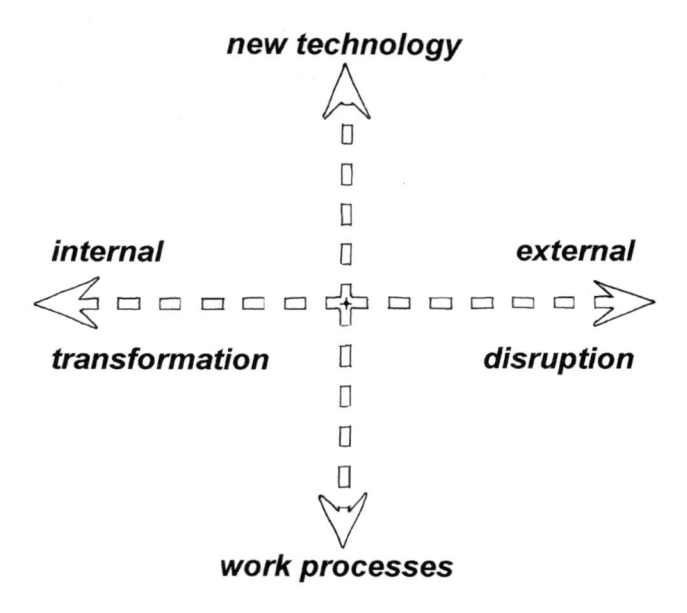

Fig 8.3: It is important for the mid-career architect to know where they stand in relation to emerging technologies and work processes

'Our profession is always evolving, whether we want it to or not,' Danei Cesario admits. 'Our clients are more sophisticated and demanding than ever, so to be able to remain inventive we must be forward-thinking. I have seen an improvement in our desire to effectively communicate, aptness to cross-pollinate with other creatives, and willingness to celebrate individualism and the varied, diverse experiences that contribute to our designs and firms. The implications of this mean that saying things like "this is the way we have always done it" becomes a more archaic, unacceptable retort, which will hopefully soon fall into obsolescence. All architects, regardless of their status or career point, will be held to a new standard of care if we plan on practising in the future. I reckon mid-career architects will continue to lead that charge.'

Fig 8.4: One of a variety of informal and formal meeting spaces at the London office of senior associate and design director Philip Twiss's firm, Gensler

'The process of design and architecture is constantly evolving, particularly with the advent and influence of AI and parametric digital design,' says Philip Twiss. 'But at architecture's heart are people and communities responding to the basic human need for shelter and sustainable environments. While the methodology and tools might change, the need to provide sustainable homes and communities, safe and engaging working environments, remains the same. The biggest change is that we need to be thought- and practice-leaders in relation to sustainability and sustainable design. It's not enough to design a one-off zero-carbon house in the countryside. Architects need to demonstrate how sustainable design can be successfully applied to dense urban communities.'

### The current model for the mid-career architect

Eek, what is the current model? I do not know what that means. Stay in a firm for a couple of years and make partner? That is not for everyone.
– Emily Grandstaff-Rice

It's interesting, until your questions I had not really thought of 'mid-career' as a thing. There is a lot of thought given to how to transition young people into leadership positions, but there isn't as much thought about what they do when they get there. I'm not sure what the current model is, if there is one.
– Duane Carter

Ted Hyman has always encouraged young architects to try everything and anything they think they might be interested in. 'There are so many challenges in the world, the need for great design solutions is more important than ever,' says Hyman. 'One of my mentors early in my career would ask me at every annual review "what role do you envision for yourself in the firm?" and my answer was always "I don't know, I'm excited about what I'm doing today, but I'm not ready to commit to my entire career", which was the right answer – at least he would say that. At some point though, I think the biggest challenge as you approach that mid-level point in your career is the pressure from yourself and others "to decide what you want to be when you grow up". After the mid-career decisions I had made, I continued to surprise myself, as my role has transitioned many more times. When people ask me why I like being an architect today, it's a pretty simple answer. "I was never clever enough to become a doctor saving children's lives, a geneticist discovering the cures for disease, or a Nobel Prize winning chemist solving the energy crisis, but those are my clients, and for three to four years I get to live in their world, knowing that my work is going to help them do what they do better". Who could ask for a better job, really?'

Fig 8.5: Even during a pandemic, important one-on-one connections and mentoring moments continue at ZGF

Hyman continues: 'One of the biggest fears that many mid-level architects face is [dealing with] the rapidly changing tools with which we practice. In the 1980s, I saw the "revolution" from pencils on vellum to the use of "pin bars" to register sheets of mylar in layers to build drawings. The belief was that by eliminating so much of the repetition work, we might reduce the need for intern and mid-level architects. In the early 1990s we saw the adoption of MicroStation, and we were all forced to learn the new tool again; however, within a few years we moved to AutoCAD – a completely different approach to CAD. At the time, we worked split shifts because it was thought that no one could sit in front of a monitor for more than three hours and remain productive or healthy. These tools were useful for a long enough period that made it possible for everyone to learn and adopt to the new tools. The speed in the introduction of Revit, Grasshopper, and every other software coming along to improve our ability to go faster and better, is making it harder for those mid-level architects to adapt. I see this as one of the biggest challenges: not only to how we use tools to produce the work, but how we think about the design process. I remain optimistic that the passion for solving problems with elegant solutions will transcend the latest tools we use to solve them.'

There are (at least) two types of mid-career architects/professions operating today. 'One is traditional, the other is adapting and innovating,' says Lora Teagarden. 'The traditional, architecture-only profession and firm structure likely leaves the mid-career architect pigeonholed into a very narrow knowledge and expertise space. If the architect is required to move into a new role, or if the firm suffers a loss of projects or income, it is harder for the traditional mid-career architect to adapt. Those in firms who are diversifying the work they do or the services they offer will be able to adapt better to economic changes or trends in work.'

## The model for mid-career architects is at risk

It is challenging to be a mid-career architect in our profession unless you become an integral part of the management structure. For the most part the profession rewards either strong managers/principals, strong designers, or those who have become specialists. To just have strong technical knowledge is not enough to open doors to leadership. I do think the model is sustainable, but perhaps not rewarding.
– David Swain

I'm not sure there is a standard "current model" for the mid-career architect. The profession is diverse; approximately 60% of all architects in the UK are sole practitioners, a further 10% have only two employees; contrast this with the global mega-practices such as Gensler, SOM and others, and everything in between. Practice structures are diverse and therefore career opportunities equally so.
– Philip Twiss

The world is changing fast. The industries that have advanced this change are primarily communications and electronics, while the AEC industry is operating in much the same way it has for decades. 'Not only is the model for a mid-career architect at risk, the model for all architects is at risk,' says Justin Martinkovic. 'Despite some technological innovations, how we design and build has not fundamentally changed. Investment in research and development in the AEC industry globally, as a percentage of net sales, is one of the lowest of any industry. The construction industry's steady decline in productivity over the past several decades is in no small part a reflection of this lack of investment and innovation. By any measure, data-driven or anecdotal, architecture as an industry is slow to adapt to change and anaemic in its desire or ability to advance the state of the art, both in terms of what we do and how we do it. This makes our industry ripe for disruption, for someone who can produce what we produce but do it better, faster and less expensive. Disruptors typically come from outside of an industry, and recent history is riddled with examples. For this reason, I feel all architects are all at risk, mid-career and otherwise.'

Martinkovic continues: 'The contradiction here is that most architects are very intelligent, creative and forward-thinking individuals. When it comes to applying this mindset to designing buildings and environments, we seem to excel. When it comes to focusing these energies on advancing our own art, and in so doing advancing our industry, we seem to be stuck in the mud. To thrive means to catch up with the advancing world, and fast. It means stepping into the role of visionary, innovator and entrepreneur. It means confronting the brutal facts and listening to what really is being asked of us. It means making investments and taking risks. It means stepping into immense discomfort and disrupting ourselves lest we be disrupted. A sea change in our industry will happen, it's just a matter of how soon and by whom.'

Mid-career professionals are well positioned to lead industry change. 'We understand the old world of architectural design and production, and we understand the new and ever-changing digital world and the potential therein,' says Martinkovic. 'We have enough experience to be realistic and pragmatic, and hopefully we still have a few precious ounces of idealism available to us. We are the bridge of the old and new, and we can play a significant role in shaping the future of our profession, if we choose to.'

## What is the model for mid-career architects?

We've long had an idea of what the roles of an emerging professional and a late-career architect are. But is there a model for mid-career architects? If so, what is it? 'Part of the problem is that there is no singular model for the mid-career architect,' says Danei Cesario. 'Once you're licensed, the only metrics to abide by are your continuing education credits. You can handle those however you see fit to remain licensed. This does not spur the kind of engagement that would yield sustainability. Imagine if there were a requirement for mid-career professionals to pay it forward to the following generation of architects as a continuing education requirement? That would create the environment of knowledge-sharing and community that nods to the sustainable apprenticeship model of other trades.'

AIA's Code of Ethics requires architects to pay it forward and give back by teaching and helping the next generation. 'I am fortunate to have mentors that helped me navigate my career and follow my passions,' says Matt Dumich. 'They instilled [in me] the notion that, beyond my individual contributions, I could make a greater impact by helping others succeed. I am committed to mentoring, connecting across generations, and reinforcing a pipeline of talent. These efforts continue to fuel my passion, inform my own practice, and give [me] great optimism for the future of our profession.'

## Conduits, connectors and bridges

The role of the mid-career architect in this transition is to serve as a bridge between the generation before and the generation after. Mid-career architects help transfer knowledge and are the bridge between generations. 'The profession has evolved in ways that have transformed the role of architects from not just designers of buildings but also to be designers of experiences, materials, process and protocols, among other things,' says Randy Guillot. 'Subject matter experts have siloed our profession from the tradition of the enlightened generalist towards a market expertise model. And all of this in a time of unprecedented technological change that has taken us from two-dimensional drawing on physical objects to a completely digital and often asynchronous 3D and 4D modelling environment. As a mid-career professional it's entirely possible, as I have done, to have practised through all of these phases of change in your career. To do this it has required an evolution of work style and tools just to be able to keep up. It's exhausting and at times I feel like if I miss the "next improvement" to this technology or the next, I will be forever behind the curve. Fortunately, like a lot of catastrophising thinking, this rarely plays out this way.'

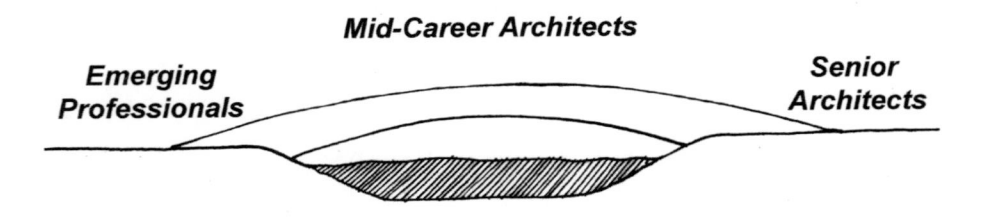

Fig 8.6: Mid-career architects serve as the bridge between emerging professionals and senior architects

Guillot continues: 'Many mid-career professionals I know are leading these technology transformations in their organisations, just as mid-career professionals did when we went from drawing on physical objects to working digitally. Having the understanding of where you are going and an understanding of where you have been gives mid-career professionals a perspective that others may not have. I do believe that this is different than past "changing of the guards". Technology has created the ability for firms to run in different ways, with different outputs and value propositions than in the past. The prevalence of modelling workflows has created a point where it is difficult for most senior architects to produce on the same platforms as the younger staff. But the transfer of knowledge is essential between those that have successfully built work and those who are learning if we are to create a sustainable model of built excellence. This takes different approaches to teaching and to learning and a different appreciation of each other's value to the entire process of design and documentation of a project today.'

'Those who can speak "digital and analogue" offer great skills for our offices,' says Trina Sandschafer. 'They bridge the gap between those who are more comfortable sketching with pen and paper and those who move as adeptly with technology. They can bridge between the communication and working styles of baby boomers and millennials. Bringing people and skills together has a very strong effect on a practice.'

It may appear to some that nothing has changed. Angela Watson doesn't think what we are experiencing today is any different than previous generations' experience. 'Tools have always changed,' says Watson. 'There's always been "the way we do it". This comes back to my belief that communication is at the heart of all of it.' And yet there is one difference: the rate of change is faster. 'As mid-career architects we don't have the same knowledge that those in the later stages of their career have in their area of expertise,' continues Watson. 'We also don't have the skills with new technology that recent graduates have. The position we find ourselves in is one that requires us to connect the two. And that transition is an ever more rapid cycle as technology increasingly drives our work.' Mid-career architects are the connectors between generations.

## Advantage: mid-career architect

Don't let fear get in the way of your growth and professional advancement. Like Watson, Aurélie de Boissieu is not sure the digital transformation we are facing today (whether BIM, computational design or AI-related) is that different from other transformations faced by architects in the past. 'Mario Carpo in his book *The Second Digital Turn* for example set [out] very clearly how architects somehow always struggled with embracing new technologies, but also were sometimes very early adopters and are setting new working standards,' says de Boissieu. 'Fear is the worst adviser one can have: fear of being outdated, being less efficient or being got rid of, for example. Fear makes it difficult to take risks, to get out of our comfort zone. What we need to teach people today is to trust their own ability to learn, to change and adapt.

## Mentoring and training in decline

It's hard for me to judge if there is a trend of this. In my career I've spent most of my time in a sink or swim situation. For me that was helpful and there were some great growth opportunities. That's not to say that those are necessarily good growth opportunities for others.
– Angela Watson

I have been involved deeply in training and mentoring for my entire career. One obligation of a great mentor is to help younger architects see their strengths and help guide them towards those – hoping that that is where they will find the greatest fulfilment. And yet, if a mentor cannot offer a path towards success – a path to leadership or to rain-making – mentorship just doesn't seem that useful. Young people crave it yet see clearly the need for political advantage.
– Rob Rothblatt

You've heard the one where the CFO asks the CEO: What happens if we invest in developing our people and then they leave us? And the CEO responds: What happens if we don't and they stay? It's a dilemma a number of firms, and not a few architecture schools, are facing – to train or not to train? In those that don't offer training and mentoring, the assumption is you will seek these out on your own. But the reality is that this creates a sink or swim culture, where you are expected to learn on the job as you go.

At a roundtable discussion at Accelerate AEC in New York City in May 2019 with design professionals who are passionate about mentoring in architecture and technology, the consensus was that there is not as much mentoring happening today as in the past. Why that is might be due to a number of factors: it is harder to mentor with certainty in a whitewater world; the next generation works in tools the previous generation cannot speak to; and, doing the work of two or three people doesn't leave much time for mentoring.

There are firmwide mentoring programmes and professional mentoring groups (such as the Chicago AIA Bridge mentoring scheme) for emerging professionals, but is there less mentoring today of mid-career architects than in the recent past? Trina Sandschafer sees mentorship vary from firm to firm. 'At my prior firm, there was not a mentorship programme – so I set to work with some colleagues, and we started one,' says Sandschafer. 'This was primarily focused on emerging professionals, as are most mentorship programmes. I do think there is a void for mid-career professionals. I was searching for a mentor and they were hard to find. I specifically wanted someone outside of my office for a broader perspective. Everyone can benefit from mentorship, no matter their age or seniority level. At my current firm we are working to broaden the role of mentorship to include everyone from senior leadership to emerging professionals. The leaders of our firm have executive coaches, and I value the importance that has been placed on continued growth and mentorship.'

Elliot Glassman enjoys providing mentoring for students and emerging professionals. 'But I don't feel that I have really been mentored that much myself, especially at this stage,' says Glassman. 'Part of it is that I don't think I am very good at asking for guidance; I very much act as a lone wolf instinctively. But I'd like to think that if someone showed an interest in providing some mentorship, I would be receptive. I have always been very interested in developing myself as a leader and have read books to help me develop those skills (inspired by my organisational psychologist wife). I even was the one to suggest leadership training at my quarterly reviews. While my company was receptive to the idea, nothing has really materialised.'

'I do believe the idea of mentorship has been on the decline over the last 10–15 years,' says David Swain. 'Ironically, many offices start "mentorship" programmes but often interest dies after kicking off the process. There no longer is the time available to mentor younger staff. At the end of the day it comes down to "it will take x number of hours to do it myself, or two times x to mentor someone else". Office leaders want to commit the time to the mentor, but the reality is the time just does not exist. Basically, either adapt, learn and embrace new technology, or a career will stagnate.'

As the speed of practice has increased, Matt Dumich believes mentoring has suffered. 'Mentoring in the office is inconsistent and often depends on the project team leaders to identify teachable moments in daily practice. It can be difficult to find broader, impartial career guidance within firms,' says Dumich. 'After earning my licence, I had many questions about the next steps in navigating my career path. Two colleagues and I co-founded an AIA Chicago programme to address these questions for ourselves and our peers. Bridge is a leadership programme pairing young architects with FAIA mentors to discuss career advancement and the future of the profession. Since its inception in 2009, Bridge has formed lasting multi-generational mentoring relationships and provided leadership development for more than 150 emerging architects.'

There is another reason for the decline in mentoring. Evan Troxel believes there has been less mentoring in recent years because there is a misunderstanding around how mentorship works. 'It's my perception that emerging professionals often wait for mentorship to happen to them,' says Troxel. 'Rather, I've found the most successful team members proactively seek it out. They ask good questions and find the right people to ask. They are always observing the learning, and they are thirsty for knowledge and won't stop until they get what they need. There is no excuse, in our information-filled society, to be waiting around to hopefully get what you need to level up in your career. Don't wait for the official mentorship programme to start (because it probably won't). Figure out what you need and go get it yourself. There are more than enough resources and people out there willing to help, but take it upon yourself to ask and do the work to find it.'

Is there less mentoring because there is less loyalty? Is there a 'why train the competition' attitude? Do mid-career architects need to self-mentor? To find out, do we need to ask an executive coach? 'There has been a trend in most recent years among all professionals and business networks [promoting the need for] "mentoring", and lots of business coaches willing to take your cash [in exchange for] such services. How successful some of these initiatives are remains to be seen,' says Zoe Hooton. 'I participated in the RIBA national rollout of the mentoring training and it had surprising results. While most practices were there to focus on the younger staff and students, it highlighted the need for leaders to really develop their own skills, and the importance of mid-career architects training and looking for mentors themselves. Unlike their younger counterparts, mid-career architects need to take more ownership in looking for ways in which mentors can influence and navigate their own performance. Cross-professional networks can be a vital source for this direction. I have found Women in Property, local Chambers of Commerce and Local Enterprise Partnerships to be great sources of brains to pick. I have then approached those that would be helpful to me and arranged informal sessions to meet.'

Emily Grandstaff-Rice has been troubled by this trend, which she believes is a function of the 2008 recession. 'For the architects that survived, we had to maintain the same level of productivity with fewer resources,' says

Grandstaff-Rice. 'As a result, the demands of our performance remain, or even have grown, without compensatory support. There is less administrative support, smaller project teams, and increased expectations from clients – all for the same fees. The greatest resource one can give is time. I see leaders being overworked, and therefore having less ability to slow down and provide the mentoring that mid-career professionals need. Sometimes I feel like I am in a netherworld – not a shareholder, and too experienced to be emerging. To use the metaphor of sinking or swimming, I am comfortably treading water. I am thriving but also without a clear direction of where I might find the island.'

## Training and learning at mid-career

There is less training, but the newer generation of senior management is recognising this as an issue and working to reverse the trend.
– Michael Riley

My sense of training issues is not specific to early-, mid- or later-career architects. I suspect the lack of training may have more to do with larger, corporate firms: budget constraints, establishing uniformity across a large organisation, challenge with standards, lack of consistent staff, varying benchmark quality between offices, and differences in clients, project types and scale.
– Joe Cliggott

After qualifying in 1991 Alison Brooks never had in-practice training, but in 1999 one of her employees taught her to draw using CAD. 'Practising architecture is nonstop learning – architects have an individual professional duty to constantly reinforce their expertise,' says Brooks. 'You cannot simply ride the wave of practice. I invest a lot in my architects. They have huge amounts of BIM/Revit training and teach each other. I encourage my architects to attend conferences and other learning initiatives that relate to our work and our mission. I firmly believe that architects should take the initiative, not wait around. If you want something, go for it, just make it happen.'

*skills*
*knowledge*
*expertise*

*unlearning*
*letting go*
*abandoning ideas*

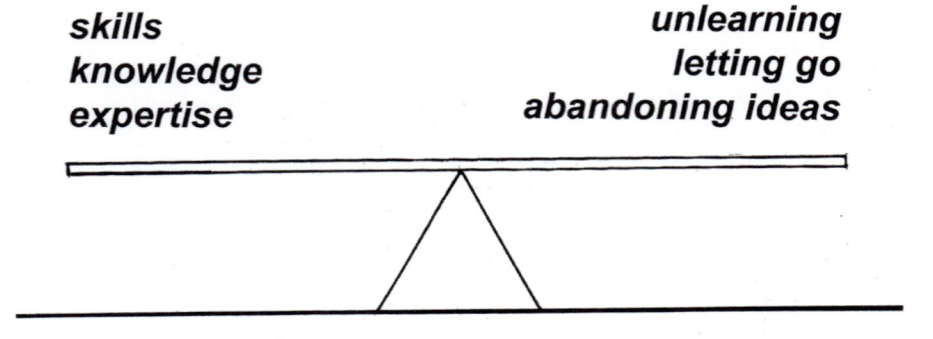

Fig 8.7: By mid-career, what we know and learn has to be balanced with what we know and need to unlearn

Mid-career architects know it is not enough to just show up and do the work. They have to attend training and events that relate to the company's mission, not necessarily their own. In this case you need to align your mission with that of your company, and ideally the two overlap a great deal. There is learning, but also recognise the importance of *unlearning* (which of course is not the same as forgetting); this comes to mid-career architects with surprising ease as their lives become more complicated, and at mid-career they continue to age. Architects adapt, stay current and avoid becoming obsolete by first unlearning then relearning.[32]

'The increased focus on quality workplaces has been helpful to staff seeking mentorship, but not all firms have been quick to provide opportunities or change bad habits,' says Lora Teagarden. 'The sink or swim mentality, in my experience, comes out in two main situations: bad workplace in general, and instances where money or time is tight. In lean economies, the easy way out is for a firm to cut all auxiliary spending – including mentorship and leadership training opportunities (everything from conference and out-of-office opportunities to non-billable internal development) – in an effort to allow the firm to get through rough spots. This can work for very short periods of time but is troubling when firms don't re-initiate these development opportunities as quickly as they are able. Sometimes the fear of spending money prevents a bad boss from seeing that not training their employees makes for bad employees, or employees lost to other companies who actually want to invest in their team.'

There are reasons why there may be less training. In school there's the availability of tutorials, but the question is whether school is the right place for training in tools. School expects graduates to learn in practice, and practitioners wonder why employees aren't trained in school. 'There is a noticeable discrepancy between learning at university and learning in practice,' says Andy Watts. 'This can relate both to project processes but also to more technical and digital skills. Some institutions – the Architectural Association, the Bartlett, Pratt – have put in place measures that seek to bridge the gap regarding these latter skills through dedicated courses and research groups. However, the demand is outstripping the supply. As the industry moves fast, it also requires senior staff to stay abreast of current practices and not live by rules of thumb established over the past decade or two. It places an onus on practice to fulfil those training needs. Take digital competency, for example. At Grimshaw, we have a strong training agenda where we offer all staff – from new starters to project leaders to partners – training, in both skill and theory, across a wide spectrum of the services that we provide in-house.'

'Approach your firm to discuss potential training and mentoring and the context of your work; they will be critical to your growth as a new leader,' suggests senior design manager at Laing O'Rourke John Edwards. 'Firms need to develop leaders to support younger members of their teams in their development.'

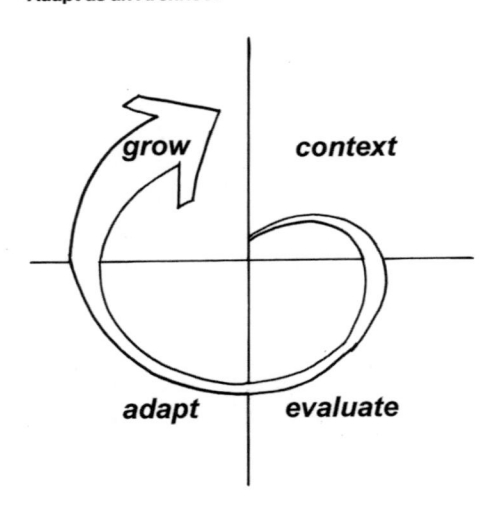

Fig 8.8: To rewire and grow, you must understand and evaluate your situation while adapting to change

Angela Watson makes an excellent point by asking what it means to 'train' in leadership and in mid-career issues. 'Training is very efficient for processes and standards,' says Watson. 'Training to be a good manager, a good designer, a good colleague or a good leader is much more difficult, and has to do with evolving capability of individuals to grow into their fullest capacity. Maybe the biggest gap in our profession has been the lack of growth opportunities or education for those in mid-career and beyond. We should always get better at what we do. I'm lucky to work for a firm where those opportunities are available, although they still have to be discovered by the individual. One of our goals is to develop a more deliberate way of helping individuals on their own path to becoming better at what they want to do.'

'There's much that we learn simply on the job about the transition from production to project management, from project management to business development, and from leading by doing to leading by empowering,' says associate partner at BKV Group Susan Morgan. 'It's that last bridging that would benefit from more insight and guidance. The learning-to-let-go moment, and the embracing the value and outcomes of using time and talents to ensure our staff and teams are empowered to do their best work. What many people struggle with, or don't realise they're struggling with, is that they view the value and reward of production as being greater than the value and the reward of empowering your teams to do their best work. Because production is one last vestige of architecture as an act of making, it is difficult to let go; oddly enough, while many people enter architecture because of their facility with drawing or with abstract and conceptual thought, these are also individuals who are suited to leadership through vision and practice, but they don't identify those skills as being "architecture". One of the challenges of navigating evolving roles in architecture is how we adjust internal narratives for what counts as participation in the dialogue of design: coming to a place where we can appreciate that setting a vision or providing course corrections is equally valuable as being the hands that mark the page or screen.'

Earlier in his career Randy Guillot saw more formalised training. 'The computer was a largely unfamiliar tool, and training seemed like the right model to bring people up to speed as quickly as possible,' says Guillot. '"Tools based" technical training like this has largely gone away, replaced with self-directed online tutorials, much in the way education has "flipped the classroom", watching lectures online and discussing in groups. What has not gone away in most successful offices is a strong mentor/protégé relationship model, where you learn from those who have done it previously on the job. As project fees have slimmed down there's been a natural tendency to minimise this perceived "overlap" in function of team members. Couple this with the ability to generate design solutions and construction drawings using digital information passed from one project to the next, and it is easy to lose focus around the idea that transfer of information digitally is not the same thing as a teaching relationship between one person to the next.'

## From mentoring to coaching

To Randy Guillot, coaching and leadership skill development are among the most important aspects of successful mid-career transition. Like many of his peers, he was generally educated around learning design and technical skills at the most fundamental levels. 'Early career is spent honing those skills, learning to work in teams and understand clients and context and the other things motivating the work,' explains Guillot. 'My experience was always on-the-job training, working with more senior designers and learning from them. What I didn't fully appreciate at the time was that I was learning far more than design and technical excellence. I was learning how to navigate the profession. I was learning how to relate to people and develop influence by understanding what motivates people. In my opinion, leadership training as a mid-career architect is essential in taking your early career experiences and applying them to be the most effective leader you can going forward. This is different than a focus on the work exclusively. It's something that's not taught in school, and something that at the time appears to be yet another thing I have to do in addition to getting my project work done. But I believe a successful mid-career has as much to do with how you relate to people as it does to how you relate to the work. Learning what kind of leader you are by being part of a good strength-based coaching programme can make all the difference in setting you up for success, helping you focus on what you're really good at and what brings you joy. During the early part of your career you are amassing experiences. At some point these experiences stop shaping you and you start shaping them. It's at that inflection point where you begin to understand what kind of leader you are. When you realise you have the power and the potential to positively influence not just clients and their projects but the broader team and the world around you. I was never offered coaching to any significant degree. I invested in myself so I could be a better leader. For me that looks like a balance of human empathy and a rigorous focus on design excellence. It involves leading people in a supportive creative culture around design excellence and client service. What I learned through strength-based coaching was that the unique balance of these two things in my life allowed me to be a more authentic leader and translated into more genuine team and client relationships.'

**be connected to the world around you**

**continue learning**

**hone your skills**

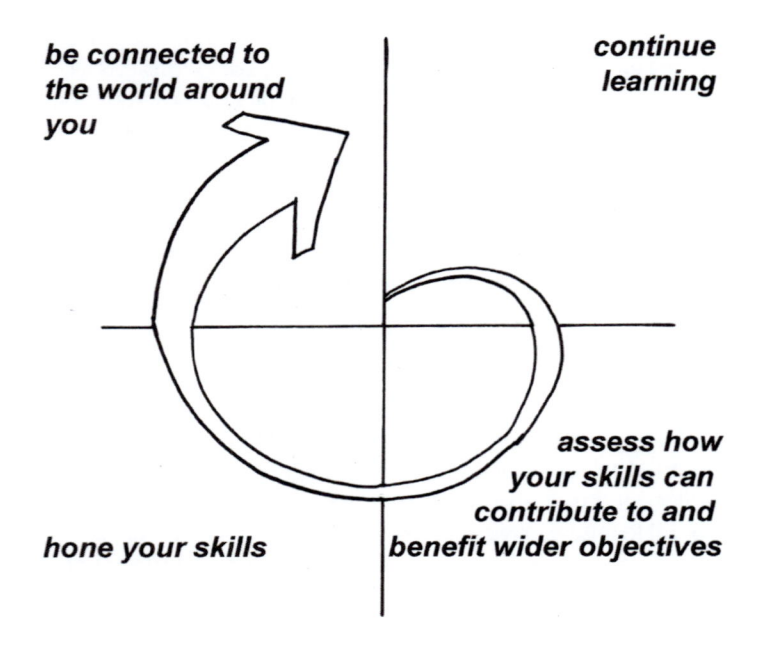

**assess how your skills can contribute to and benefit wider objectives**

Fig 8.9: To rewire, you must continue learning, assess and hone your strengths, and connect with those who might benefit from your skills and interests

At the firm where Angela Mazzi works, GBBN, mentoring and training of staff at all levels is a high priority. 'While training and mentoring are certainly essential to emerging architects, you never stop needing them,' says Mazzi. 'We must all either evolve or stagnate, and continuing to be accountable for your evolution to another person is perhaps more valuable at mid-career. I've sought out quite a bit of private coaching on my own as well. Currently, my company has our leadership working with a career coach who helps us specifically focus not just on our development but on how we can work most effectively with others and optimise our leadership skills.'

### ASK THIS

I have in the past [mentored] and continue to mentor a few individuals. More often than not they struggle to accumulate field experience in one firm setting and struggle to accumulate a variety of design sectors/types in another setting. My litmus test continues to be, "Do you feel confident you could walk out of here tomorrow and run your own firm; do you have the skills and knowhow to accomplish this with minimal competence?" This is often a wake-up call for what the traditional role of architect demands. **[Henry David Louth]**

## ASK THIS

To believe our profession will continue to practise as it has for the past century, with principal architects directing young staff to produce monumental award-winning designs, is a nostalgic and narrow-minded perception. The changes to practice through globalisation and the information revolution in which we live will have far more impact. The architecture profession is not unique to these changes, but as visionaries we can identify outside forces and adapt if we are willing to embrace them as they are recognised. A few thoughts are as follows:

- How can we leverage prefabrication of building components/systems for mass production to reduce construction cost and construction duration, to design healthier/resilient spaces, to engage with sophisticated and intellectual intelligence technology?
- How can we collect data from our buildings and the occupants (clients) to better understand components and systems, to better [design our] indoor environment to relate to the end user?
- What is the next-generation business model? How will the design profession continue to evolve and engage with the next generation of architects, clients, built environment [professionals], etc?
- How can we better partner with the construction industry and how [can] we leverage our partnership and collaboration with them to produce a well-designed building that exceeds the client's expectation and deliver an outstanding project that is within budget and on schedule, and profitable for all?

[Virginia E Marquardt]

## ASK THIS

Trina Sandschafer recognises that architecture is changing. 'There is no question about that,' she acknowledges. Here are some questions Sandschafer has been thinking about:

**Community** – In a world that is more connected than ever, we have also become disconnected. How can architecture promote community – in a residential building? In a school? In an office? In an institution? In a neighbourhood? How does physical space influence connection to place at various scales?

**Wellness** – Human beings spend almost 90% of their time indoors – in buildings and spaces we create. It is our responsibility to make that space in sync with what human bodies need to thrive. Biorhythms, biomechanics, light, air and connection are all critical.

**Sustainability** – Beautiful buildings are no longer enough. We must do more. We are running out of time and resources to make a difference. Buildings are among the largest users of energy and producers of greenhouse gases on the planet. The time to act is now. How can we lead by example?

**Innovation** – How can we foster innovation? How can we use VR to change the design process? How do we put our clients in the driver's seat of design? How can we use technology innovation to create drawings sets faster? How can we work with our construction partners to adapt and evolve construction?

**Storytelling** – Storytelling is in our DNA. It is part of what makes us human. How can architects support this? Yes, we want to tell our own stories, but most importantly, how do we use design to help our clients tell their stories? 'As I write this, the world is in the grips of the COVID-19 pandemic,' says Sandschafer. 'There will be implications across all built spaces based on this incident. As a profession, we are still learning and evaluating what those will be. The firms and leaders that adapt will be best poised to lead what is on the other side of this pandemic.'

## TRY THIS

Personally, I chose very early in my career to engage in shorter-duration, faster-turnaround projects as a means to accumulate experiences, confidence and credibility quickly. I was travelling regionally on behalf of the firm I worked with in the States leading various additions, renovations and retrofits because I could hold a conversation, problem-solve, and could traverse uncertain situations with limited oversight, not because I could hold a mouse (which I can do as well). **[Henry David Louth]**

## TRY THIS

It is important to continue to follow your passions to remain excited and engaged throughout your career. This is a regular process of critical self-reflection and situational awareness to keep evaluating, adapting and growing. It also requires finding new ways to create value as one advances. As experienced architects, our value is in our ideas and ability to synthesise complex problems. **[Matt Dumich]**

## TRY THIS

Early career development is about seeing a broad spectrum of capacities to make informed decisions early (not just technical, not just software, not just delivery, not just design acumen, not just academic).

Generalist skills shared across disciplines are invaluable, as they reinforce core skills, they are versatile, they are adaptable, they are problem-solvers, and when the worst hits they are dependable and [you] are better prepared to negotiate a lot of variables simultaneously. **[Henry David Louth]**

## TRY THIS

Embrace and continuously immerse yourself in emerging architecture and design technologies. The more you know and understand these tools of our industry, the more value you will add to your firm's projects. Think about emerging technologies – like augmented reality – and how they can transform your practice of architecture, and challenge yourself to integrate these tools into your work. **[Mary Shaffer]**

## TRY THIS

To accomplish this, we need to learn how to ask the right questions of those who know things that we don't. Maybe most importantly, we need to recognise what we don't know and accept the need to collaborate and to be dependent on the performance of others. This is an important skill. How we ask is going to have a direct impact on how willing somebody will be to share their knowledge with us. **[Angela Watson]**

# 9: Reinforce

Fig 9.1: Adapting to near-constant change in your career requires you to balance competing forces

## Staff of any gender will not stay for long in a company that adversely affects their work-life balance.

Fundamentally we're part of a time-hungry creative profession that operates on tight timeframes and low profit margins. Taking a year out for maternity leave (a statutory right in the UK) is inevitably a career interruption. This is true for any person in any career. It's particularly onerous for architects. Competition deadlines and project schedules wait for no one.
– Alison Brooks

This is one of our great questions. As one of the few larger architecture firms that is a women-owned business, this is something we should be able to answer, but it's not so simple to pin down.
– Angela Watson

Support us.
– Virginia E Marquardt


Female architects leave the profession at a higher rate than male architects. What can firms do to help female architects stay? What can professional organisations do to help female architects remain when the economics just don't compute? 'It takes a long time and is expensive to become an architect in comparison to how much average architects are typically paid – and compared to other professions with similar educational durations,' says Sara Beardsley. 'This makes it a difficult profession to pursue for anyone but affects women more profoundly because there is a lot of pressure and early career demands, as well as low pay, at the same time as they may be considering having a family. For many young women, the economics of working while paying for daycare, especially early in a career, simply do not compute, and when overtime and licensure requirements are factored in, it becomes even more difficult. Some young mothers actually do not have much "net income" at all for a period of time, when daycare costs, transportation and other work-related expenses are factored in.'

Beardsley continues: 'In order for a larger number of women [with or without children] to choose to stay, it not only requires a career that pays the bills, but one that is rewarding, accommodates for work-life balance when needed, and where there is a path upward into leadership roles. Issues like unconscious bias, and less availability of mentorship among women and minorities [partially due to comparatively smaller numbers of existing leaders who are women and minorities] are well documented. Studies have also shown that women do not primarily leave the profession due to work-life balance concerns; they also leave due to lack of fulfilment or overall satisfaction with their career, which may occur for a variety of reasons. In project teams or with clients that have a strong top-down hierarchy and are not structured to foster collaborative design, some women feel that they struggle to be "heard".'

'Professional organisations can continue to advocate for and promote the importance of architecture as a profession, so that all architects can realise fair fees and better stability and respect as professionals,' continues Beardsley. 'Architecture schools and the leaders of the licensure process need to consider how they can be more cost-effective and accessible to all. Firms can be supportive of each employee and work with them in consideration of their individual needs. Remote working, part-time opportunities and flexible work schedules are very important to young mothers in particular, and should not be obstacles to long-term advancement. Young women can advocate for themselves and seek out effective mentors, whether they be male, or female.'

Fig 9.2: Team meeting at director Sara Beardsley's firm, Adrian Smith + Gordon Gill

Women are leaving the field, and those who stay in many cases aren't thriving. That said, this is not strictly a female architect question, as we'll reference issues facing parents – particularly but not by any means exclusively women – at this critical time of their career, when they are also most likely to be starting families.

## Managing parental responsibilities

At the graduate level and throughout their twenties the male/female split among architects is 50/50, but then the rate falls off for female students and professionals, with the overall split in the UK being approximately 72/28 (ARB-registered architects) in favour of men. Within the RIBA the proportion of men to women is even higher. 'Firms need to actively aspire and aim for a gender-balanced workforce; they need to employ female staff and then ensure there are equal opportunities for career progression and equal pay,' says Philip Twiss, who cited these statistics. 'Encourage and facilitate flexible working and recognise that the family comes first; increasingly this applies to male as well as female staff. Staff of any gender will not stay for long in a company that significantly adversely affects their work-life balance. Staff of any gender need to see role models at senior management levels to know that there is a path for them. Firms can ensure there are appropriate mentoring schemes and establish links with women's networks even if that means they need to connect to other companies. Professional

# 9: Reinforce

bodies need to lead by example: three of the last six presidents of the RIBA have been female; the director of my local RIBA region is female, and the president, vice-president and secretary of my local branch of the RIBA, the Birmingham Architectural Association, are female. Governance bodies can include policies in their professional codes of conduct to enforce diversity of all kinds, whether gender, sexuality or ethnicity, and where necessary investigate practices for non-compliance. The change is not something that will happen overnight but it is happening, albeit painfully slowly.'

Fig 9.3: The London office of senior associate and design director Philip Twiss's firm, Gensler, is conducive to spontaneous interpersonal interaction and engagement

'The biggest thing firms can do to help women stay is hire women architects – immediately after graduation,' suggests Trina Sandschafer, who practises what she preaches. '50% of architectural graduates are women. 50% of all new hires are not women. We can start there. If the playing field is even from the beginning, we will not be facing such discrepancy in later years. When we fill architecture roles at every level, insist that the candidate pool include women. Do not stop until the offices we work in reflect the population we design for. This applies to all the ways in which we can better reflect the diversity of the people who occupy our buildings.'

Another solution is for firms to work smart: i.e. fewer but better (more flexible) hours. Virginia E Marquardt provides a slightly different perspective from some other mid-career female architects, as she doesn't have children. 'With my husband being autistic, I am his support system and sometimes caregiver,' explains Marquardt. 'Many older architects are their parents' and older children's support system, too. We need to open up our discussion and talk about not just females but about all types of support that is needed within the firms to support our employees at different stages of their careers and lives. To keep good team members/employees, maintain morale and have a healthy work environment, a good boss – whether the employee is female or male – needs to be supportive and understanding of all of their employees' needs. Because it's not just females that are the caregivers, males are, too. And at different stages of our lives, we are caregivers for our children, spouses, parents, siblings, and maybe grandparents, too.'

Just the other day Marquardt reminded her team to pace themselves when she noticed after a deadline that they were continuing to work 50–60 hours a week. 'It's easy to start putting in a few hours here and there, and then working weekends, too,' says Marquardt. 'To remember we'll be working anywhere from 25–40-plus years in our careers; the project schedule is a marathon, not a race. We need to maintain a balanced life, to find time for family and friends, exercise, hobbies, eating healthily and sleep. Our brains need time to rest and we will be better for it. I would rather see my team work 40 hours a week – that is more intense and gratifying – than 50 or 60 hours a week and burning out.'

## What firms can do

We have a long way to go to be more inclusive as a profession, by recruiting and retaining diverse talent that reflects the society we serve. Greater inclusivity is everyone's responsibility, and I believe that the results benefit all architects.
– Matt Dumich

Firms must make their teams feel well supported and allow them to work in flexible ways: being as flexible as possible, allowing female architects to set the level of the work they want to do, allowing them to fit their working week around other responsibilities and work from home at different times when needed.
– John Edwards

Female architects deal with the burden of burnout culture of the profession along with biological pressures of motherhood. Licensure and the mental load of caregiving while balancing full-time employment isn't an ideal situation without the privilege of a proper support system. The dropout rate can be slowed by providing part-time and remote working opportunities as well as educating firm leaders about the diverse needs of female architects to thrive in the profession.
– Meghana Joshi

## 9: Reinforce

Firms could give female architects one less thing to fight for. But what is that one thing? If only we could all agree. Danei Cesario is passionate about this topic as a feminist, a woman of colour from another country, and as a mother of two young daughters. 'You cannot flourish where you're not welcome,' says Cesario. 'There is historic undermining and lack of celebration for women's contributions, in architecture, in the home, everywhere. Most of the "credit" we have been given has been an outcome of protest or fight. One major shift firms can make would be to give us one less thing to fight about. If our male counterparts are able to achieve without a similar battle, why can't women? We don't want a battle on every one of life's frontiers. Making women feel welcome, appreciated, elevated, seen and celebrated makes us stay. My current boss has been a proponent of that even prior to us working together. She advocates for talent and acknowledges it publicly. In turn, that influences how other members of leadership regard the staff.'

Fig 9.4: Danei Cesario was invited as a guest critic to Pratt Institute's Master's in Architecture final review by her friend and frequent collaborator Professor Irina Schneid

There is a lot that firms can do to make workplaces fairer and more inclusive, says Chithra Marsh. 'Things are improving, but there is still some way to go to removing the barriers to career progression and equality in pay. Most notably there is a tendency for female architects to step away from their careers once they become parents. This usually coincides with them reaching mid-career and a level of responsibility which makes the break from career harder. Even after the shortest maternity leave it might be perceived that the world has moved on without them and [this] can knock their confidence.'

Marsh continues: 'Good workplace policies should [make] this transition back into the workplace as easy as possible, and allow them to feel confident in taking up where they left off. Organised KIT (keep in touch) days are a great way for a woman to ease back into the working environment.' (As is SPLIT, for shared parental leave in touch.) 'Once back to work, allowing agreed part-time or flexible working can provide balance at a time when every part of their lives feels disrupted,' says Marsh. 'Open communication between the senior management and the individual would help them to know that support is available and that they will not be penalised for having the added responsibilities at home.'

For female architects with kids, the onus is on the firm. 'Females tend to be the main caretakers of children and elderly relatives, which can often put them in a compromised position, not being able to balance work and family life,' says Zoe Hooton. 'Professional organisations should be adaptable, honest and work with women and parents to balance the demands of both. Our experience is that it has to be a reciprocal relationship, but practice must be the first to offer a hand. The demands of parenthood, if looked at over a longer time period, are also a short time in an employee's career, so therefore organisations must support staff in order to be rewarded with loyal employees.'

We also need to support working mothers far better, says Tom Lee. 'As a new father myself, I can still go to work and focus without much interruption. For a new mother, especially if breastfeeding, time and energy are taxed in ways that society doesn't fully embrace. Though appropriately equipped "mothering" rooms are great, an equally necessary accommodation is time and flexibility tailored to each new mother, while providing assurances that opportunities for growth will be carefully preserved and not just delegated to others with fewer time constraints.'

A big inflection point for female architects is when they start a family, says Evelyn Lee. 'Once architects figure out a way to increase their profit margin, they can then offer to female employees similar benefits that are offered in the tech world, including long-term paid maternity leave, beyond the minimum that is required. If your firm is bringing in more money, there are definitely things they can do with that money to attract and retain female architects. Look for ways to do asynchronous project scheduling so people are working when they are able to work. And figure out a way to accommodate people on a part-time schedule. If you give them that flexibility and ability, they may very well come back full-time. Firms need to figure out how to have permanent part-time employees and allow people to do that.'

Another solution is to pay women more; for firms to show support in the form of higher salaries. Women in architecture earn 80% of what men in architecture earn.[33] Firms recognise this and should do something about it. 'In many cases, simply paying women more (or at least the equivalent of their male counterparts) can make a big difference,' says Alexandra Pollock. 'Childcare, especially in urban areas, is very expensive. Since women typically make less than men, they may make the choice to stay home after looking at the maths. Providing as much flexibility as possible is very important as well. Some parents may feel comfortable coming back to work full-time after having a child, while others may not. Allowing parents the freedom to take the time they need, or to return back on a reduced schedule, can help make that transition easier. Flexible work hours and/or the option to work from home can make a big difference as well. As I write this, our whole firm is working from home, as is the majority of the country. Coming out of this public health crisis, I think the comfort level with working from home in our industry will be much higher – I am hopeful this will help retain more women in the industry.'

There is the reality that firms have been working with reduced fees since the last recession, and that many architecture firms operate on low profit margins. Now we have to wonder what the impact will be of the recession brought about by the pandemic. 'As I understand it, female architects leave primarily because the salary/childcare cost/time equation doesn't stack up,' says Alison Brooks. 'Pay levels in architecture are quite low because fee levels are so low. The lack of fixed fee scales has made architecture one of the most brutally competitive professions – not only in design terms but in fee-bidding. If architects stopped fee-undercutting, and professional fee scales were established as in Germany, average salaries would increase. If salaries were higher, female architects wouldn't feel that they're "paying out most of their salary in childcare", a perspective that makes working seem less worthwhile. We need to be clearer about the principle that the cost (and burden) of childcare should be apportioned equally between both parents. Working through the COVID-19 pandemic has proven that home working and flexible hours is an effective solution for all employees, regardless of gender or the fact of parenthood. But it will certainly help female architects, and parents generally, spend less time travelling and more time with their children.'

Another solution is to promote women more, providing them with support in the form of voice, leadership, status and recognition. Support women in architecture by keeping them engaged, addressing this not as a female architect problem but as an employee engagement problem. 'We need to continue to promote women in architecture, and that includes doing a much better job supporting working mums,' says Tom Lee. 'Women bring a very valuable perspective to a practice, and as evidenced by the fact that the majority of my more recent clients – the decision-makers – are female; women make great leaders and should be better represented among leadership in architecture as a whole. We're behind the curve as a profession.'

'When firms limit exposure and opportunity for female employees, they will find themselves obsolete,' says Emily Grandstaff-Rice. 'There has long been an affinity bias among architects that female designers have to work hard to assimilate to. Some of us do it better than others. Firms that do not limit potential of women to lead teams, design and pursue technical pathways see greater retention. This is something practitioners need to work hard at, but it is essential to keeping female employees engaged and contributing at the highest levels.'

'The one thing I can think of that causes people in general, and maybe female architects in particular, to stay is to give them responsibility and opportunity early,' says Angela Watson. 'When anybody is engaged in their work and it becomes something that is meaningful to them, not only as a job but as something that gives them balance in their life, they are a lot more likely to stay. Of course, that needs to be supported by flexibility and control over work-life balance.'

Another solution is to mentor equally. 'We are seeing a real transition in the profession in terms of numbers. Our office is at least 50% woman, and at last we have gone from one woman partner among 10 to five out of 14,' says Ted Hyman. 'They are some of the best programmers, managers and technical architects; the issue we continue to struggle with is the number of women in design leadership roles (those conceptual designers). This may have more to do with the way gender plays into conversations, and we are working hard to try and unravel why this is so prevalent, not only in our firm but nationally. Mentorship is the single biggest thing we can all do to help change the face of the profession for both gender and race inequality.'

Fig 9.5: ZGF's work teams often become a second family of sorts. Even when separated due to a global pandemic, it is still important to celebrate birthdays and anniversaries. And, perhaps even more importantly, to embrace the fact that a kiddo or two will take over the call from time to time!

Fig 9.6: Virtual meeting platforms like Microsoft Teams and Zoom make it not only possible but incredibly simple to bring ZGF's teams together, even when they span six offices across the US and Canada

'Mentor equally while understanding the differences in each person's personality and background,' says Lora Teagarden. 'Give equal access to project opportunities, management opportunities, client interaction, meeting attendance, construction phase oversight, contract training, etc. Treat them like a skilled employee that you want to keep around, and they'll give you loyalty in return.'

## What professional organisations can do

Professional organisations can only do so much. They can create language around culture, creating a culture that is more inclusive.
– Evelyn Lee

The Equality and Human Rights Commission provides helpful guidance to employers if they sign up to its 'Working Forward' pledges. This [shows] how to support all your staff, making the workplace inclusive for everyone regardless of background or circumstance.
– Chithra Marsh

Organisations such as Women in Property are a great source of support, according to Chithra Marsh. 'Employers can fund membership for their female members of staff. They can then benefit from joining the mentoring programme available for women at all stages of their career. They can meet and learn from like-minded individuals. They offer a series of organised opportunities where females within the property and development community can get together, network and share their stories. They have branches nationwide. I have been a member of the North West committee for a number of years and am a former NW branch chairman. The support I have gained throughout this time has been invaluable and continues to this day.'

Angela Mazzi has been particularly pondering this issue as a new AIA Fellow and as a local AIA chapter board member when a Women in Architecture group formed. 'This topic is clearly not the only point of discussion, but maybe talking more about how to say yes to what you really want and letting go of guilt as you find YOUR way through what having a career means is worth putting out there,' suggests Mazzi.

Professional organisations can assist in multiple ways: celebrate those firms that are providing the right blueprint, call out those firms that are not, train and educate young female architects for the difficult conversation around salary negotiations, and provide greater salary transparency across the profession so that everyone understands how they fit within the structure, says Joe Cliggott. 'Firms need to treat family obligations for men and women equally – generous parental leave, not just maternity leave, needs to be the norm,' says Nicole Semple. 'We can't expect to elevate women if they are still expected to bear the largest parenting burdens. Mentor, promote and provide opportunities for women as often as men. When young professionals see themselves reflected in leadership, not only will that organisation start to reflect their values, but they'll see a place for themselves as well. Once an organisation's leadership reflects the diversity of the profession, more people will see a role for themselves.'

An architectural practice soapbox Donna Sink often stands on is this: workplace policies that are good for women are good for families, and every gender benefits from a community made of strong, happy families. 'It really should be commonly accepted that employees with young children in daycare need flexibility in their schedules to allow for sick days and whatnot; it should also be commonly accepted that parents attending soccer games or school plays for their children is a benefit to everyone, and the flexibility to do so should not be difficult to achieve,' says Sink. 'Rather than consider workplace flexibility to be tagged as a "women's issue" we need to think of it as a family, community issue, and recognise that healthy communities are built on people being able to build valuable, balanced lives that include both work and home life.'

## Family and work-life balance

Balance is a joke – you can work hard and live hard, but not always at the same time. If we have the assumption that candidates need to suffer to achieve professional status, female architects will continue to leave.
– Emily Grandstaff-Rice

Yes, work-life balance is achievable, but you need to work for a firm that values it. I believe that the firms that value work-life balance have a much richer and more diverse workforce, and that in turn has a positive impact on the work they do and the designs they generate.
– Alexandra Pollock

There is nothing as humbling as a personal health emergency to put things into perspective.
– Emily Grandstaff-Rice

Just as adaptive learning systems are personalised – tailoring instruction to the needs of each student – so too responses to this question are different for each individual. And again, is work-life balance strictly a female architect question? 'No, it is not,' responded several of the architects I spoke with. There are other questions we need to consider. Work–life balance: Is this a key driver for many at this stage of their careers? (Yes, it is.) Do we work to live or live to work? Are architects all-in at mid-career versus seeking balance? 60% of female architects have left the industry (in the UK) in between completing Part 3 and the five- to ten-year period leading up to them becoming associates.

When was the last time a male architect was asked how he achieves work-life balance? asks Trina Sandschafer. 'My female colleagues and I are asked all the time. My male colleagues? Almost never. Women are asked this work–life question in the thinly veiled question of how do you work and have a family? If men are asked how they work and maintain life balance, it is more likely to be how do they find time to go to the gym, not how do they have a family. We will never solve life–work if it is viewed as a women's question. Men and women both have families. We both have careers. We both contribute on both fronts. It is challenging, yes, but we both do it. We will only solve this question when men and women are viewed equally at work and at home. Work–life balance is important to everyone – not just those (women and men) with families. I would hope that everyone strives to have a work-life balance. If that means spending time with your children, excellent. If it means spending time with your pet, gardening, painting, travelling, playing an instrument or reading a book – great. All creative minds need time away from the office to recharge. Good ideas come in the space we give our minds to rest. We should all strive for this balance.'

Zoe Hooton works in a female-supportive practice, 'but it is difficult to work within a professional atmosphere and be pregnant, never mind a parent,' says Hooton. 'The early-morning/late-night networking events, the awkwardness of revising my director's contract which didn't include maternity leave, or the disappointment of winning a job but knowing you're not going to lead it, thrown in with the physical strains of being pregnant, are exhausting. However, what I have found most difficult are my own feelings about my work-life balance and the weight of responsibility I have for my practice. I start maternity leave tomorrow and I am conflicted. I feel sick to my stomach about leaving my practice, work, clients, ongoing projects. I trust my staff and am confident in their abilities, but it's my own guilt that I am wrestling with. My work is my first baby, so how do I cope with this second? We have many parents in our office and the only real way to achieve a life balance is by asking yourself what your priorities are and talking through your needs with your employer. Allowing a staff member a late start once a week so they can take their children to school, or the independence to get a longer holiday each year is worth so much more to many than motivating them with a pay raise. Employers need to be adaptable and employees need to be bold in making clear what their priorities are. So, will work-life balance be achievable for myself in my new chapter? Gosh, I hope so.'

## Is work-life balance achievable? Is it desirable?

I don't believe in the concept of 'work-life balance' if you have a vocation: I am an architect; I structure my life around who I am.
– Alison Brooks

Job candidates have more power than they think. If every candidate asked during their interviews what the firm's policy is on work-life balance, the industry would change.
– John Gresko

Practices have a professional duty of care to their staff, and therefore should bid for jobs at an appropriate level of fees to enable them to resource the project to adequately carry out their professional duties.
– Philip Twiss

Over the last few years, Virginia E Marquardt has had to evaluate what is important in her life, and learn how to balance work and life. 'It's really easy to let architecture and the work take over and become your life,' admits Marquardt. 'In particular, since the economic downturn in the mid-2000s, many of us in our mid-career, Generation X, have had to play multiple roles because of lay-offs. And because of the lay-offs we had our role and responsibilities, and roles and responsibilities of positions above and below us. We worked many hours, many times six to seven days a week and 10–12 (or more) hours a day. Work became our life.'

Marquardt continues: 'Since the economic downturn, many of us have continued to have to play multiple roles, because the middle is missing. Many of the individuals laid-off found alternate careers. And we have had to learn to produce more work with fewer team members. At the same time our clients are requiring faster schedules with reduced fees. After about 10 years of this, I became burned out. I became overwhelmed and lost sight of who I was and what was important in my life, family. Over last few years, I have been refocusing on myself, my husband, my dog and my family as a whole. I'm practising gratitude, mindfulness and meditation, [I've] taken up Pilates, [I'm] eating healthier, getting six to eight hours of sleep. It is not easy, and I have fallen back into old habits quite often, but with the help of my therapist, my husband and my parents I'm starting to have a more balanced life and work.'

Danei Cesario has likened the work-life balance to riding a jet-ski. 'Sometimes you have to lean right, other times left, but the goal is ultimately to stay aboard the jet-ski,' says Cesario. 'It helps tremendously to have support within the home as well as within our workplace. It is not always possible to do all of the things all of the time at an exceptional level. I believe that treating ourselves with grace and patience is achievable. Feeling like we are doing our best and contributing effectively is desirable. How we go about that as life partners, as colleagues, reinforces whether this elusive balance is attainable or not.'

Fig 9.7: Danei Cesario addressing the United Nations General Assembly's Cities + SDGs Panel on the correlation between zero-hunger goals and health in our cities

'It is achievable,' says Diane Reicher Jacobs, 'but you need a team. We seem to forget, as a profession, as human beings, that we thrive on teams. The go-it-alone strategy that pulls us away from the extended family as a unit has been detrimental. It has been an asset for centuries, erased perhaps during the Industrial Revolution. I could not have achieved professional success and raised such good kids without a committed partner and a host of friends and family to share in the joy and responsibility of raising kids, along with creating a vibrant home. It was desirable for me – my kids have watched their parents struggle and succeed and have embraced our professional accomplishments as their own. They know that we are in this together. This is not only work-life balance, but life balance. Viktor Frankl reminds us that our purpose in life is to work and to love. This balance fulfils that purpose harmoniously. As firm leaders we must help others achieve similar successful outcomes as well – however they define it.'

Angela Mazzi believes work-life balance is both desirable and achievable. 'Most firms offer flexible schedules, provide laptops and remote working access to servers, allowing work to happen from anywhere, accommodating for kid transport or getting to a doctor appointment,' says Mazzi. 'Your responsibility is to make the boundaries. A flexible schedule should never mean you are available to everyone on demand, just as it shouldn't mean that you don't have to account for your whereabouts. I have learned the hard way that I need to schedule everything, from the vacation six months out (that I have not yet planned but need to hold a week off on my calendar), to personal appointments and kid pick-ups. Since it's on my calendar, anyone looking to schedule my time has the heads-up to work around those dates and times – and I get to say "no" if they try and schedule me anyway. I am currently attempting, with less success, to schedule blocks of time to work so my whole day won't get consumed with meetings.'

## 'Balance' is different to every person

If the COVID-19 pandemic has a silver lining it may be that firm owners are able to see that working from home or working on flexible schedules is not only possible but beneficial to employee satisfaction, and thus to firm profitability and success.
**– Donna Sink**

COVID-19 is proving that there can be a reasonable work-life balance.
**– Alistair Kell**

The change in working practices enforced by COVID-19 will affect the workforce for years to come. Practices that have resisted working from home have almost overnight been forced to introduce infrastructure to facilitate remote working and trust their staff with the new home working environments.
**– Philip Twiss**

Randy Guillot is a man with four children that range from eighteen to six years of age in a blended family. His particular narrative around work-life balance typically has these responsibilities at the centre. 'But my experience is that whether you have a large family or not, each of us has their own individual struggles with prioritisation and balance in the profession of architecture,' says Guillot. 'In fact, attitudes about work, specifically the number of hours you spend at work, have changed over the years that I've been practising. And I would argue for the better. When I began practice the amount of hours you worked was a badge of honour. Long hours spent at the office created wonderful memories for me with my teammates, but would be seen as extreme by today's standards. I do believe that hard work helped me to establish myself in this profession, but the world has changed and grown in so many ways outside of "work" that the development of well-rounded young professionals is far more balanced today, between life pursuits and work pursuits and everything in between. I write this from my home office as we ride out the COVID-19 crisis in quarantine. Certainly, in this situation, the boundaries between work and life are as blurred as they ever have been in my career. But it does point out that there are many ways that this profession can thrive, and sitting in the studio with your teammates is only one of them. I've always worked a lot of hours; to me that balance of family and work was reasonable. It never left a lot of free time, but that was a trade-off I was willing to make.'

'This is a question that would be answered differently by each individual or family,' says Angela Watson. 'Fulfilment and financial constraints are only two of the many factors at work. Providing flexibility and opportunities to design your own balance is the only viable answer. If a firm can support that and encourage it, they're much more likely to help families and individuals be able to manage those seemingly conflicting pieces of their lives.'

'The biggest aspect to realise around the discussion of work-life balance is that "balance" is different to every person,' says Lora Teagarden. 'My childcare requirements, home situation and financial stresses look completely different from [those of] my co-workers, which makes my work-life balance look different as compared to them. Every person's home life, priorities and background are different and creating a work environment that sees these differences as knowledge assets to a collective team should be a priority for a firm. Women historically have left the profession for a variety of reasons, most of which boil down to the profession being built to fit the personality and needs of a very narrow type of (male) worker. Work–life balance is only achievable when the assumption of a single type of worker is removed and each person is given the freedom and tools to succeed, as well as the time to do so. When a firm gives an employee their trust that they will complete the tasks given to them, without judgement of timing, an employee can succeed without the stressors of home life weighing on them while they sit at work. When a parent is able to leave work early to pick a child up from school or practice and then remotely complete the work from home at a later time, they perform both their work and home functions with less stress or concerns of "letting their team down", because the leadership has created an environment that shows value both to work and to personal responsibilities. A work setting built on mutual trust and strong work ethic mixed with flexible work time/location options has the greatest chance of [offering] work-life balance.'

## Work smart not long

Unfortunately, there's a long-held myth in the profession that the more you work the better the architect you are: 'a masochist bent that gets ingrained in us starting in studio during our college years,' says associate principal at Krueck Sexton Partners Don Semple, who invited his architect wife, Nicole Semple, principal at Kuklinski + Rappe Architects and quoted earlier, to respond to some questions for this book. 'We learn to devalue our own time. Which is a tough thing to un-learn, and is part of the reason most architects are bad at business. It's hard to justify your value to a client when you don't even value your own time. Certainly, what we do as architects has its challenges and requires dedication and time. But that time is worth something. For me work-life balance is about optimising and prioritising. I am constantly challenging myself to learn ways to be faster and to stay more focused while at work so that I can go home at the end of the workday to spend time being a good husband and father.'

I've worked in architecture firms where the chief design principal would come into the office at 10.30 am and – unaware or uninterested that you have been at your desk since 7.30 am – expect you to work until 10.30 pm and in offices where the firm culture is such that you are considered to be leaving 'early' at 7 pm. 'Like any art-form, architecture is a creative discipline, can be all-consuming, and as such does not lend itself seamlessly to a traditional "nine-to-five" workday,' admits Sara Beardsley. 'Therefore, I would say that "work-life balance" is not always fully achievable, desirable or possible. Work is always a big part of the life of an architect, and it is about finding the balance that works for each particular individual, depending on many factors in play. The goal is that the profession as a whole has enough opportunity where there can be a variety of work situations with varying degrees of flexibility, depending on the role and type of firm. Architects are very dedicated to their craft and tend to work, at times, in great spurts of creativity and/or production effort. There will always be times where there is a big deadline, or an intense period of working. But even as a creative discipline, architects can make an effort to be better managers, and collaborate in such a way that is more organised and respectful of people's time – and allows them to have their creative time and creative freedom – in a flexible way – so that the intense periods of work or overtime hours are the exception, and not the daily norm.'

## Alternatives to work-life balance

One thing you discover at mid-career is that you have less energy and time – or the same amount of time, but increasing demands on it. To Tom Lee, it's not about working only 40 hours a week, but rather it means sometimes work takes priority and sometimes life does. Early in Lee's career, he worked seven days a week and had the energy, passion and time to do it. 'I was also learning a great deal, so the more I could work, the faster I could learn – there was no balancing: work came first for years with little exception,' says Lee. 'At mid-career, I find myself at a pivotal time where I have to make some choices about the trajectory of my career while balancing some significant life changes, including marriage and now our first son. Today, balance means that on certain days, work comes first and on others, life does. As for the work, it's forced me to be more mindful as to how I spend my increasingly limited time and energy and taught me to be more selective when it comes to evaluating opportunities.'

Matt Dumich prefers the term 'work–life integration', because the two are not always truly balanced. 'This integration is uniquely individual; to know one's priorities and flex appropriately,' says Dumich. 'It is a constant juggle but very possible to achieve. Our professional culture must support greater flexibility to allow work–life integration. If we are successful, I believe architecture will be even more attractive as a career and will result in better equity, diversity and inclusion in the profession. Architecture is a difficult profession requiring a great deal of passion and patience. It can take a long time to establish yourself as an architect. Other pressures and priorities often become a factor as one advances and gets older. I was fortunate to have an early start in my ongoing leadership journey. I had found my path and felt more established in my career by the time my wife and I had our son, now almost five years old. It is incredible to become a parent and really puts personal and family priorities in focus. This is another inflection point in an architect's career, to re-evaluate one's job and firm culture to support greater work–life integration.'

## ASK THIS

Joe Cliggott abhors the phrase 'work-life balance', which seems to suggest that we are two different people. 'It also supposes that work is work, and life is life, when in reality for most if not all architects, the two are totally intertwined,' says Cliggott. 'I also do not believe that a "job" is equal to "career", as one may be about the bi-weekly paycheck and benefits, and the other is a complete story of one's contributions to society. I am not only an architect from nine to five each workday. I am always an architect. And I know that I am not alone in this feeling. The question at hand should be, are the demands and expectations of the job extending and interfering with the other aspects of life that make us a complete person?

## TRY THIS

Listen. Understand. Listen more. There needs to be real accommodation without reprisal. There need to be more role models in leadership positions to show the possibility of where a career can take one. There needs to be equal pay for equal work. **[Joe Cliggott]**

## TRY THIS

A few examples of how we at HMC Architects support work-life balance:

- We have an alternate work schedule, so that if you like, you can take every other Friday off.
- We encourage our staff to take vacations and use their PTO [paid time off].
- We have gyms either in our office and/or building for the staff to use.
- We allow employees, who want to, to donate some of their PTO to others who might be in need due to an illness or other emergency. Employees have the option to donate to a central PTO bank that can be used for people who are in need due to a medical hardship (self or family) or other emergencies if they run out of their own PTO. HMC is a family firm, and it's about supporting each other … our family members.

**[Virginia E Marquardt]**

## TRY THIS

Some companies invest in having more staff with balanced hours, and others go at it very lean, work the employees more, and make money off the salaried employees over time. It's important for architects to choose their prospective employers wisely and ask questions about work-life balance. **[John Gresko]**

# 10:
# Reintegrate

Fig 10.1: Some architects are able to visualise a successful outcome (and *in*come) for themselves, while others make it up as they go

# Wisdom more than makes up for decrease in speed.

> One of the great midlife pressures people don't discuss is the great stress of Constantly Starting Over – needing to prove oneself in new jobs with new people. As much as we discuss the dexterity of architects and their ability to adapt, we should not forget the toll this takes: a little at a time, but nonetheless a toll.
> – Rob Rothblatt

> Paying back student loans; family; mortgage; saving for your kid's college education: these have a tremendous impact (on how one experiences work as an architect), especially if there is a family of children that are counting on the 'architect' as the main breadwinner. The commitment and sacrifice required to balance all of these demands is a burden that none of us can really prepare for.
> – Joe Cliggott

Internal forces and midlife pressures that were not there at the start of your architectural career – paying back student loans, family, mortgage, saving for your kid's college education: what impact, if any, do these have on how you experience your work? Midlife pressures are not unique to architects – but architects experience their fair share. Some even make you a better architect. 'Life appears a little simpler in the early stages of your career,' says Chithra Marsh. 'Once you take on the responsibilities during midlife, the pressures most definitely have an impact on your career, both good and bad. Family responsibilities, finance pressures and the need to keep your children safe and well can be difficult in their own right. Combining that with the day-to-day responsibility as a practising architect doubles the pressure to be in two places at once. Life becomes a little more unpredictable, and learning to juggle becomes a brand new skillset.'

Marsh continues: 'If the firm you work for is flexible and supportive, this can alleviate this pressure to a certain degree. However, it's not all bad. You also learn resilience, adaptability and how to prioritise, and this contributes to how you work. Having children affords you much greater compassion and patience for others. It helps you see other points of view and builds your skills as a team player and good leader. You learn to nurture your team to get the most out of them.'

'Becoming a parent made me a better employee, mainly because I had to become more focused and efficient with my work,' says Danei Cesario. 'I couldn't count on working until midnight to get my work done any more. The responsibility of adequately providing for myself, eventually my family and our future gave me perspective; I began to understand my value more when negotiating a salary. In essence, my "midlife pressures" (alternatively titled: "personal maturation") pushed me to always make the juice worth the squeeze in anything I built – from actual building to my personal life. This made me a more compassionate, decisive and effective architect.'

Fig 10.2: Danei Cesario on a panel organised by SEAoNY on how architects lead and expand their reach through diversity, inclusion and equity

Midlife often coincides with increased conservatism and unwillingness to take on risk. You may find that you stay put due to the responsibilities and burdens of midlife. Mid-career coincides with a lull in one's midlife – a point that has been identified as the low point in the happiness curve.[34] The mid-career architect resides first in a downward trend, then at the bottom of the 'U'. What's more – the lack of support; the lack of understanding, sympathy, empathy; the lack of direction and feeling lost; and, finding oneself at the bottom of the so-called happiness curve – all hit the mid-career architect at the same time. There's that feeling that you're on your own. What's a mid-career architect to do? But there is one resounding message: life gets better. In late mid-career, the curve gradually lifts you out of the depths. And we learn from Marsh and Cesario that having children and other mid-career responsibilities can make you a better architect (though starting and raising a family has stresses of its own).

One outcome is you become more sensitive to choices before you, and instead of working longer you try to work smarter. 'You become a lot more conscious of the impact of the decisions you make,' says Andy Watts. 'The creativity and the fun is still there, but you appreciate the practical aspects of what you do as well; the financial implications of a certain creative choice, or the impact on the business. That does not have to rule you. In fact, you can turn it to your advantage. I've seen this happen at Grimshaw. As well as solving design problems using technology, we can also work to identify pain points – those inefficiencies in our processes – and work to solve them too.'

## Money

This is a big issue within the profession, especially when it comes to attracting a more diverse group of young architects, says Ted Hyman. 'With the cost of education, the time and energy it takes to earn a five-, six-, or seven-year degree, the arduous licensing process, then only to be faced with non-competitive wages for the early years on the job. It is becoming untenable for smart people without a lot of financial resources to stay in architecture. This is one of the biggest reasons we still only have 2% African American representation in a profession that should be especially attractive to individuals who want the opportunity to improve their own communities. I personally could not have survived financially without the second income of my wife, and it has only gotten harder for young architects. It is easy to say we just need to pay people more, but that can only happen if our clients see the value proposition of design and pay accordingly. It is shocking that architects will take on projects at 6% of the construction cost and work for one to three years to produce design and construction documents, and at the same time a real-estate broker is compensated at the same level for simply facilitating the sale or lease of that very same project.'

About 10–15 years ago, Virginia E Marquardt and her husband decided to pay off all of their debt. 'We do not have children,' Marquardt explained. 'That was a decision we made early on, because of the time the profession of architecture requires one to devote to learning the craft, and because of autism and anxiety in my husband's family. At that time, my husband quit his job because he was experiencing lots of anxiety and we could survive on my salary alone ... we didn't know that he was autistic – we just knew he was different and had lots of anxiety. My husband was diagnosed with autism spectrum disorder (ASD) and general anxiety in his mid-forties. Because we only had the one income, we went down to one car, and started to really buckle down on our finances, focusing on paying off our student loans faster. (Several years before that, we had started paying off our credit card debit from college and when we were first married, and only spending what we could pay off each month.) For the last eight to ten years we have been debt free. It has been the most freeing experience! We are now saving and able to really save and plan for our future. Especially since the field of architecture sees its ups and downs, we have saved enough for a year. And now that we are in this pandemic, if anything happens to my job we are ready and can survive it.'

## Health insurance

Healthcare in the UK is provided by the government and funded by taxpayers. Not so in the United States. 'Without a doubt, architects in the United States are faced with one significant and limiting midlife pressure: health insurance being tied to employment,' says Donna Sink. 'Many times over the years I have been in the position of having enough "side project" opportunities to consider cobbling them together into starting my own firm, and every time the main limiting factor has been needing health insurance through an employer. Over the two decades of our marriage my spouse and I have traded off having the "real job" that comes with health insurance: one of us can be freelance or self-employed and exploring personal passions through our work, while the other is shackled to "the system". If health insurance was not employment-based I am certain that both of us would currently be running our own businesses; as it is, because we have a child we do not feel we are able to be without health insurance, and both of us being self-employed never seems to bring in enough income to cover mortgage, student debt, groceries, education, retirement savings and health insurance (our health insurance is our second-highest monthly expense, after our mortgage, even with a generous employer-sponsored plan). The especially sad part of this situation, to me, is that there is so much pro-bono work I would like to do as an architect: helping churches upgrade their facilities, working with community groups on public spaces, creating well-designed and safe ramp access at homes and businesses without them. Doing this work at no cost is impossible to do through a firm that has a specific billable rate to maintain, and impossible to do as a "side job" when one is employed at a firm that doesn't allow it or is fearful of liability (never mind that after working a 40-plus-hour week, the energy to devote to volunteering is minimal).'

## Becoming a parent

Mid-career workers have many outside factors weighing in on their careers. I like to focus on what I have learned from these forces: focus, prioritisation, compassion and delegation.
– Trina Sandschafer

The profession usually demands long hours and commitment to get the best results. I find this rather incompatible with family life, and have to make conscious decisions to step back from work slightly to make sure I don't miss the early years with my children and family. This does make me plan work more effectively, set daily, weekly and monthly goals, and make sure I leverage technology to do more with less.
– Michael Riley

The main midlife pressure Sara Beardsley faces has been in becoming a parent. 'This was not only an additional pressure in terms of work-life balance, but also in terms of an increased desire for stability that, as a younger architect, I did not put so much importance on,' says Beardsley. 'Geographic stability, and job security, are in general a greater concern at this point in life than they were several years ago. Becoming a parent has made me more responsible, more compassionate towards others, and helped me learn to "work smarter" and more efficiently. While I do still think it's important to be involved in professional organisations and have a social life, parenthood has driven me to be more selective about my outside-of-work professional activities, especially when they translate to after-hours obligations.'
That selectivity didn't stop her from contributing to this book, for which we are grateful.

Alexandra Pollock and her husband, both in the AEC field, have two young children. 'Before we had kids, working long hours or weekends was not a big deal to us (although maybe it should have been),' says Pollock. 'Starting a family had a big impact on our priorities and the time we could dedicate to work. I found the most challenging thing was that I no longer had the "extra" time when I could focus on trying a different approach to something I was working on, or learning something new. I have found it important to try to schedule this time in, as it is important to career growth.'

## The architect at mid-career

What happens to architects when they age is similar to what happens to everybody when they age – though architects tend to wear glasses sooner. But this is perhaps where the biological analogy ends. While people as they age aren't able to protect themselves as well from outside forces, architects become stronger and wiser, improving over time. It is a truism in the industry that architects don't really come into their own until their fifties. Even if you feel you aren't adapting as well as in the past, your brain remains adaptable and flexible throughout your career.[35] There is no reason the architect can't adapt as well.

There are challenges to this optimistic thinking. Younger employees, for example, may be quicker at adapting to new technologies, and our ability to do so may decrease with each decade.[36]

But the role of wisdom – adaptive behaviour – that comes with years and experience can be said to more than make up for any decrease in speed. That is why as architects age they learn to cut to the chase and ask more pertinent questions – zeroing in on the underlying problem that needs addressing – and the aforementioned working smarter over working longer.

With age comes perspective. Duane Carter is a good example of this phenomenon. 'I am slower to learn – particularly with technology,' admits Carter. 'It's also harder to work long hours and be productive. I've had to accept that I won't get much done after 3.00 pm. I do think that I am more productive than when I was younger because I tend to not get caught up in the minutiae.'

There is evidence that a career in architecture – just by remaining an architect – will keep your brain agile and adaptable, as neuroplasticity apparently does not slow down nearly as much in older adults who make consistent demands on their brains to think differently. Architects who regularly exercise and challenge their brain by working on projects that require them to undertake new adaptations – new ways of looking at and solving problems – tend not to slow down as much as they age.[37]

## Acquired wisdom

I learn faster today than I used to. I have a better understanding of the wider AEC industry landscape; it allows me to use what I already know to balance, put in perspective and understand better what I want to learn. I also get less 'lost in details'.
– Aurélie de Boissieu

Older = wiser, smarter, more at ease and clearer-thinking. In our culture age equates to authority. As a female architect this authority is hard-won, so it's important to take advantage of those years. The clarity that comes with experience means you can make good design decisions quickly.
– Alison Brooks

Less exposure on a regular basis with certain technologies means slower. Not sure that it is a result of age. With age, there is simply a greater repository of experiences to draw from as reference.
– Joe Cliggott

Acknowledging your limitations – whether you are physically slower, slower to learn, or have trouble keeping up with the deluge of information – is probably wise, because each person is different and knows themselves best. 'I am definitely finding it hard to keep up with everything that is on the horizon,' says Evelyn Lee. 'All of the new things students are learning in school that we haven't quite yet figured out how to apply to practice. There is just a lot of movement right now. Even the building tech sector has taken off in a way that I find quite surprising. So I lean on others. And have a lot more exploratory conversations to learn about what I don't know. And leverage my network better to connect people to move those things forward, progressing them through my network. Especially those things I don't understand. Rather than trying to do it all on my own. Because I can't do it all on my own.'

One advantage of being a mid-career architect is that with age comes perspective. 'I may be slower to pick up new programs, but the confidence [with which I] approach and tackle a problem is of much greater value,' says Emily Grandstaff-Rice. 'I have a greater confidence to handle [seemingly] insurmountable problems. I can handle complexity in a way that would crush me as an emerging professional. It is important to know … how much work to do, when to ask the right questions, [sit] with uncertainty. I would not give that up for the ability to do amazing renderings at the drop of a hat.'

By mid-career the belief that you can learn to play any role gives way to the reality that some roles are best left to others. As he's grown older, Tom Lee has learned to acknowledge his limitations, and that some aspects of the profession – such as operations and project management – are not for him. 'That said, I've probably slowed down in many areas, including cutting back on my hours so I can spend more time with my family, but I've also learned to slow down the design process, because I have found that a thoughtful, rigorous and collaborative design process almost always leads to better results in the end,' says Lee. 'To that end, I've also learned to be more patient – we have high aspirations as a practice, but to make meaningful and lasting change requires taking one step at a time. Sometimes it's more constructive to measure the progress made from a series of small steps rather than how far you are from achieving the end goal.'

One way to adapt in mid-career is to participate in mutual mentoring and rely more on one's network. About three years into her professional career, Mary Shaffer thought she knew all she needed to know to be a good architect. 'Such naive confidence!' says Shaffer. 'Thirty-plus years into my career, I am a voracious consumer of information and learning, and I have so much more to learn. There is constant change in technology, building codes, materials, products, trends, work processes – if I didn't keep up with the changes and design trends, I would not be a valued resource to my team and our clients. Certainly, digital natives have the advantage of having technology in their lives from the day they were born. There is a comfort and fluency with technology and software that those of us born earlier will probably never have. I value the trust built in cross-mentoring relationships at all levels – you can teach me how to run clash detection on our building model, and I'll share my project management knowledge with you; an intern can teach me a fresh perspective on design, and I can teach them how to turn that design into a constructible detail. Over my years in the design industry, I have learned that mutual respect for what each of us brings to each project is exponentially more important than a specific skillset or a certain number of years of experience.'

A career in architecture is actually several careers. 'At this point in my career, I might be slower, but I perceive it as being more "steadied",' says Lora Teagarden. 'I'm still eager to learn, while understanding that it's not always me who has to do the thing (learning delegation). I'm eager to get a task complete, but I'm more patient with myself and co-workers. I'm eager to change the world, but I have a better understanding of the systems at play.'

Head of technology at Ayre Chamberlain Gaunt Allister Lewis feels that anything is possible, no matter the age of the individual; what is important is an interest in the subject at hand. 'Understanding the reasoning behind a new technology, software or process is also required,' says Lewis. 'Very often BIM is taught as a software solution, when in actual fact it is a process. Understanding this context, and the requirements for professionals to be more efficient, effective and productive to benefit clients and then users, would help with the understanding as to why new software is required.'

As a mid-career architect you can be seen as expensive, especially if you have previously asked for and received a leap in salary – you may have unwittingly priced yourself out of your position. It can then feel as though there is a target on your back, especially during an economic downturn. Because of cost pressures in the industry Michael Riley finds there is a predisposition against architects and senior architects later in their career. 'They are perceived as slower, less engaged and too expensive,' says Riley.

'They have tended to be an "under pressure" group when the industry contracts. This is unfortunate, and we need to devote more time to training, engagement and career enrichment for these talented and experienced individuals. We can't rely too much on younger, "energetic" staff, as they need advice and guidance to develop their experience.'

## Hands-on versus hands-off

I don't feel I'm slower at all at this point in my career. If anything, I've become so much more efficient at everything I do.
– Nicole Semple

I joke with my peers that we could never get hired today with the skills we graduated with.
– Randy Guillot

I wrote this in my application for graduate school: 'Everyone can stretch and grow at any point in their career – if we stop learning we will not just stand still; we will lose ground.' That philosophy has been with me from early in my career.
– Mary Shaffer

The Catch-22 of mid-career: to be hands-on or hands-off? The hands-on phase of your career can go by so quickly. It can feel that just as you gain confidence producing, you suddenly find yourself managing others who are the doers. This is one of the things Evan Troxel sees colleagues in his firm struggle with most. 'Because our profession rewards those with so-called "experience" much more than youthful energy, it takes a long time for individuals to get to a position where we are calling the shots,' says Troxel. 'Yet once we are calling the shots, we long to still be doing the actual work on projects. This creates a Catch-22, where we should be leading but have a really hard time letting go of doing the day-to-day tasks to maintain control of the inner workings of the project. We are slower to learn new ways of working, for sure. We are less prone to acknowledge the new ways might in fact be better ways of working because we can't invest the time to really figuring that out. But my view of this topic is that we must step back and enable others to do the work. We must remove the red tape so they can accomplish more than we did in a shorter amount of time. This helps the entire profession! It's a fundamental aspect of leadership – finding and training our replacements so they can take their trajectory higher than they could on their own.'

The Peter principle states that you rise in a hierarchy beyond your level of competence. Today, mid-career architects find that they design less, but serve more of an "editor" role. Both are necessary, and as an editor and not the sole project designer one is able to touch and thus influence many more projects. Still, you must determine for yourself whether you want to do more and manage less and, if so, at what price. John Gresko doesn't subscribe to the theory that as architects age, they should lose touch with technology

– Revit, for example. 'As long as I am practising architecture, I want to be knowledgeable in all my available tools and resources,' says Gresko. 'One never knows when those skills will be needed. I'll stop keeping up once I retire. This is how one can stay relevant and hedge against being out of work for too long, should lay-offs or downsizing occur.'

## The age of decisiveness

'Age does not make you slower,' says Danei Cesario. 'It makes you sharper, more decisive. I am slower now to be flattered, to accept nonsense and mediocrity, to doubt myself, to become impatient or frustrated. My career is a long game, so my approach is to act and react in accordance with what I will be proud of a decade from now. Fortunately, I am still young enough to embrace novelty and innovation. My younger colleagues are a source of energy and nostalgia. I appreciate their struggles of inexperience, and often see my slightly younger self in them. I impart my growing wisdom when I'm asked without beginning the statement with "In my day …". My day is actually not that far removed from right now, and what good does it do to alienate the people who need the most support?'

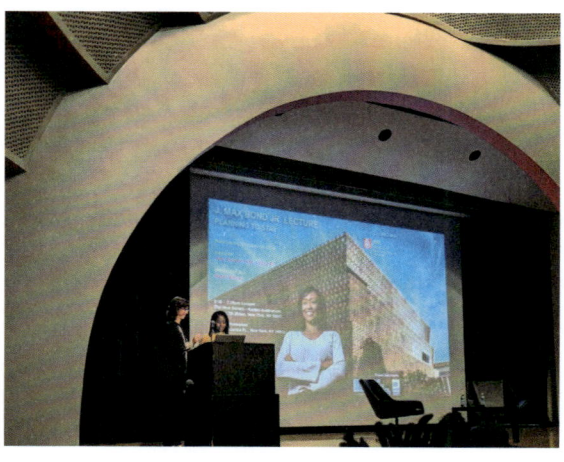

Fig 10.3: Danei Cesario presenting the opening remarks at the annual J Max Bond Jr memorial lecture in October 2019 to welcome keynote speaker Zena Howard FAIA

In terms of the implications of ageing, Andy Watts says: 'I am not sure that it inevitably means any of these things; these things relate to the attitude of the individual. Working in a technology team, where a large part of our remit is the training and upskilling of our design teams, you might expect us to see senior members of the team as being more reluctant to change their working methods. This is not always the case. We see recent graduates not wanting to learn new ways of working, and we see leaders wanting to discover new tricks.'

Watts continues: 'In terms of ways in which I myself may be getting slower, I would say that this relates to my own changing circumstance. Rather than being able to throw myself into a specific specialism or project, I have to spread across multiple outlets. The wisdom – which I am still trying to discover – is about how to prioritise what to work on.'

'This question is a bit of myth we all tell ourselves in order to justify not learning something new,' says Don Semple. 'It's always difficult to learn something new, no matter your age. We just all come from a point of not knowing much early in our careers and being forced to learn, to a point where we know enough to get things done. It becomes easier for us (less risky, less initial mental effort) to focus on getting our tasks done the way we know how as opposed to learning a better way. Much of maintaining relevance is continually challenging yourself to improve and learn. I would hope any slowing on cognitive function isn't until much later in life.'

Semple continues: 'When we came into the profession in the mid-2000s it was a very age-divided profession; divided by digital knowhow. Most of our peers were hired because they could 3D-model, render and utilise Revit. Senior staff at the time had very limited digital abilities and found little value in investing in developing digital skills when they could hire someone just out of school for relatively cheap, allowing them to focus on those things they felt were better uses of their time. I generally feel like the profession is less divided now. Or at least the divide has shifted back. Most mid-career professionals I know have far more digital skills than anyone we can hire directly out of school. Given this digital proclivity, my sense is that most mid-career architects are relatively adept in learning new tech, which helps us stay relevant.'

'Your mind thinks that you are still like you were in your twenties, but age has indeed brought wisdom, being knowledge, experience and contacts,' says managing director at BAM Design Andrew Pryke. 'You can therefore evaluate things better and quicker than in your early years to make a better-judged decision. Some people can become more risk-averse, but this needs a mindset to assess these risks with a positive attitude to look for a way to move forward, not a reason to remain in your comfort zone.'

## Slow down to speed up

The longer John Gresko is in this profession the wiser he feels he becomes in specific areas. 'Conflict avoidance; I've had my fair share of construction experience and lived through some conflict,' says Gresko. 'Applying lessons learned in design to avoid mistakes and misunderstandings later has helped. Also, learning how to go slow to go fast. Architecture can be very methodical and sequential. If we do not manage our process carefully, on large projects, we can get super turned around quickly with external pressures. Saying no is another thing I have learned. Saying no to riskier projects, specifying untested products, and saying no to quicker deadlines and turnarounds. All of these are intended to reduce risk, time and cost on projects. As I age, I am able to be on defence more and protect our interests.'

Trina Sandschafer views mid-level and senior-level leaders with great respect. 'You learn by doing and having walked this career path,' says Sandschafer. 'There is great knowledge in that experience. I do not view myself as slower. The only exception may be in reacting when the moment is tense. I find that younger people tend to react very quickly to tense situations. Employees with more tenure tend to pause, analyse and respond. I think that is a skill that is necessary when leading. Yes, we need to be instinctual, and that is often the case, but when things get heated, a slower response can be healthy.'

'I joke with my peers that we could never get hired today with the skills we graduated with,' says Randy Guillot. 'The skills of recent graduates around visualisation and complex problem-solving are extraordinary. Recent graduates have the ability to move between platforms and ideas and between social groups with speed and agility unlike anything graduates of my generation had the ability or the digital means to do. That said, I do find the things that helped to make me successful even as a young architect are still many of the things that give my perspective value as a more senior member of the team. As someone educated "pre-computer" (I used my first computer in the first few years of my career), drawing was a considered activity. If for no other reason than taking time to erase it took almost as much time as it did to draw it, so perhaps there was more consideration about what went down on the paper. That consideration also extended to really defining what problem you were trying to solve. Today, you can do anything, digitally you can create worlds that never could have existed in the past.'

Guillot continues: 'Now that you can do anything, what will you do? I find myself asking my studio to slow down. Not because I can't keep up, but because I want them to consider what they are really doing. What are our clients' sensibilities? How are you going to build it? How much will it cost? What is the value of our time in developing this idea? Can it have a broader social impact?

Now that we can do anything, it's easy to do lots of things. But the value of a great idea, well executed, that's in alignment with our clients' values and our goals as a firm and a society often requires more thinking than drawing at the beginning. I love to draw. It's a part of my thinking process – and I often draw to work through fundamental questions on a problem I am facing. It's here that wisdom can be transferred, where ideas are their most malleable.'

## Time as a factor

Ask a mid-career architect what they need – time? support? opportunity? – and you might be surprised by how they respond. 'What I've noticed the most is that I'm running out of time,' says Angela Watson. 'My responsibilities are mostly tied to communication and collaboration. For me, the most important tools and technologies are those that let me do all of that better. This is where learning new tricks makes a big difference in how effective I can be. Here I can invest the time to learn new tools and explore new ways of using them. I often miss the ability to learn new tools that have to do with design and visualisation. I would love to explore more. But as I said, I seem to be running out of time – all the time.'

Fig 10.4: Partners Michael Jacobs AIA and Diane Reicher Jacobs AIA of Holly Street Studio working together on the early stages of a project, exchanging leadership roles as projects evolve in development, circling back from conceptual to detailed discussions and back again throughout the full process

Diane Reicher Jacobs finds it harder to take time for exploration, as she feels the pressure to produce, take care of others or cross things off her list more. 'I am physically stronger in some ways, as I have maintained fitness as a priority throughout my career – something I wish more would do. However, sleep is non-negotiable, and I need greater quantities of that now. So, it's hard to build up to that block of midnight magical inspiration that was so fruitful during the earlier years. I love learning new technology. One time, after seeing someone perhaps younger than me exclaim that they were too old for "this stuff" and asking a younger staff member to start up a PowerPoint, I promised myself I would never use age as an excuse to stop learning new things – technology or otherwise. How else can we share our ideas, that are often weathered and valuable? But I have to fight to make time for these nevertheless. (This is actually a silver lining during this time of quarantine.) I am slower in that I have too many things in my head – so it's hard to prioritise and avoid multi-tasking, which slows the best of us down. I am always working on finding a singular path in the middle of each endeavour, but it's tough.'

All of that hard-earned knowledge mid-career architects have accumulated over time can be a double-edged sword. Philip Twiss doesn't believe you get any slower to learn, although he believes you do have to unlearn and adapt to new technologies and software and be open to different and new approaches. 'Just because someone else's way of doing something is different doesn't make it wrong,' says Twiss. 'Generally, as an architect's career progresses their role as an architect evolves with it; similar to many professional services. As [I have progressed] through middle/senior management I do less and less drawing and more and more "management"; resource planning, business strategy and development; oversight of multiple projects rather than being embedded with just one as a project architect. The experience and wisdom brought about by failures as much as successes informs what you do. You also have to be open to new ideas, to let the young guns off the leash and let them teach you a thing or two. You might not be able to teach an old dog new tricks, but they do know some good ones!'

'It is certainly more challenging to learn new technology and "tricks" as you grow older, but I think the reason is related more to just generally having less time in life to adapt to change,' says David Swain. 'While we may be slower in picking up new technology, we do become much quicker in pulling from our memory bank of experience to resolve issues as they come up during the course of the project.'

Mid-career architects are still very much learning. 'Physically I am slower than when I started out in the profession,' admits Zoe Hooton. 'I can't pull those long nights any more, but should I? I've learned to work smarter [rather] than harder. However, technology, CAD and Revit skills I once acquired have now gone. My take-up of technology is slow, but it doesn't mean that I don't spend the time learning how it can benefit the office. If anything, because I know that this is now my weakness, I make an effort to understand it so that I can relate to my staff problems and ensure that our practice is moving forward with its application of technology. Experience speeds up decision-making. So, my experience and time spent compensates for my depleted technology skills. However, as I look to my professional role models, I see how they have and are still continuing to learn, adapt and challenge themselves – so while the pace isn't what it was, the acquisition of new knowledge is only just beginning.'

## TRY THIS

The pressures you are feeling are probably different from those others in the office are experiencing. Because modern firms are multi-generational (there are five in ours), I believe it's important to bring it to others' attention throughout your career that what you are feeling pressure from is probably different than what others are feeling simply due to the station they are at in their life and career. I've found that most individuals treat others as if they have the same circumstances as they do, and have to be reminded – constantly, it seems – that there are differences. Some have kids in college, while others are just having their first. Some have teenagers with extracurricular activities each night of the week, while others are empty-nesters. Some don't have

kids at all and prioritise weekend experiences outdoors, while others who have been in the profession for a long time long to always be in the studio. The lack of these differences being top-of-mind often creates unrealistic expectations between roles and generations. Misunderstandings over expectations and priorities rear their ugly heads a lot, and the outcome is often a damaged relationship. I think it's really important to treat people appropriately based on their life circumstances, and be flexible to other ways of living that may not align with my own. Not everyone on the team needs to have the same working hours, perceived "dedication" or the same amount of experience to create rich and successful project outcomes.
[Evan Troxel]

# Epilogue: Thrive

Fig 11.1: Each architect has to determine for themselves what it will take for them to thrive throughout their career

**What we can plan – we plan for, what we can't – we adapt**

A career is a chess match … against 1,000 players. We need to have a strategy, a goal. However, there is another side that is also playing, and we need to be able to react and adapt. These opposing forces are innumerable, but we cannot become overwhelmed.
– Joe Cliggott

I am a believer of listening to my gut and my mother's voice. For my relatively short life, neither of these have led me astray. I have visualised my life, but there have been joyous accidents and curveballs along the way. I trust the process. It's vital to have goals to work towards and a roadmap to follow. I know when I'm on the right track when I feel it. Learning to trust your intuition is the greatest gift you can give yourself.
– Danei Cesario

It is hard to plan a straight-line path and look far ahead. Consider roles on projects, and looking to build experience and seniority at the same time will allow you to define the steps you want to take, but the opportunity then needs to exist before you can progress. A plan is a good thing to have, but if it's too rigid or looks too far ahead it's likely not to be achieved.
– Alistair Kell

We don't always know what others have in store for us – whether in addition to mentors we have sponsors who, like career guardian angels, are looking out for us, removing obstacles, assuring our growth. To a great extent we can control our education and training, what we focus on in our careers, and as we continue on our career journey how much control we have over our work. But, as the pandemic and associated economic recession have proven, we can't have the same level of control over external circumstances.

When opportunities arise – say someone leaves the office and you are offered the chance to fill in for them – they can be a one-time thing that you discover you enjoy and want to continue, or you may be rewarded with another unrelated opportunity you cannot refuse. What we can plan – we plan for, what we can't – we adapt.

Have architects visualised outcomes for where they are today, or would they describe their career as a happy accident? Everything Nicole Semple is doing today in the profession she put in writing in a high school essay. 'I realise this is rare, but I decided very early in life to become an architect and centred every decision around achieving that goal,' says Semple. 'The path to achieving those goals hasn't always looked as I envisioned, but the goals remain unchanged. I'm a firm believer in figuring out what you want, writing it down, and making an action plan to follow through. A large part of it is luck, and there will be difficulties, but if you work hard enough, you'll find some kind of success. Also, there is no arrival – if you're complacent then you've become lazy. There is always room for growth.'

I've had students who kept the career timeline assignment I gave them in our professional practice course write to me years later to say they were curious to see how accurate their predictions were, and find they are living their timeline more or less as designed. This speaks to the power of planning and visualising – but admittedly as much to chance.

Fig 11.2: A ZGF design team gathers in a meeting room to review and mark up drawings with the project's partner-in-charge

'There is no doubt a mid-career architect needs to have a keen sense of what they like, where their strengths lie, and have their antennae up for opportunities,' says Rob Rothblatt. 'In an overarching way, one can have a career plan whether one is going to be in design, or technical, or digital, or management, or large firm, or residential, or client-side, etc. Some of these things may seem to happen by chance, but we are open to some things, and other opportunities we ignore. And mid-career architects who are adept at adapting often have to weigh interesting choices about whether to jump, follow a boss or colleague to a new gig, or stay put. The questions mid-career architects need to ask, and which they can't really know, is when there is a fork in the road, will the road they take lead them to their destination? There's some luck in that – given that there are no overall mentors in architecture who can map out a career path or guarantee one for a young architect.'

## Planning versus leaving things to chance

I've absolutely planned out many variants to my potential career(s).
– Evan Troxel

This is the single biggest cause of friction between my partner and me. I am nourished, propelled and inspired by a clear vision; he is all about successful completion of the task in front of him. Mostly this is a key ingredient for our success, but when these two things are not in sync – it is difficult firing on all cylinders.
– Diane Reicher Jacobs

To some degree my career and its path has been planned, and to some degree I've been in the right place at the right time.
– Virginia E Marquardt

Architects envision – it's what we do – and leaders communicate vision. But how much of one's career can be envisioned? How much is preparing yourself – hustling and striving versus learning to recognise opportunities when they appear? Emily Grandstaff-Rice is a planner by nature. 'I am always running through future scenarios – many of which never materialise,' says Grandstaff-Rice. 'But I find it a useful process to help envision what could be. I also set multi-year deadlines for myself. This sometimes helps me get through the more difficult times, knowing that I have a cut-off date in the future to remind myself to walk away if the situation does not improve. One of my favourite quotes comes from a well-known female engineer in response to another female professional saying that she had been "lucky in career". She stated [that] she "worked hard to be lucky". Things do not just happen; you must be ready for them. Part of being ready is knowing when a chance (even one masked in serendipity) is something to pursue. At the beginning of my career, I felt like I had to hustle a lot more. Now I see opportunities as coming easier because, in part, I am more prepared to received them. The other side of this coin is that I must be selective to ensure I have enough capacity to take additional efforts on.'

Trina Sandschafer has been a planner most of her life. 'Sometimes that means making measurable one-year and three-year goals,' says Sandschafer. 'Sometimes that means thinking critically about where I wanted to go – sometimes it was a gut feeling. Not everyone has the same planning strategy, but I do think it is important to know where you would like to end up. Then, you will be able to make thoughtful decisions when challenges or opportunities come your way.'

Fig 11.3: Work session at Holly Street Studio with (L to R) Sergio Carrasco Assoc. AIA, Tyler Wothers Assoc. AIA, A. Ben Perrone AIA, Michael Jacobs AIA. The firm typically employs 8–12 staff, working in full studio charrette at key project milestones

But what role does deliberate choice play versus serendipity? According to Diane Reicher Jacobs, deliberate choice sets the scene. 'It helps you clarify what you will not do – so you have more horsepower to evade distraction (the world conspires against us with this) and do the things you are "meant" to do. The only caveat is that you must remain "open to grace", allow the deliberate choice to be a backdrop for your efforts, not a prescription.' But how important is it to visualise one's career outcomes? 'I am confident that it is why I've landed here. Just where I want to be,' says Jacobs.

'I definitely visualised outcomes, but it has ended up being very different,' says Duane Carter. 'Part of this is because things just didn't work out, but mostly it was that I haven't fit into the paths that I saw around me. At some point, I started to feel much more confident in my knowledge about things, and started to be freer to express my enthusiasm for things that others didn't think were important. This is when I started to feel like I had "arrived", where I wasn't just doing what people told me but creating value.'

People have a hard time thinking more than a few years into the future. A case in point can be demonstrated by the career timeline exercise mentioned previously. The career timeline is an experiment I do with my graduate students, where I ask them to place their career goals along a timeline with birth at one end and the proverbial milk truck on the other: graduation; employment; taking exams and licensure; falling in love; getting married; finding a home; starting a family; starting a firm; winning recognition, etc.

Here's what I discovered: they inevitably placed all of their career milestones in the first seven years. And who can blame them? Who can really say what will happen beyond the seven-year time horizon? No one knows what will happen even a decade ahead. The future is fuzzy.

Creating a career is like writing a novel. As we saw in Chapter 3, EL Doctorow said that 'Writing is like driving at night in the fog. You can only see as far as your headlights, but you can make the whole trip that way.' Careers are long, and it makes sense to break them into chunks.

## Celebrate the small wins

Careers are part planned, part circumstantial or serendipitous. And some take a design approach. 'A career, and a life, in my mind is a combination of deliberate plans and serendipity plus numerous outside influences well beyond one's control,' says Joe Cliggott. 'A "happy accident" befell a colleague and I back in 1998 that would change both of our careers. Working on an office tower project that had come off being on hold, we decided to switch roles: he would take over the lobby design and I would take over the typical floor plans. Little did we know that this meant I would be the one to stay with the project for the next four years, and he would go on to other important projects after nine months. I would ultimately go on to the next few projects with the same client, and the client would then hire me to work on projects in the Middle East. That simple choice between two young architects who only had four years of experience changed the trajectory of both of our careers. Luckily, we both benefited from the decision. [Then] there have been clear moments throughout my career where either firms, projects or roles have come along, and by merging what was being offered with where I wanted the journey to take me, I've been able to find success. The vision of success has to be one where you celebrate accomplishments, even the small wins, while staying focused on the next challenge ahead.'

'It seems like people are naturally inclined toward one or the other category – those who have destinations in mind and plan how to get there, and those who made the next move that feels right and are content to let serendipity take them where it will,' says Oscia Wilson. 'There's no use trying to force yourself to change your fundamental makeup. Whichever approach you take, you'll have a full and varied career and you'll contribute your brilliance to the collective good.'

'I'm a planner and controller (I have to be as a project manager, principal, operations person),' says Virginia E Marquardt. 'I needed to see and plan out my career and its path. However, I can only plan and see so much. I only know what I know at the time, and as the profession continues to change, I had to adapt my plan and my path as the profession as changed.'

Allister Lewis's approach has always been to ensure that he enjoys the work that he does. 'If this is the case, then opportunities will arise as an individual will be performing a good job in the role that is rewarding,' says

Lewis. 'However, there is a certain amount of good timing to any organisation you may join and the work that you undertake. By being enthusiastic and willing this may support better outcomes across time spent at a certain organisation. Having an outline plan is useful to understand where you would like to go as a professional. However, being adaptable and willing to change based on circumstance, opportunity and organisational needs is helpful.'

## Knowing when you've arrived

I don't think anyone knows when they have 'arrived'! You have to keep going and pushing forward to the next challenge.
– Allister Lewis

To describe yourself as 'arrived' is far too American for my liking. Yes, reflect on your successes but drive forward every day, because in a profession which evolves as quickly as architecture you can't take your arrival for granted. Tim Minchin, an Australian comedian and Broadway show producer, describes the danger of those chasing goals and long-term dreams. He advocates a passionate dedication to the pursuit of short-term goals, and to be micro-ambitious.
– Zoe Hooton

'Where I have got to has been a function of both setting goals and happy accidents,' says Elliot Glassman. 'I definitely wanted a career focused on combining design with environmental sustainability, and because of the serendipitous timing of the Great Recession, I went back to school at a time where I brought with me some architectural maturity, and in addition to sustainability was able to acquire new skills I did not anticipate when I was making that choice, namely computational design analysis. It is an important part of my career today. Since I graduated nearly eight years ago, I have been promoted a few times and have established myself as a known technical leader in a very large global company. But I still do not feel that I have arrived. I do have an image in my mind of what I hope to do in my career and the impact I want to have and it all still seems very remote to me.'

'How do you know when you've arrived?' asks Alexandra Pollock. 'This is a matter of perspective – it can be something that you might never feel like you attain. How can you really ever arrive if you keep moving? I do believe that as you arrive at milestones in your career, you should celebrate them – such as finishing your first project, getting licensed or being promoted.'

'In 2008 after 10 years at my first practice I left, moving to a new satellite office for a national firm,' says Philip Twiss. 'I wanted change and wanted to grow and experience other approaches to architecture, which I did, working on some amazing projects in the UK and abroad with Make. Subsequently, in 2014, I moved to a newly set-up practice in London, but it didn't work out as planned and I left after only a year. This change meant that I had to pause, be self-reflective and work out what it was that hadn't worked, and what had gone right previously. What were the circumstances that had enabled me to flourish in my early career, and what was it that I needed to continue to do so? And so in my search for a new job, the opportunity came to join Gensler and set up the new office in Birmingham (my home city), which 12 months later we did. In reality the opportunity with Gensler came about through a series of chance circumstances; the previous role didn't work out and Gensler happened to be looking at that time. It was serendipitous but sometimes you do need a bit of luck!'

Matt Dumich never had a specific career goal that he targeted, but has periodically consulted peers and mentors to evaluate his career trajectory. 'Any success I have found has come through a strong network, opportunistic mindset, some good timing, and a little luck,' says Dumich. 'I know others who tried to intentionally curate their experiences, understanding what skills or opportunities a firm could provide before moving on to another firm to round out their skillset with an end goal in mind.'

Andrew Pryke's career has been influenced by luck, but with a passion for high-end design opportunities at its heart. 'It has never been a straight path,' admits Pryke. 'On occasion I have taken a risk, but always with a plan B (and C in some instances) and with an idea to explore opportunity, experience and a challenge. I am not sure there ever is an arrival, but an ever-continuous journey, not knowing what will come around the corner next.'

'Where I am today is definitely a happy accident,' says Andy Watts. 'I never had a clear picture of my ideal career beyond it being within the somewhat fluid realm of architecture. That said, there were always signs that might have indicated that my final route was an option; I always enjoyed problem solving over design execution, I can't stand for inefficiencies and I have always had at least one eye on the future. Perhaps I should have paid closer attention early on!'

'I have more of a deliberate career trajectory than a visualised plan,' says Tom Lee. 'For me, the exercise of visualising my career is frightening, as it becomes too prescriptive and doesn't allow for serendipity, and just letting it all to chance (or an employer) can be a very slippery slope. I think it's critical to have direction in one's career, but with a willingness to adapt as the world and our interests evolve.'

One's career becomes a balancing act between being acting deliberately and leaving things to chance. A need to have direction but adapt as you go. Or, adapt as the world changes. But also adapt as you – and your interests and passions – change. Angela Watson did not visualise outcomes for where she is today. 'In fact, even when I was trying to imagine what my future would be like, I've been fairly besides the mark,' says Watson. 'My career has been very much like my design approach. I don't go in with a preconceived idea of what it should be. I do determine what values are important to me and I do determine what's important not only to me but also to others. This gives me a framework of values that guide me in how I respond to the situations that I find myself in. Think about a sketch model or even one of those junk models. I remember dumpster diving when we were in school and making little sculptures on top of a site map and then interpreting those to become a building. It's that interpretation that allows you to see things you might not have imagined. Recognising opportunities in unexpected situations creates these happy accidents, even though they are not really accidents, but rather opportunities for new perspectives.'

## What thriving looks like

If you asked me what thriving looked like five years ago, I would have [had] a different answer then. Today, thriving means balancing my life with my work. Making sure I'm taking care of myself first, then my family, friends and my team. Because I cannot thrive and succeed without my health and my tribe.
– Virginia E Marquardt

A lot of successful people wonder when they have arrived. It comes with the territory to keep striving for the next thing. I think you know when you have arrived when you feel inspired by your work and eager to contribute to projects and the growth of your firm. Thriving is feeling like you are moving forward – it is stopping to take stock of how far you have come.
– Trina Sandschafer

Fig 11.4: The Alison Brooks Architects studio is a place for research, design experimentation, discussion and technical development

Alexandra Pollock had no idea when she started her career where she would end up. 'I worked hard, and I followed my passion – and it led me to where I am today,' says Pollock. 'Being focused on technology, there have not

**Epilogue: Thrive**

been many people that I could look to [to] know what my career path was supposed to look like, and what the next "right" step might be. In a way, this has been a positive factor in my growth, as it has forced me to carve my own way. Where you choose to create your path is just as important as the path itself. Being at a firm that shares your values is critical.'

'I know that I have arrived when others are working in the same mental and physical space toward the same thing; when the situation or circumstance becomes much bigger than me,' says Diane Reicher Jacobs. 'Thriving looks like your ideas and purpose taking flight outside of yourself. Our studio is starting to reflect that. It is very exciting. But I didn't realise it until this question – thank you, Randy! Also, both of our kids are pursuing careers in similar fields. It's pretty cool to see important causes continue to be pursued, when they started out as inklings in a lecture hall for me during college. [My kids] are much smarter than I was at their age – gives me hope and a great deal of satisfaction. Also, when people say thank you (for my work).'

Success is part drive to succeed, part opportunity and part luck, according to Mary Shaffer. 'If you have drive to succeed, but there are no opportunities, you are left in limbo,' says Shaffer. 'If you leave everything to chance, you may get lucky and someone sees your potential and offers you an opportunity for growth. Opportunity is key to a successful job hunt. You could be the best architect to ever live, but if no one is hiring, where would you find a job?'

You create one?

Fig 11.5: At the end of mid-career, what is it that you want to hand over to the next generation of architects?

### ASK THIS

What gets you up in the morning and inspires you to give your best self every day? Would you describe your current position as your ideal job? If you do not see opportunity in your current situation, take some time to think about whether there is potential for you within in your firm, or if a change of firms is needed for you to thrive, and take the steps to get yourself there. **[Mary Shaffer]**

### TRY THIS

Even before visualisation has to come clarity. Once you know what you want, visualisation is a critical step in developing positive emotions around what it would feel like to achieve it. Our senses receive and process billions of inputs daily. We are consciously aware of very few of them. Getting clarity and visualising helps tell your brain which inputs should be flagged for attention, which is why it can feel like synchronicity – where attention goes, energy flows. Take time each morning to direct your day and watch what happens! **[Angela Mazzi]**

Fig 11.6: What you hand over to the next generation of architects at the end of mid-career will be your legacy

# APPENDIX

# Appendix: Reboot

Fig 12.1: What makes architects especially good at adaptation may not be enough to ensure career longevity

## Think of each chunk of your career as an arc or sigmoid curve

Here's what worked for me over my 42-year career. Think of each chunk of your career as an arc or sigmoid curve. You start by learning something new, get discouraged, then gradually improve and in time become something of an expert. There comes a time when you peak – and thereafter your output becomes less and less effective.

At the same time your interest wanes or you get burned out, and you're looking for something else to keep you engaged – and your interest active. You cannot earn a high income just by showing up on time and doing an average job, so you must constantly improve throughout your career. The goal should be to jump off on to something new, starting the whole process over. But when?

## Successive sigmoid curves

Ideally you would do that before your effectiveness starts to plateau or decline and your expiration date arrives.

The problem with jumping from one career arc to another – successive sigmoid curves – is knowing when the inflection point occurs: you can't! No one knows when that pesky inflection point occurs. A lot of times you don't know until after you look back, in retrospect, and say 'I should have gotten off earlier' – and it is just too late.

Since you can never know when the best time is to move on, I decided – while remaining an architect – to jump off and on to a new interest every seven years.

## My walk home from the train

To illustrate, I like to think of a career path as being like a concrete sidewalk. Doing this has ensured that I've adapted, remained relevant, become resilient and flourished throughout my career. How so?

In 20 years, I made the walk to and from our local train stop 6,000 times (for those keeping score with a Fitbit, that's 60 million steps).

Sidewalks aren't made in one long ribbon, why should our careers be? So, let's look a little more closely at our career path.

On inspection, sidewalks are not quite as smooth as we were led to believe. We build sidewalks over all sorts of things: roots, rocks, utilities. Metaphorically, what are the roots underneath your career?

- Ever-shifting technological trends?
- Fickle employers?
- An unpredictable economy?

We're building the foundations of our careers over roots!

One of the dirty little secrets I share with my architecture students is this: All concrete cracks. We confront microscopic cracks every day. Like a concrete sidewalk, our careers need to accommodate these cracks. Otherwise, the cracks will take over.

Cracks will sometimes appear in careers due to:

- your interests waning
- you getting burned out doing one thing
- your salary pricing you out of a position
- emerging talent taking your place.

When cracks do occur in our career, we can try to hide or mask them.

But sometimes there are just too many to try and hide them.

Cracks appear when:

- we aren't happy in our career
- we can't be ourselves
- we can't speak our mind
- we're playing by someone else's set of rules
- we're biting our tongues
- we're swallowing our pride.

Constantly addressing these forces can drain our psychic energy and take its toll.

Concrete inevitably cracks – but you can control where the cracks occur. (We do this in architecture by creating control joints. By creating a break, we induce a crack. The crack goes where we want it to go, not randomly where it can catch us by surprise.)

In your career path, doing this leaves you in control. You can cut a seam in your career path. Think of it as creating a career control joint.

I relieved these tensions in my career by creating a career control joint every seven years. You can do so however often suits you.

In my career I maintained my main job (architect), and every seven years changed my side job (urban planner, public speaker, consultant, etc.).

On a regular basis – at the control joint or inflection point – you jump off one track on to another.

If you are working at one career – say, renderer or modelmaker, start planning for your next – say, urban planner or façade specialist, either once your current one has played out or to run alongside it as a parallel track.

Careers can be long. To ensure that yours remains that way, do these two things:

- Always have two careers, and
- Change one of them every x years.

You should change your side career every x years:

- to avoid an existential crisis midway through your career
- to keep from becoming complacent and bored
- to keep from falling behind and becoming obsolete
- to keep from falling into the trap of living someone else's idea of who you are.

You can look at having two careers two ways: as an unfortunate economic and social reality, or as an opportunity to expand meaning, purpose and possibility in your life.

By changing your career every few years, you are in essence, with each iteration, creating a better version of your former self.

And in that way, you can ensure that you are always evolving and improving, always doing what you love, always doing what it takes to sustain a long, fulfilling career.

Author's note: A portion of the appendix text was originally published as the transcript for the author's 26 April 2015 TEDx talk, *The 7-Year Career.*

# Notes

1. James Boswell, *The Life of Samuel Johnson, LL.D.*, vol. 3 (1791).
2. The author is grateful to William Worn for suggesting this topic and related questions.
3. Sumita Singha. *Autotelic Architect* (Routledge, 2016), p 162.
4. David Lee, *Design Thinking in the Classroom* (Ulysses Press, 2018), p 11.
5. Dawn Graham, *Switchers* (AMACOM, 2018), p 45.
6. Catherine Sanderson, *The Positive Shift* (BenBella Books, 2019), p 37.
7. Rod Judkins, *The Art of Creative Thinking* (Penguin Publishing Group, 2015), p 36.
8. Emily Balcetis, *Clearer, Closer, Better* (Random House Publishing Group, 2020), p 4.
9. Reid Hoffman and Ben Casnocha, *The Start-up of You: Adapt to the Future, Invest in Yourself, and Transform Your Career* (Random House, 2012).
10. Enrico Moretti, *The New Geography of Jobs* (HMH Books, 2013), p 28.
11. George Couros, *The Innovator's Mindset: Empower Learning, Unleash Talent, and Lead a Culture of Creativity* (Dave Burgess Consulting, 2015), p 180.
12. Andrew McAfee, *More from Less: The Surprising Story of How We Learned to Prosper Using Fewer Resources – and What Happens Next* (Scribner, 2019), p 12.
13. Jonathan Levi, *The Only Skill that Matters: The Proven Methodology to Read Faster, Remember More, and Become a Super Learner,* (Lioncrest Publishing, 2019).
14. Vitruvius, *The Ten Books on Architecture: Books I–X* (Dover Architecture, 1998), p 193.
15. Steven Novella, *The Skeptics' Guide to the Universe* (Grand Central Publishing, 2019), p 446.
16. Gernot Wagner, *Climate Shock* (Princeton University Press, 2015), p 7.
17. Nir Eyal, *Indistractable* (BenBella Books, 2020), p 31.
18. Andrew Yang, *Smart People Should Build Things* (Harper Business, 2014), p 127.
19. Sumita Singha. *Autotelic Architect* (Routledge, 2016), p 45.
20. '4 in 5 Employees Want Benefits or Perks More Than a Pay Raise', Glassdoor Employment Confidence Survey (2 October, 2015), https://www.glassdoor.com/blog/ecs-q3-2015/, accessed 12 October 2020.
21. 'Everyone must be an entrepreneur as traditional paths of doing business disintegrate across professions', *Architect Magazine* (16 December, 2011), https://www.architectmagazine.com/practice/everyone-must-be-an-entrepreneur-as-traditional-paths-of-doing-business-disintegrate-across-professions_o, accessed 12 October 2020.
22. Rod Judkins, *The Art of Creative Thinking* (Penguin Publishing Group, 2015), p 171.
23. Kelly Leonard and Tom Yorton, *Yes, And* (Harper Business, 2015), pp 7–8.
24. Daniel Levitin, *Successful Aging* (Penguin Publishing Group, 2020), p 281.
25. Ibid, p 112.
26. Jacob Bronowski, *The Ascent of Man* (Ebury Publishing, 2011).
27. Abhijit Banerjee and Esther Duflo, *Good Economics for Hard Times* (Juggernaut, 2019), p 48.
28. knowledge-architecture.com, accessed 16 October 2020.
29. pechakucha.com, accessed 16 October 2020.
30. Daniel Levitin, *Successful Aging* (Penguin Publishing Group, 2020), p 164.
31. Steven Johnson, *Farsighted* (Penguin Publishing Group, 2019), p 116.
32. Karie Willyerd and Barbara Mistick, *Stretch: How to Future-Proof Yourself for Tomorrow's Workplace* (Wiley, 2015), p 55.
33. Sara Johnson, 'Female Architects Earn $14,877 Less Than Male Architects', *Architect,* 17 March 2015, https://www.architectmagazine.com/practice/market-intel/female-architects-earn-14-877-less-than-male-architects_o, accessed 21 October 2020.
34. Jonathan Rauch, *The Happiness Curve: Why Life Gets Better After Midlife* (Thomas Dunne Books, 2018).
35. Michael Gelb and Kelly Howell, *Brain Power* (New World Library, 2011), p 7.
36. Daniel Levitin, *Successful Aging* (Penguin Publishing Group, 2020), p 20.
37. Ibid, pp 85–86.

# Index

Page numbers in **bold** indicate figures.

adaptability 10–24, **21**
Adrian Smith + Gordon Gill Architecture 8, **8, 36, 172**
Alison Brooks Architects 67, **67, 152**
American Institute of Architects (AIA) 23, **85,** 95, 135, 137, 143–145, **145,** 146, 148–149, 157, 161, 179
architecture profession
    future of 151–162, **153,** 167–169
    remaining in 46–62, **51**
    salaries 49, 176, 177
    support for female architects 49–50, 171–187
    work-life balance 49–50, 137, 171–187
    *see also* career paths
Arrowstreet 7
Ayers Saint Gross 49
Ayre Chamberlain Gaunt 195

BAM Design 198
BDP 5, **5**
Beardsley, Sara 8, **8,** 9, 35, **36,** 36, 41, 57, 70, 73, 77, 100, 113, 114–115, 119–120, **120,** 171–172, **172,** 185, 192
Berlin, Isaiah 28
Black Lives Matter 52
brilliance 71–74
Brooks, Alison 6, 30, 34, 37, 39, 60, **67,** 67, 71, 78, 89, **89,** 93–94, 105–106, 143, 148, 152, **152,** 162, 171, 177, 181, 194
burnout 88–89, 174
Buttress Architects 32, **33,** 124, 138

career longevity 46–62, **51**
career paths
    architecture-related fields and roles 61, 132
    career reinvention 135–149
    diversification 66–67
    firm ownership 111, 129–131, 140–141, 142
    getting unstuck 92–94
    inflection points 118–133
    parallel roles 143–149
    paths to leadership 98–115
    pivoting roles 123–129, 132, 141–142
    pivoting to leadership 125–127, 143
    planning versus happy accidents 203–212
    rebranding 138–140
    remaining an architect 46–62, **51**
    singular versus multiple 55–58
    switching firms 98–115
Carpo, Mario 159
Carter, Duane 49, 57, 61, 82, 101, 109, 154, 193, 206
Cesario, Danei 1, 12, 28, 41–42, **50,** 50, 72, **72,** 76, 77, 84–85, 89, 92, 106, 122, **122,** 127, 135, **145,** 145, 153, 157, 175, **175,** 182, **182,** 189, **190,** 197, **197,** 203
Cliggott, Joe 8, 22, 36, 47, 48, 57–58, 67, 73, 77, 82, 90, 92–93, 106, 121, 124–125, 141–142, 162, 179, 186–187, 189, 194, 203, 207
coaching 165–166
communication skills 3, 90–91
company ownership 111, 129–131, 140–141, 142
complacency 84–87

COVID-19 pandemic 1–4, 8, 9, 10–12, 13, 16, 29, **29, 30,** 52, 75, **155,** 177, 183
curiosity 19–20, 71

de Boissieu, Aurélie 21, 53, 92, 140, 159, 194
digital transformation 14, 37–38, 53, 128, 141, 152–154, **153,** 157–159, 195, 198, 199
diversification 66–67
Dobson, Adrian 35
Doctorow, E.L. 71, 207
Drew, Stephen 6, 46, 62, 80, 91, 118
Dumich, Matt 105, **105,** 129, 143, 144, **144,** 157, 161, 168, 174, 186, 209

economic recessions 4–6, 16, 55, 75, 119, 129, 132, 161–162, 177, 182, 195–196
Edwards, John 74, 77, 84, 146, 163, 174
employability 82–83

family responsibilities 49–50, 137, 171–187, 189, 192–193
female architects, support for 49–50, 171–187
financial planning 49, 191
firm ownership 111, 129–131, 140–141, 142
flourishing 80–96
Floyd, George 52
focus 71
Frankl, Viktor 183
FXCollaborative 83

GBBN 40, 166
generalists 35–36, **35,** 53–54, 56
Gensler 22, 38, **56, 69, 86, 154, 173,** 209
Giacometti, Alberto 19
Glassman, Elliot 53, 68–69, 75, 102, 110–111, 118–119, 160, 208
Google 49–50
Grandstaff-Rice, Emily 2, 7, 18, 19, 38, 49, 57, 64, 68, 70, 74, 76, 84, 85, 88–89, 92, 98, 110, 121, 127–128, 139, 148, 154, 161–162, 177, 180, 194, 205
Gresko, John 24, 33–34, 42, 53–54, 55, 70, 71, 76, 82, 93, 102, 110, 111, 139, 181, 187, 196–197, 198
Grimshaw 38, 51, 66, 92, 122, 140–141, 163, 190
Growing Sudley 132–133
Guillot, Randy 22, 37, 44, 73–74, 80–81, 123, 139–140, 157–158, 165–166, 184, 196, 199

Harrison, Sarah 130, 132–133
Harrison Stringfellow Architects 130
HDR Architecture 22, 52
health insurance 191–192
HMC Architects 6, **7,** 10–12, **11, 83, 107,** 187
Holly Street Studio 4, 5, **54, 200, 206**
Hooton, Zoe 3, 47, 51, 65, 67, 72, 88, 91–92, 106, 124, 140, 161, 176, 181, 201, 208
HPA Chartered Architects 3
Hyman, Ted 6, 29–30, 81, 113–114, 125–127, **126,** 154–156, 191

influence 38–39

Jacobs, Diane Reicher 4, 5, 20–21, 24, 41, 54–55, **54,** 65, 71, 76–77, 94, 96, 113, 114, 148–149, 183, 200, **200,** 205, 206, 211
Joshi, Meghana 34, 51, 80, 104, 109, 123, 148, 151, 174

# Index

KA Connect 122–123
Kahler Slater 22
Kell, Alistair 2, 5, **5,** 19, 87, 103, 183, 203
Krueck + Sexton Architects 185
Kuklinski + Rappe Architects 185

Laing O'Rourke 163
leadership
    pivoting to 125–127, 143
    training 165–166
    women in 178–179
learning *see* training and learning
Lee, Evelyn 28, 58, 60, 85, 98, 176, 179, 194
Lee, Tom 52, 59, 84, 93, 108, 111, 120–121, 132, 143, 152–153, 176, 177, 178, 185–186, 194–195, 209
Lewis, Allister 55, 60, 195, 207–208
lifelong learning 53–55, 60, 83, 87–88, 95
Little Diversified Architectural Consulting 109
Louth, Henry David 141, 166, 168–169

Macdonald & Company 6
Marquardt, Virginia E. 2, 6, **7,** 10–12, **11,** 56–57, 59, 82–83, **83,** 91, 107, **107,** 143–144, 167, 171, 174, 182, 187, 191, 205, 207, 210
Marsh, Chithra 32–33, **33,** 98, 112, 124, 138, 175–176, 179, 189
Martinkovic, Justin 6, 7, 31–32, 41, 46, 52, 58, 65–66, 70, 71, 99, 131, 142, 156–157
Martinkovic Milford Architects 6
maternity leave 130, 171, 175, 176, 179, 181
Mazzi, Angela 40, 43, 54, 58, 86, 87, 114, 146, 166, 179, 183, 212
Mead & Hunt 66
mental health 88–89
mentoring 90, 157, 159–162, 163, 166, 178–179
mid-career architects
    ageing 193–201
    anchors for 39–42, **41**
    as bridge between generations 157–159, **158**
    current model for 154–157
    mid-career defined 6–8
    midlife pressures 189–202
    support for female 49–50, 171–187
    *see also* career paths; training and learning
money issues 49, 176, 177, 191
Morgan, Susan 164
Mozina, Tom 56, 70, 72, 99–100, 104

parallel roles 143–149
passion 51, **51,** 81–82
Perkins & Will 56
perseverance 22, 67–71, 80
PLACED 138
Pollock, Alexandra 24, 83, 128, 147, 176–177, 180, 193, 208, 210–211
prescience 74–77
Pryke, Andrew 198, 209

RATIO 57
Red Leaf Architects 19
relevance 28–44, **35,** 51, **51**
resilience 55, 57, 64, 65–67
RIBA 35, 95, 146, 148, 161, 172, 173
Riley, Michael 20, 53, 87–88, 114, 162, 192, 195–196
role models 91–92, 172–173

Rothblatt, Rob 19–20, 39, 46–47, 108, 151, 159, 189, 205
Rowland Design 7

Sandschafer, Trina 22, 40, 43, 55, 61, 65, 67, 73, 86, 94, 95–96, 102, 108, 118, 147, 158, 160, 167–168, 173, 192, 199, 206, 210
self-awareness 84, 90
Semple, Don 185, 198
Semple, Nicole 179–180, 185, 196, 204
Shaffer, Mary 23, 24, 61, 66, 74, 75, 78, 85–86, 95, 103, 140, 169, 195, 196, 211, 212
Shepley Bulfinch 3, **3, 48, 69, 90, 101, 147**
Sink, Donna 7, 104, 130–131, 145–146, 180, 183, 191–192
Skidmore, Owings & Merrill 1
Slack Technologies 85
SmithGroup 105, **105, 144**
specialists 35–36, **35,** 53–54, 55, 56
strategic foresight 76–77
Stringfellow, Su 130, 132–133
Studio Gang 90
sunk costs 84–85
Swain, David 30, 48, 64, 90, 135, 156, 160, 201

talent 71–74
Taylor Design Architects 33
Teagarden, Lora 43, 57, 59, 66–67, 68, 83, 95, 102, 132, 156, 163, 179, 184–185, 195
training and learning
coaching 165–166
leadership training 165–166
lifelong learning 53–55, 60, 83, 87–88, 95
mentoring 90, 157, 159–162, 163, 166, 178–179
at mid-career 162–166, **162, 164, 166,** 198, 200–201
Troxel, Evan 66, 86, 94, 128, 141, 161, 196, 201–202, 205
Twiss, Philip 6, 20, 37–38, 42, 54, 55–56, **56,** 59, 68, **69,** 76, **86,** 86, 93, 112, 146, 154, **154,** 156, 172–173, **173,** 181, 183, 200–201, 208–209

Vitruvius 16

WALLEN + daub 1, **50, 72, 85,** 145
Watson, Angela 3, **3,** 21, 23, 32, 37, 48, **48,** 53, 58, 69–70, **69,** 72, 73, 90–91, **90,** 95, 100, **101,** 125, 147, **147,** 148, 151, 159, 164, 169, 171, 177–178, 184, 199–200, 209–210
Watts, Andy 18, 38, 51, 66, 71, 75, 89, 91, 106, 122, 128, 140–141, 142, 163, 190, 197–198, 209
Wilson, Oscia 32, 49–50, 88, 102, 103, 104, 129–130, 137, 207
Women in Property 161, 179
work ethic 68–70, 71–73
work-life balance 49–50, 137, 171–187
writing books 66–67
WSP Built Ecology 53, 68

Yang, Andrew 18
Young Architect Forum 143–144

Zaha Hadid Architects 141
ZGF Architects 29, **29, 30, 81, 109, 112,** 125, **126, 155, 178, 204**

# Image Credits

Figures 0.4, 2.2, 3.4, 4.7, 5.2, 7.4
Shepley Bulfinch

Figure 0.5
BDP (Building Design Partnership)

Figures 0.6, 0.9, 4.3, 5.4
HMC Architects

Figures 0.7, 1.8, 6.2, 9.2
Adrian Smith + Gordon Gill Architecture

Figures 1.3, 1.4, 4.2, 5.5, 5.6, 6.4, 6.5, 8.5, 9.5, 9.6, 11.2
ZGF Architects

Figure 1.5
Buttress Chithra Marsh

Figures 2.3, 3.5, 4.4, 6.3, 7.3, 9.4, 9.7, 10.2, 10.3
WALLEN + daub

Figure 2.5
Diane Reicher Jacobs of Holly Street Studio

Figures 2.6, 2.7, 3.3, 4.5, 8.4, 9.3
Gensler

Figures 3.2, 4.6, 8.2
Alison Brooks Architects

Figures 5.3, 7.2
SmithGroup,
Photograph: Travis Frangie

Figure 10.4
Diane Reicher Jacobs of Holly Street Studio,
Photograph: Brad Reed Photography

Figure 11.3
Diane Reicher Jacobs of Holly Street Studio,
Photograph: Diane R. Jacobs, AIA

Figure 11.4
Alison Brooks Architects,
Photograph: Paul Riddle

All other illustrations by Bruce Bondy